Spirituality and Wellbeing

SPIRITUALITY AND WELLBEING

Interdisciplinary Approaches to the Study of
Religious Experience and Health

Edited by Bettina E. Schmidt and Jeff Leonardi

equinox

SHEFFIELD UK   BRISTOL CT

Published by Equinox Publishing Ltd.

UK: Office 415, The Workstation, 15 Paternoster Row, Sheffield, South Yorkshire S1 2BX
USA: ISD, 70 Enterprise Drive, Bristol, CT 06010

www.equinoxpub.com

First published 2020

© Bettina E. Schmidt, Jeff Leonardi and contributors 2020

All rights reserved. No part of this publication may be reproduced or transmitted in any form or by any means, electronic or mechanical, including photocopying, recording or any information storage or retrieval system, without prior permission in writing from the publishers.

British Library Cataloguing-in-Publication Data

A catalogue record for this book is available from the British Library.

ISBN-13 978 1 78179 764 8 (hardback)
         978 1 78179 765 5 (paperback)
         978 1 78179 766 2 (ePDF)

Library of Congress Cataloging-in-Publication Data

Names: Schmidt, Bettina E., editor.
Title: Spirituality and wellbeing : interdisciplinary approaches to the study of religious experience and health / edited by Bettina E. Schmidt and Jeff Leonardi.
Description: Bristol : Equinox Publishing Ltd., 2020. | Includes bibliographical references and index.
Identifiers: LCCN 2019011193 (print) | ISBN 9781781797648 (hb) | ISBN 9781781797655 (pb)
Subjects: LCSH: Health--Religious aspects.
Classification: LCC BL65.M4 S6784 2020 (print) | LCC BL65.M4 (ebook) | DDC 201/.661--dc23
LC record available at https://lccn.loc.gov/2019011193
LC ebook record available at https://lccn.loc.gov/2019981008

Typeset by JS Typesetting Ltd, Porthcawl

Contents

Acknowledgements   vii
List of Figures   viii

Introduction
  Jeff Leonardi and Bettina E. Schmidt   1

Section One:
Setting the Scene

Chapter 1
  Spirituality and Wellbeing: Is There a Necessary Link? Toward a Critical Approach to the Study of Spirituality
  Everton de Oliveira Maraldi   19

Chapter 2
  Clinical Parapsychology: The Interface Between Anomalous Experiences and Psychological Wellbeing
  Chris Roe   44

Section Two:
The Body in Focus

Chapter 3
  Made in the Image: The Christian Understanding of the Body
  Jeff Leonardi   67

Chapter 4
  Spirituality and Wellbeing in Traditional China: Food, Self-Sacrifice, and Spiritual Practice in a Chinese Buddhist Legend
  Thomas Jansen   87

Chapter 5
Spiritus contra spiritum: Spirituality, Belief and Discipline in
Alcoholics Anonymous
Wendy Dossett   113

Section Three:
The Diversity of Perspectives

Chapter 6
Narratives of Spirituality and Wellbeing: Cultural Differences and
Similarities between Brazil and the UK
Bettina E. Schmidt   137

Chapter 7
Using Autoethnography to Explore the Experience of Spirituality
in Epilepsy
Louise N. Spiers   158

Chapter 8
To Thine Own Self Be True: Alcoholics Anonymous, Recovery and
Care of the Self
Lymarie Rodriguez-Morales   181

Section Four:
Applied Practice

Chapter 9
Religiosity, Spirituality and Wellbeing in the Perception of Brazilian
Health and Mental Health Professionals
Marta Helena de Freitas   199

Chapter 10
Compassionate Presence: Buddhist Practice and the
Person-Centred Approach to Counselling and Psychotherapy
Becky Seale   225

Index   245

Acknowledgements

We wish to thank the Alister Hardy Trust for its ongoing support of the Religious Experience Research Centre (RERC) in Lampeter. The Trust co-funds the annual RERC conferences and supported some of the research seminar series which led to the development of this book. We also want to thank the colleagues of the Faculty of Humanities and Performing Arts for their ongoing support of the RERC. The conversations between the two editors about spirituality and wellbeing were further inspired by INSPIRE, at the University of Wales Trinity Saint David, that offered funds to kick-start research pertaining to the Well-being of Future Generations (Wales) Act.

List of Figures

7.1 'Normal' me—Blenheim Palace, Oxford, UK, 1988.
7.2 'Abnormal' me—Louvre, Paris, France, 1989.
7.3 MRI scan, 30 June 2014.
7.4 Consultant letter, 25 September 2014.
8.1 The Twelve Steps of Alcoholics Anonymous
8.2 Twelve AA traditions

INTRODUCTION

Jeff Leonardi and Bettina E. Schmidt

The study of religious and spiritual experience is a growing field of studies, though with methodological challenges. The editors of this volume, Bettina Schmidt and Jeff Leonardi, are both attached to the Religious Experience Research Centre at the University of Wales Trinity St David at Lampeter, Bettina as Director and Jeff as Honorary Research Fellow. The Centre has an archive of over 6,000 accounts of individual religious or spiritual experiences and these are often impressive in themselves. The Centre has long been a focus for research in this field, ever since its foundation by Sir Alister Hardy. When we begin to read and study these accounts and others like them, we cannot but be struck by the impressive depth of meaning the experiencer finds in them, and often the significant consequences for them in their future lives. In so far as their experiences may have communicated deep truths about the nature and meaning of life and relationships, often with a sense of peace, unity and love, one can well imagine that some of these consequences might be found in terms of beneficial effects on the experiencers' sense of wellbeing, and that this in turn might have positive impacts on their health. This is, effectively, the territory this volume seeks to address, from a wide variety of viewpoints. Bettina is an anthropologist of religion and Jeff a Person-centred Counsellor and Anglican priest, and this collection reflects the different foci of their work and research, but also the extent of meeting points, especially in terms of the study of spiritual and religious experience and therapeutic approaches to being present and receptive in relationships.

Our starting point is a broad definition of spirituality as 'that which gives meaning, value and purpose to a person's life'. We argue that spirituality is crucial for any consideration of human wellbeing. Although spirituality is not always represented as a central focus in the health and wellbeing literature, there is a growing understanding in many quarters of its vital role in many people's lives and therefore for their wellbeing, across cultures. The following quote, from the Dalai Lama, illustrates well the necessary challenge that the study of spirituality presents to the pursuit of wellbeing in a materialistic culture:

> Material progress and a higher standard of living improve comfort and health but do not lead to a transformation of the mind, the only thing capable of providing lasting peace. Profound happiness, unlike fleeting pleasures, is spiritual by nature. It depends on the happiness of others, and it is based on love and tenderness. We would be wrong to think that being happy consists of grasping the best at others' expense. The lack of altruism, which causes family discord and disturbance, causes solitude. We should take care not to be excessively concerned with the external world, realising that grasping and owning material goods reinforce self-centredness ... Of course, one can cultivate human qualities without having a religion. But as a general rule, religion allows us to increase these qualities more effectively. (Dalai Lama 2011, 88)

We distinguish between *spirituality, faith* and *religion*, recognizing that each can operate independently of the other, and that none inevitably implies adherence to the others, although there are clear connections and a natural sequence between them. Spirituality will be defined below; we take *faith* to mean the body of beliefs associated with the individual's spirituality; and *religion* to mean the organization of beliefs and practices in a collective body or institution. In contemporary Britain far more people assert that they have a spirituality than do a commitment to a particular religion. 'Faith' occupies a midpoint between spirituality and religion, as a kind of adherence to a religion but without active practice. By way of contrast, in South America for example, there is a far wider engagement with the practice of religions. The authors represented in this book make links to a range of religious and spiritual traditions. Consequently the book makes a contribution to interfaith dialogue by enhancing the understanding of spirituality and wellbeing from different faith perspectives.

Leonardi has developed a more detailed definition and explication of spirituality as follows:

1. Spirituality refers to a level or dimension of experiencing, which overlaps with the common sense and everyday, but which is distinctive, special and seems to connect with a wider or higher level of awareness and being.
2. Spirituality is fundamentally relational.
3. Spiritual experience may include a sense of the presence of, and relationship with, the divine or transcendent.
4. Spiritual experience tends to convey a sense of profound meaning and purpose and connectedness with creation, life and other

human beings, and a corresponding sense of responsibility for one's own part in it all.
5. Spiritual experience tends to confirm the value of the subject, and, by extension, all other human beings.
6. In spiritual experience, the senses, feelings, imagination and intuition are all equally important, alongside thought and interpretation.
7. Spiritual experience tends to have the quality of revelation or external event—and this leads to a sense that one participates in a wider and higher scheme of things.
8. Spirituality is informed by the repeated experience of the interconnectedness—and at times synchronicity—of events and relationships.
9. Spirituality is related to sexuality, which is another kind of energy of relationship and connectedness.
10. Spirituality tends to evoke a sense of the super-sensible—both positive and negative—and of life beyond death.
11. Spirituality tends to evoke joy.
12. Spiritual experience can, for some, be a negative experience, either in its nature (as in 10.) or in terms of other people's response.

But not only spirituality needs to be conceptualized; wellbeing does as well. The recent wave of publications on wellbeing seems to indicate that the concept of wellness is relatively new. But the opposite is true, as Richard Woods shows. Reflecting on the etymology of the term in the English language, Woods links the concept of wellness to the English term *wealnesse* that was used in the middle of the seventeenth century 'to refer to a general state of well-being or healthiness' (2008, 9). Wealnesse, meaning wellness, is connected to the much older term 'welfare' that had originally the meaning of 'fare' or go well. Etymologically 'well' is related to 'wealth' that originally meant happiness. But Woods goes further and highlights the spiritual dimension to his research on wellbeing. Woods writes that 'spiritual health is not a state but a dynamic transactional alliance with the physical environment, the social system and the divine milieu in which we live, move and have our being. No one is either holy or healthy in isolation' (Woods 2008, 21).

Despite this etymologic link to spiritual health, wellbeing is usually seen in relation to health. Already in 1948 the WHO uses the term 'physical, mental and social wellbeing' in its definition of the global health of a person: 'health is a state of complete physical, mental and social well-being and not merely the absence of disease or infirmity' (WHO 1948, 2). In the following years this definition was amended and linked to an excess of positive over negative affect (Bradburn 1969) or the ability to fulfil goals (Foresight Mental Capital and Wellbeing Project 2008), though wellbeing is still commonly linked to aspects of health and other measurable aspects of quality of life. For instance, Shin and Johnson define wellbeing as 'a global assessment of a person's quality of life according to his own chosen criteria' (Shin and Johnson 1978, 478). But what exactly is 'quality of life' and can it really be measured? Most scholars agree today on the multifaceted nature of wellbeing and criticize that it is not possible to equate it with only one aspect such as health or life satisfaction (Forgeard et al. 2011, 81). Hence, it is widely accepted today that wellbeing, as well as its siblings (or, perhaps better, components) happiness and life satisfaction, are differently perceived depending on a range of factors (Dodge, Daly, Huyton and Sanders 2012). Nonetheless, most studies try to measure wellbeing by identifying apparent 'objective' features that can be measured across cultures and societies while acknowledging at the same time some 'subjective' components. Tambyah and Tan, for instance, write that 'subjective wellbeing research focuses on measuring an individual's cognitive and affective reactions to her or his whole life as well as to specific domains of life' (2013, 17). While they acknowledge that subjective wellbeing is a multi-faceted concept (Tambyah and Tan 2013, 33), the majority of data is presented in tables with statistical data and the study lacks a discussion of what matters to people. And though the authors include religious belonging and spirituality in their data set, which shows the importance of spirituality, they do not even mention spirituality in passing in the discussion of the impact of value orientation on life satisfaction (Tambyah and Tan 2013, 128).

The term 'subjective wellbeing' is the predominant approach to measuring happiness and wellbeing and reflects its orientation towards utility. It indicates that it is possible to measure happiness and wellbeing by a single question such as 'how happy are you with your life' (see White 2016b, 16). The term 'psychological wellbeing' is used to indicate a much closer connection to health and reflects therefore much more the WHO definition. Common is the tendency to measure wellbeing with presumed 'objective' features, as White outlines: 'Happiness tends to be identified more with emotion or feelings, and with the individual while wellbeing may indicate "objective" elements such as standard of living, access to health care or education – in addition to "subjective" elements such as satisfaction with life' (White 2016b, 5).

As Theodore J. Chamberlain and Christopher H. Hall write, psychologists seem to need a tool with which to define and measure even such an abstract term as wellbeing (Chamberlain and Hall 2000, 118). However, as Sarah C. White criticizes in contemporary studies on wellbeing, especially in psychology and economics, the identification of the empirical with measurement is problematic. She writes 'Sample size may be large but the data are thin, compromising numerical scores by which people rate their emotional experience or satisfaction with their lives' (White 2016a, xi). Her frustration of this ongoing need to measure is understandable as it leads to an oversight to understand what matters to people. In particular the subjective variables such as religious belonging and commitment are still neglected within studies of life satisfaction and wellbeing. As several scientists argue, these subjective features of wellbeing are difficult to measure and evidence is therefore largely anecdotal.[1]

Consequently little attention has been given to religion and spirituality within studies on wellbeing and life satisfaction despite the fact that some studies have highlighted the positive impact that religious commitment, conceptualized as 'meaning' and 'belonging', has on a subjective feeling of satisfaction with life (Hadaway and Roof 1978, 295). Christopher Kirk Hadaway and Wade Clark Roof even stated that religion is the best of eight elements to predict the perception of quality of life. Following this line of argument David G. Myers and Ed Diener state that in order to find out 'Who is happy? Knowing a person's age, sex, race, and income (assuming the person has enough to afford life's necessities) hardly gives a clue. Better clues come from knowing a person's traits, whether the person enjoys a supportive network of close relationships, whether the person's culture offers positive interpretations for most daily events, whether the person is engaged by work and leisure, and whether the person has a faith that entails social support, purpose, and hope' (Myers and Diener 1995, 17). Their argument reflects a shifted focus on 'positive functioning' within the debate of wellbeing that can be linked back to William James' early writings on healthy mindedness (1902) and continued with Carl Rogers's work (1961). Rogers defines wellbeing in terms of 'the good life' and becoming 'a fully functioning person'. Rogers' approach to wellbeing has therefore strong similarities to the notion of wellbeing as 'living well together'. In later work (e.g., 1980) he also acknowledged the importance of spirituality for wellbeing (see Leonardi 2010).

If we examine different aspects of the psychological study of wellbeing, we will find perspectives which cohere with the approach we are suggesting: in developmental psychology, psychological wellbeing may be analyzed in terms of a pattern of growth across the lifetime of the person; in personality psychology, it is possible to apply Maslow's concept of self-actualization, Rogers' concept of the fully functioning person, Jung's concept of individuation, and Allport's concept of maturity to account for psychological wellbeing. In all of them, the following general factors are likely to be considered significant for wellbeing:

1. self-acceptance
2. personal growth
3. purpose in life
4. situational competence
5. autonomy
6. relationships.

This particular list is adapted from the work of Carol Ryff (1989, *Six-factor Model of Psychological Well-being*), but there is considerable coherence between many writers in the field, especially of humanistic psychology in general, and of positive psychology in particular. All factors listed here can be seen to be closely related to spirituality as we have defined it in the broad sense, especially 1–3 and 6.

There is an interesting overlap in research into the outcomes for individuals in terms of psychological wellbeing and functioning of, on the one hand, significant spiritual experiences and, on the other, of effective counselling and psychotherapy. Both Hardy (1979, 98–103) and Hay (1987, 157–9) report on outcomes of distinctive spiritual experiences. Hardy reports three particular effects or outcomes: (a) a new or renewed sense of purpose or meaning to life; (b) changes in religious beliefs; and (c) changes in attitudes to others, especially closer relations to persons and to nature. Hay reports that such experiences confirmed or intensified the person's beliefs, made them more optimistic, gave more insight into life and encouraged moral behaviour.

By comparison, Carl Rogers, in a chapter entitled A Process Conception of Psychotherapy (Rogers 1961, 125–158), offers a summary of the outcomes of successful therapy, in which a person moves away from *fixity*—of feelings, conceptions and behaviour—and towards openness and fluidity; from incongruence to congruence; from self-concealment to self-disclosure; from the avoidance of intimacy in relationships to its embracing: 'the person becomes a unity of flow, of motion ... he has become an integrated process of changingness' (Rogers 1961, 158). The person so described is not only to be viewed in terms of the successful outcome of therapy, but also as a well-adjusted and well-functioning human being in every other sense. There is clearly an overlap here between Hardy's (c) above and Rogers' claims about relational growth and development that also reflect the following contributions to this volume.

The Contributions of this Volume

As has been suggested earlier, the common theme uniting the diverse contributions to this volume is a recognition and affirmation of the profound significance of spiritual and religious experience across cultures, for individuals, families, communities and societies, and this is evidenced by much of the research conducted by our contributors, or by others and referred to here. This affirmation is in the context of an uncomfortable and sometimes dismissive scientific and intellectual culture among academics, scientists and professions like medicine, social work and even counselling and psychotherapy. Schmidt describes it well in her chapter:

> the apparently unbreachable wall between the medical sector and faith, whether it is spirituality or religion, makes it so difficult to challenge the dominance of the Western understanding of wellbeing. ... Studies about wellbeing rarely mention religion or spirituality. The common understanding is that healing is achieved by a scientific medical practice. ... the underlying secular framework of the wider medical sector which features two assumptions: that religion is backward and should be (or will be) replaced by more reasonable worldviews and that religion is a private matter.

She also cautions against a reduction and diminishment of the contribution made by spirituality and religion to a person's life to purely functional benefits in terms of health and wellbeing:

> It is also important to avoid a purely functionalist or instrumentalist approach and look at religions only as a possible resource for healing or other aspects of life satisfaction. To just study 'what can religion do for people's wellbeing' limits the understanding of both, religion and wellbeing as it would judge, as Eyber highlights, religious participation 'purely on what it contributes on material and social levels' (Ager and Ager 2011).

Chris Roe's chapter deals with the implications for psychological wellbeing of 'anomalous' or 'paranormal', experience, and he also recognizes and critiques the scientific establishment for discounting the serious study of such phenomena: 'there is a great taboo associated with paranormal phenomena. They are often regarded as obviously false because they are deemed to contravene fundamental principles that have been repeatedly demonstrated in other areas of science'. As a result, members of the public often feel disinclined to share their experiences of this kind:

> In turn, this silence has encouraged members of the public to be reticent about sharing their experiences with others (especially members of the health professions) for fear of seeming, at best, naive or gullible (Evenden, Cooper and Mitchell 2013) or, at worst, as suffering from some underlying psychopathology (Roxburgh and Roe 2014).

He concludes that any negative impacts or outcomes of such anomalous experiences are almost entirely derived from negative responses to any declaration of them to significant others or health professionals: 'such experiences and their disclosure to others can have consequences for the wellbeing of the experient, particularly in terms of concerns the experient might have about being labelled as psychologically deficient or unwell by virtue of having had them, and especially because of the psychological distress that can be caused when trying to make sense of and come to terms with events for which no satisfactory explanatory framework is offered by the scientific community or psychological support services'.

Conversely, when, for example, a counsellor listens with quiet receptivity and alert acceptance, the experient feels received and validated and can proceed to comprehend and integrate the experience/s in positive ways for their psychological wellbeing: 'Braud (2012) argued that if exceptional experiences are not dismissed or bracketed as anomalous, deviant or irregular, but rather are worked with sufficiently, they can foster beneficial and transformative changes in the experiencer, including shifts in one's sense of self and one's connection with others. Indeed, Braud argues that the value of self disclosure about personally significant experiences and of confiding in others underpins counselling and therapeutic traditions that can lead to personal growth and acceptance'.

The widespread caution about voicing such experience to professionals is also borne out by both Schmidt and Freitas in their chapters. Indeed, Freitas found that interviewing health professionals in Brazil about their own spiritual or religious beliefs could indirectly confront them with their own ambivalences or even avoidance in this area. We quote from her work at some length because it is so eloquent about this issue:

> Being invited to talk about the subject of SR (Spiritual and Religious experience: eds.) in a work context was very unusual in the experience of practically all the professionals covered in the three surveys. The initial reactions to this experience were far from unanimous. There were those who refused to take part in the research, though quite an insignificant number (most commonly physicians and social workers), even those who interpreted the invitation as a kind of 'sign', through which they would be called upon to come back to an experience they had shunned for years, which was making them 'sceptical' and 'emptied' (this happened with psychologists, doctors, and nurses). There were those who were very tense at the beginning and much more at ease at the end of the interview (more common among nurses), as well as those who, during the course of the interview, were more discreet about some subjects (especially in relation to their own religiosity) but at the end

of the interview, after turning off the tape recorder, spoke in a more spontaneous manner, revealing their own religious and spiritual beliefs and experiences more naturally, or expressing their real opinions about various situations experienced in the work context. There were also those, especially among psychologists, who were so touched during the interviews, to the point of bursting into tears or convulsive crying.

This last response seems to have indicated how important such experience was to the professionals concerned, and perhaps how pent up and unexpressed they were, and how releasing and moving it was for them to be able to voice them to an interested and non-judgemental listener.

Many of our contributors declare or imply the need for a better culture and training in these matters for health and other professionals. This concurs with Leonardi's ongoing research into spirituality for various therapists, and often the neglect of it in their training. Vieten and Scammell's recent (2015) work *Spiritual and Religious Competencies in Clinical Practice* (also quoted by Freitas in her chapter) makes a very clear and comprehensive case for the need for such training and support.

Spiers' chapter deals with the experience of *epilepsy*, both from the view of it as a medical condition, and as a potentially spiritual condition. Her argument resonates with what we have suggested about Roe's work with regard to the negative impact of a negative view of the condition by medical personnel and other people, even though they are also associated with heightened states of unitive awareness:

> It has been noted that those in the helping professions are often ill-equipped to provide support for the emotional reactions that individuals have to spiritual experiences (Braud 2012) and I would add EFEs (*Epileptiform Events,* eds.) to this ... Descriptions and experiences of EFEs share a phenomenological similarity with other mystical and spiritual experiences (Neppe 1983; Persinger and Marakec 1993). Anomalous experiences in non-epileptic populations are also seen as irrational or pathological (Walsh and Vaughan 1993) and can be seen as dangerous, or 'an abomination' (Michael 1999, 53). Roxburgh and Evenden (2016) observe that individuals fear mentioning anomalous experiences as they expect to be labelled as mentally ill. It is hardly surprising, therefore, that individuals with EFEs are reticent to discuss them, or keep them secret for fear of judgement (Åsheim Hansen and Brodtkorb 2003).

Spiers brings a particular insight to this work as she has the condition herself, and adopts an *autoethnographic* approach accordingly: 'Autoethnography enables the researcher to consider spiritual experiences from the perspective of those who have them and enables us to understand the role of wellbeing arising from what may be otherwise considered an illness'.

This connects with a concern or tension which is referred to in this volume by both Maraldi and Seale. This tension can be understood with reference for example to the current adoption of *mindfulness* based approaches to psychological health and wellbeing. The critique of these approaches is that they tend to utilize the *techniques* of, for example Buddhism, but without the spiritual underpinnings or the support and guidance of the relevant community of faith. The term sometimes used here is 'Buddhism Lite'. Seale refers to this lack directly:

> Reconciling a Western emphasis on strengthening the ego through therapy with the notion of transcending the self in a Buddhist practice is one example of clashing world-views. ... Batchelor (2015: 255) writes that a secular approach to meditation could end up losing 'any sense of sublimity, mystery, awe or wonder', therefore, mindfulness is in danger of being simply a technique to feel better rather than a spiritual practice. ... Wellbeing is not a hedonistic experience to be found through the pursuit of pleasure but rather an inner state not contingent on transient external experiences. ... Wellbeing can be found through staying awake to an inherent desire to 'live in harmony with the universe'. This concept points to the ethical underpinning of Buddhist practice; in seeing and knowing our inseparability in this way, living an ethical life becomes inseparable from our wellbeing.

Maraldi's overview of the fields of spirituality and religion in contemporary societies argues that traditional religion has lost its appeal for many who therefore find their focus has shifted to spirituality. He also suggests that spirituality properly understood has a larger significance than even the focus on health and wellbeing outcomes, because it partakes of the transcendent source of meaning and experience. 'In an era in which organized religions are no longer the main sources of cultural values and meanings, and in which metaphysical speculations concerning a transcendent reality are discouraged by science and technology, it is not surprising to find that spirituality was reduced to abstract notions such as "purpose in life" or "feelings of inner peace"'. Maraldi emphasizes the need for an ethical framework for any psychological therapy and connects the spiritual path to the Jungian concept of *individuation*:

> The emphasis on wellbeing has diverted us from the purposes for which spiritual practices and traditions were initially developed. In its very essence, spirituality might be best defined as a quest for self-knowledge, a quest toward finding our place in this world (which includes our relationship with others), but which is often portrayed simplistically by self-help as a harmless and 'make it yourself' product one can buy to achieve happiness and wellbeing (Carrette and King 2005). This spiritual

quest may sometimes involve therapeutic benefits, but challenges and difficulties comprise an essential part of the spiritual growth process as well. I define spiritual growth in terms of the Jungian concept of individuation (Jung 1933, 1969), that is, the challenging but rewarding path in the search for who we are.

We have two writers, Lymarie Rodriguez-Morales and Wendy Dossett, who focus on their research with the Alcoholics Anonymous (AA) 12 Step recovery programme, and both give accounts of the origins and developments of the programme. While Dossett's chapter focuses on the meaning of spirituality for participants in the 12 Step Programme, Rodriguez-Morales' research addresses the practical aspects of how the young adults in her study make sense of the process of recovery and learn to implement self-care. It is not surprising, perhaps, that we should find some salient evidence for the significance for health and wellbeing of spirituality in research into a therapeutic programme for those experiencing a potentially life-destroying condition. Dossett explains how the Programme rests on a need for the participant to reach and recognize a point of pure *helplessness* in order to reach out to something beyond themselves, the *Higher Power* as variously understood:

> The claim for a spiritual dimension to addiction and recovery centres on the concept of powerlessness. Sufferers are understood within the twelve-step *epistème* to be powerless over the substance or behaviour which causes harm. Members speak of knowing, on the one hand, that their substance use results in significant adversity for themselves and others, yet, on the other, being utterly unable to desist. The momentary relief from emotional (or sometimes physical) pain offered by the substance is so overwhelmingly compelling, that no amount of ordinary willpower is sufficient to battle the compulsion. Members often talk of being strong-willed in other areas of their life, but of needing to reach a point of 'despair' of their own willpower in relation to mind-altering substances. In fact, they describe the insistence on the positive use of willpower by caring professions and family members as profoundly damaging. It is only when the limits of their own power are finally acknowledged (members speak of 'surrendering') that effective power (in their words, 'higher power' or 'power greater than myself') can be accessed. In this presentation of the addiction problem, the idea that the will might be strengthened and the problem thereby overcome is mere hubris. Despair of personal willpower, followed by the complete reliance upon a higher power is essential.

In both accounts we find evidence that members of the recovery programmes find somewhat equal support from other members as well as from the 'Higher Power'. Dossett quotes one of her interviewees making a very wide-ranging and inclusive statement about this Higher Power: 'something greater, the group, the ground of all being, the universe, the "unknown mystery of things", nature, not me—or at least, not my self-serving ego'.

Rodriguez-Morales makes clear connections between the AA participants' quest for abstinence, recovery and health, and the spiritual framework of the Programme:

> A key conceptual issue that emerged regarding AA's spiritual worldview is *recovery as care of the self*. Participants presented their drug and alcohol abuse as by-products of or indeed as secondary to their problems in self-regulation: capacities for managing feelings, self-esteem, relationships, and self-care were in perilous dearth. Drugs and alcohol were used to compensate for deficits in regulating their affective life, enabling the achievement and maintenance of states of feeling, such as soothing and calming themselves, that they could not access on their own; this naturally developed into an unhealthy dependence on such substances. Successful recovery arises as the result of a functioning care of the self, as a worldview.

A recurrent concern in the study of spiritual and religious experience is the potential confusion between genuine spiritual experience on the one hand, and psychological disturbance on the other. The extreme sceptic will of course identify any of the former phenomena with the latter description, but those working in the field with any seriousness need to make this discrimination. Vieten and Scammell, referred to earlier, devote a chapter of their book to exploring this theme (2015, 61–80). Here, Maraldi addresses this theme, as does Schmidt in her work on trance states and spirit-possession (e.g., Schmidt 2016). In his chapter here Maraldi states:

> It must be stressed, however, that dissociative experiences are not always viewed as pathological, and may occur as part of cultural activities such as religious rituals (Maraldi et al. 2017). The discussion of whether certain experiences really deserve the label of 'pathological' is of fundamental importance to the study of the relationship between spirituality and wellbeing. The study of spiritual experiences could shed light on the nature of diverse psychological processes which psychiatrists and psychologists have hitherto investigated from an almost exclusively psychopathological perspective.

Like Seale he points to the possibilities of negative effects of mindfulness-based meditative practice detached from a wider spiritual context, Maraldi suggests that even with such a structure meditative practice can engender 'disturbing emotions', and indeed might be expected to do so in the context of the personal growth and transformation aspired to by the spiritual discipline concerned; these will then be seen as challenges for development and healing, rather than as symptoms of disorder: 'It follows from this that some level of psychological strength is a pre-requisite for practising meditation, and not exactly its main (or exclusive) goal.'

Both Jansen and Leonardi address the ascetical tendencies in religion. Where Leonardi observes in Christianity the dangers of a neglect of the needs of the body, or further a denigration of those needs, Jansen's exposition of the *Legend of Miaoshan* in Chinese spirituality suggests that by an extreme act of self-sacrifice and mutilation the Princess Miaoshan reveals her transcendent and divine nature. In a patriarchal culture, this story also affirms the independence of character and saintliness of its female protagonist. Jansen makes further connections between the self-actualizing process of Miaoshan and that concept as developed in human psychology by Carl Rogers and in psycho-spiritual terms by Leonardi.

Leonardi's chapter explores the health-giving—or not—view of the body and its care—or not—in the Christian tradition. He suggests that there has been a deep ambivalence towards physicality from the early days, associated with ascetical teachings and practice. This can be taken to extremes, and there can be a debate, echoing the one above, about what is seen as *challenge* or *damage*. These tendencies can also be seen to have continued into secular thinking at the Enlightenment, as Cartesian dualism and other Mind/Body dichotomies, which serve to elevate the intellect over the other bodily and sensory awarenesses. Ultimately, though, the Christian understanding of the body has to be deeply affirmative in the light of the central doctrines of *Incarnation, Resurrection* and *Divinization*. When the body can be affirmed and even trusted, the perspective on health and wellbeing can expand to embrace the Person-centred concepts of the *actualizing tendency* and *organismic awareness*. These translate in everyday terms as 'intuition' and 'gut instincts', and deserve much greater exploration by the scientific community:

> The affirmation of the body as a wider locus of awareness and understanding than that provided by the intellect alone has profound implications for the study of spirituality. The Western emphasis upon conceptual understanding can neglect this broader territory and its riches. Indeed, it can be suggested that it is only when the study of spirituality and religion embraces such an integrative approach that real understanding of these matters can develop.

Maraldi echoes the sense of a need for a continuing expansion and exploration of these themes into the future, and his words can serve to close this Introduction and offer a perspective on the works gathered here in terms of a broad-based project of future development:

> From a health-centred approach, the definition of spirituality in terms of individuation might help us to to take a broader picture of spirituality. The implications for health, while still important, become secondary, giving rise to new forms of research, aimed at understanding spirituality in other areas of human life. If spirituality is no longer the locus of wellbeing, what can it teach us about who we are and about the world we live in? This question is actually very old, and the many answers to it are scattered throughout different spiritual traditions around the world, but a scientific, theoretically sound understanding on this regard is still lacking. This is a challenge for the future.

Biographical Notes

Jeff Leonardi is a Person-centred Counsellor, Supervisor, Trainer and Spiritual Companion, and a retired Anglican priest who was for 17 years Bishop's Adviser for Pastoral Care and Counselling in the Lichfield Diocese of the Church of England. He has been a Person-centred Counsellor for the past 40 years and has a PhD in the spirituality of Person-centred Counselling in relation to Christian spirituality, and the implications for Christian ministry and pastoral practice. He is currently undertaking research into Relational Spirituality and is an Honorary Research Fellow of the Religious Experience Research Centre at the University of Wales Trinity Saint David at Lampeter.

Bettina E. Schmidt is professor of study of religions at the University of Wales Trinity Saint David and Director of the Alister Hardy Religious Experience Research Centre in Lampeter, UK. Her research area is anthropology of religion with special focus on Latin America, the Caribbean and its diaspora. Among her more recent publication is *Spirits and Trance in Brazil: An Anthropology of Religious Experience* (Bloomsbury 2016).

Note

1. A comment made, for instance, by Chamberlain and Hall in relation to Dale Matthews' book on the power of faith and religious commitment (see Chamberlain and Hall 2000, 4, referring to Matthews 1998).

Bibliography

Ager, A. and J. Ager. 2011. 'Faith and the Discourse of Secular Humanitarianism'. *Journal of Refugee Studies* 14 (3): 456–472. https://doi.org/10.1093/jrs/fer030

Bradburn, N. 1969. *The Structure of Psychological Well-being.* Chicago, IL: Aldine. https://doi.org/10.1037/t10756-000

Chamberlain, T. J. and C. A. Hall. 2000. *Realized Religion.* Philadelphia, PA: Templeton Foundation Press.

Dodge, R., A. Daly, J. Huyton and L. Sanders. 2012. The Challenge of Defining Wellbeing. *International Journal of Wellbeing* 2 (3): 222–235. https://doi.org/10.5502/ijw.v2i3.4

Foresight Mental Capital and Wellbeing Project. 2008. *Final Project Report*. London: The Government Office for Science.

Forgeard M. J. C. et al. 2011. 'Doing the right thing: Measuring well-being for public policy'. *International Journal of Well-being* 1 (1): 79–106. https://doi.org/10.5502/ijw.v1i1.15

Hadaway, C. K. and Roof, W. C. 1978. 'Religious Commitment and the Quality of Life in American Society'. *Review of Religious Research* 19 (3): 295–307. https://doi.org/10.2307/3510129

Hardy, A. 1979. *The Spiritual Nature of Man*. Oxford, UK: Clarendon Press.

Hay, D. 1987. *Exploring Inner Space: Is God Still Possible in the Twentieth Century?* Oxford, UK: Mowbray.

James, William. 1988. *Writings 1902-1910*. New York: Library of America.

Dalai Lama. 2011. *My Spiritual Autobiography*. London: Rider.

Leonardi, J. 2010. 'What We Are Meant to Be: Evolution as the Transformation of Consciousness'. In: *The Human Being Fully Alive: Writings in Celebration of Brian Thorne*, edited by J. Leonardi, 58–75. Monmouth, UK: PCCS Books.

Myers, D. and E. Diener. 1995. 'Who is Happy?'. *Psychological Science* 6 (1): 10–19. https://doi.org/10.1111/j.1467-9280.1995.tb00298.x

Rogers, Carl. 1961. *On Becoming a Person*. Boston, MA: Houghton Mifflin.

Rogers, Carl. 1980. *A Way of Being*. New York: Houghton Mifflin.

Ryff, C. D. 1989. 'Happiness is Everything, Or Is It? Explorations on the Meaning of Psychological Well-being'. *Journal of Personality and Social Psychology* 57: 1069–1081. https://doi.org/10.1037//0022-3514.57.6.1069

Schmidt, B. E. 2016. *Spirit and Trance in Brazil: Anthropology of Religious Experiences*. London: Bloomsbury.

Shin, D. and D. Johnson. 1978. 'Avowed Happiness as an Overall Assessment of the Quality of Life'. *Social Indicators Research* 5 (1): 475–492. https://doi.org/10.1007/BF00352944

Tambyah, S. K. and S. J. Tan. 2013. *Happiness and Wellbeing: The Singaporean Experience*. London: Routledge. https://doi.org/10.4324/9780203082089

Vieten, C. and S. Scammell. 2015. *Spiritual and Religious Competencies in Clinical Practice: Guidelines for Psychotherapists and Clinical Professionals*. Oakland, CA: New Harbinger.

White, S. C. 2016a. 'Preface'. In: *Cultures of Wellbeing: Method, Place, Policy*, edited by S. C. White with C. Blackmore, xi–xiv. Basingstoke, UK: Palgrave Macmillan.

White, S. C. 2016b. 'Introduction: The Many Faces of Wellbeing'. In: *Cultures of Wellbeing: Method, Place, Policy*, edited by S. C. White with C. Blackmore, 1–44. Basingstoke, UK: Palgrave Macmillan. https://doi.org/10.1057/9781137536457_1

Woods, R. 2008. *Wellness: Life, Health and Spirituality*. Dublin, Ireland: Veritas Publications.

World Health Organization. 1948. *Constitution of the World Health Organization*. New York.

Section One:
Setting the Scene

Chapter 1

Spirituality and Wellbeing: Is There a Necessary Link? Toward a Critical Approach to the Study of Spirituality

Everton de Oliveira Maraldi

The notion of spirituality has gained widespread popularity and scholarly attention in recent decades as an expression of several factors combined, including the emergence of more individualized forms of faith, a diverse and constantly changing religious market, and greater emphasis on the personal experience of the sacred rather than on traditional beliefs, practices and rituals (Carrette and King 2005; Roof 1999). Today, organized religion is no longer the main holder of power over the discourse of the sacred; it is the individual who determines much of the characteristics of his/her relationship with whatever he/she might call transcendence by consuming and mixing various beliefs and practices and forming in this way his/her own spiritual *bricolage*, either as a member of a religious community or not. Some individuals now define themselves as 'spiritual', rather than religious, while others consider themselves as both spiritual *and* religious, or even religious *but not* spiritual (Zinnbauer et al. 1997). The demarcation between religiousness and spirituality is a much-debated issue and for the most part unresolved in the psychological literature (Willard and Norenzayan 2017; Zinnbauer and Pargament 2005).

Spirituality has been defined in many ways, including meaning in life, inner peace and harmony, feelings of hopefulness, or having transcendent experiences. Such definitions are so broad and varied in content that it is sometimes difficult to specify what exactly spirituality is (Lindeman, Blomqvist and Takada 2012). Broad definitions might be useful in everyday life and even in clinical practice. They provide individuals with a wide range of options to describe and make sense of their experiences and worldviews. However, such a variability is usually problematic in scientific research. To design a study, analyze data, share and discuss their findings, scientists must rely on objective definitions, and this is true also of concepts such as wellbeing and quality of life, which involve a good dose of subjectivity. But despite many attempts to conceptualize spirituality in a clear, scientific manner, there still exists a fair amount of divergence among researchers. Many agree, however, that definitions based on wellbeing concepts tend to tautological results, especially when measures of spirituality and mental health are positively correlated, since spirituality is conceived as inherently beneficial (Koenig 2011; Lindeman, Blomqvist and Takada 2012; Lindeman 2014).

A large and growing body of research highlights the positive effects of spirituality on mental health. In these investigations, spirituality is usually described as serving an important protective function against a series of psychopathological conditions, from substance abuse to depression and suicide attempts (Balboni and Peteet 2017; Bonelli and Koenig 2013). Based on such evidence, researchers and health organizations outlined the importance of taking patients' spiritual needs into consideration as part of a broader approach to wellbeing in clinical practice (Moreira-Almeida et al. 2016; VanderWeele, Balboni and Koh 2017). There is some controversy, however, as to the generalizability of this relationship (e.g., King et al. 2013), with some studies showing it depends on how spirituality is defined and measured (e.g., Migdal and Macdonald 2013). More investigations are also needed to understand the precise mechanisms by which spirituality impacts mental health. Although some studies suggest a causal direct influence, the findings may still be subject to unmeasured factors and confounders (Maraldi 2018).

In this chapter, I propose to define spirituality mainly in terms of individual religiousness and a secularized search for transcendence, independently of wellbeing and mental health. I start by briefly outlining some of the historical underpinnings of the concept of spirituality, as well as the contemporary terminological controversies surrounding it, with emphasis on the psychological literature. In a second section, I review and critically discuss the findings of other researchers, as well as of research I have carried out in Brazil in order to demonstrate that spirituality is not necessarily a matter of wellbeing, but that its relationship with mental health may be more complex than generally assumed. I also present evidence indicating that some popular spiritual practices, such as meditation, may involve important side effects besides their reported benefits, a relevant issue which is often left out of the picture when spiritual practices are scientifically investigated or recommended by clinicians. Most studies have concentrated their attention on the health benefits of meditation, thereby ignoring the occasions on which it did not work properly or even caused harm (Farias and Wilkhom 2015). It is of fundamental importance to recognize that there is a 'dark side' of spirituality which needs to be integrated if we want to take full advantage of spirituality's healing potential.

In my view, the main reason why spirituality is so frequently associated (both in the psychological literature and outside academia) with wellbeing and mental health has to do with a legitimization strategy. In this secularized, scientific and technological era in which we live, religion has become an expression of conservatism and regression, a pale simulacrum of the 'real' and direct experience of the divine. For many individuals in our society, the word 'religion' carries a long history of intolerance, irrationality and sectarianism, and is something with which they understandably do not feel comfortable to be associated. In a world in which the value of things is placed more on their practical implications than on their existential importance, the relationship with whatever we might call the sacred tends to be measured by its reported benefits to psychological and physical health, rather than by any metaphysical criterion. As I shall argue, the relationship between spirituality and wellbeing is but an expression of more profound changes in contemporary religiousness. In an era in which organized religions are no longer the main sources of cultural values and meanings, and in which metaphysical speculations concerning a transcendent reality are discouraged by science and technology, it is not surprising to find that spirituality has been reduced to abstract notions such as 'purpose in life' or 'feelings of inner peace'.

Contrary to what some readers might think at this point, I am not an antagonist of spirituality, a dogmatic sceptic eager to demonstrate his arguments. What I actually intend here is to help raise the scientific debate about modern spirituality to another level by showing how the emphasis on wellbeing has diverted us from the purposes for which spiritual practices and traditions were initially developed. In its very essence, spirituality might be best defined as a quest for self-knowledge, a quest toward finding our place in this world (which includes our relationship with others), but which is often portrayed simplistically by self-help as a harmless and 'make it yourself' product one can buy to achieve happiness and wellbeing (Carrette and King 2005). This spiritual quest may sometimes involve therapeutic benefits, but challenges and difficulties comprise an essential part of the spiritual growth process as well. I define spiritual growth in terms of the Jungian concept of individuation (Jung 1933, 1969), that is, the challenging but rewarding path in the search for who we are, a proposition I address in more detail later in the chapter.

In reviewing the huge amount of scientific data on spirituality, it became inevitable to mention technical, psychological concepts, which some of the readers may not be familiar with. However, I have tried to explain these concepts succinctly, as far as possible. A number of bibliographical references have also been cited in support of the definitions presented here. I hope the reader will bear with me as I review and discuss some of the many findings related to spirituality and wellbeing in an attempt to integrate the available scientific knowledge about this topic, defend my central argument and propose pathways for future investigations.

Spirituality as Disguised Religiousness?

Before reviewing the literature on spirituality and wellbeing in more detail, it is important, first, to explicate my understanding of spirituality and its implications for research on wellbeing and mental health. To me, the polyvalent functions of modern 'spirituality' (source of meaning, wellbeing, spiritual or mystical experiences etc.) resemble a layered construction, reflecting different and complex changes in the West's religious landscape over the last two centuries. One crucial change was undoubtedly the importance that people began to attribute to their own spiritual experiences to the detriment of what the religious tradition exhorted. William James ([1902] 2002) was certainly the most successful in characterizing this shift of perspective from the collective to the individual when he defined religion as the 'feelings, acts and experiences of individual men in their solitude, so far as they apprehend themselves to stand in relation to whatever they may consider the divine'. (pp. 29–30).

Reports of mystical or spiritual experiences follow human civilization for centuries, comprising an essential feature of different religious traditions (Wulff 2014). But partly due to the privatization of religion in Western societies, we began to look at those reports of extraordinary phenomena through the lens of the individual; hence the emphasis on 'experiences' rather than on a definite corpus of collective beliefs and dogmas. This was due to a long process of historical transformations, from the search for a more direct relationship with the divine in Pentecostalism and the Charismatic Movement, without the necessary and irrevocable intermediation of a priest, to counterculture and the New Age movement which exhorted a direct experience of the transcendent through a series of practices and psychedelic substances. More recently, psychologists became masters in 'exorcizing' the more metaphysical aspects of these experiences in favour of their neurophysiological, cognitive and personality correlates. The rise of popular attention devoted to practices such as meditation and mindfulness in the last decade (even if without the assumption of mysticism) suggests that this shift from the collective to the individual, from a sacralized to a secular conception of the spiritual, has partly become culturally mainstream.

This shift also determined some important terminological changes. Instead of just using 'religious' experience, researchers from many branches of psychology began to develop their own technical, secular definitions to account for experiences previously understood as belonging almost exclusively to the realms of magical, mystical or religious beliefs, such as 'parapsychological' (Rhine and Pratt 1957), 'transpersonal' (Sutich 1968), 'exceptional' (White 1997) and even 'anomalous' (Cardeña, Lynn and Krippner 2014). One of these definitions is indeed 'spiritual experience' (Underwood 2006). More recently, Walach (2015) directly referred to a 'secular spirituality'.

Despite their secular, non-religious tone, these are all different names, different expressions for virtually the same things. This becomes clearer when we look at the empirical evidence. In a survey with a representative sample of more than one thousand Americans, Steensland, Wang and Schmidt (2018) found, for example, that when people were asked to describe what the term spirituality meant to them, the responses focused on categories related to theism (higher being, deity), with only a relatively small percentage of participants offering exclusively immanent descriptions.

This finding is consistent with the results of a series of other investigations. Religious and spiritual (but not religious) individuals typically share a host of beliefs such as the idea of an afterlife and the effectiveness of different forms of spiritual healing, even though the interpretation given to these experiences may vary (Flannely et al. 2006; Goode 2000). In the Bible, for example, we find numerous accounts of exceptional or extraordinary events that could be labelled as paranormal (i.e., scientifically unexplained or 'fringe' phenomena), such as premonition dreams and spontaneous, anomalous cures (Sparks 2001).

A number of studies indicate that concepts of spirituality overlap considerably with New Age religiosity and paranormal beliefs (e.g., Farias, Claridge and Lalljee 2005; Willard and Norenzayan 2017). In a study conducted by Lindeman and colleagues (Lindeman 2014), paranormal beliefs were much better predictors of spirituality than constructs such as wellbeing and purpose in life. Similarly, MacDonald (2000) found paranormal beliefs to be one of the main dimensions underlying different measures of spirituality, a finding that proved to be consistent across different cultures (MacDonald et al. 2015). After reviewing a series of investigations on paranormal, superstitious, magical and religious beliefs, Lindeman and Svedholm (2012) concluded that they all share some of the same basic cognitive characteristics, and suggested researchers to integrate current lines of research.

This does not mean that there are no important differences between traditional religious believers and the followers of more alternative spiritualities. As a matter of fact, research has identified both commonalities and distinctions, either regarding the endorsement of specific beliefs or in terms of their psychological profile (e.g., Schofield et al. 2016). But some authors have suggested that, instead of differing significantly from religious beliefs, spirituality and New Age ideas are in great part substitutes for traditional religiosity (Persinger and Makarec 1990), or just one step on the path between religion and non-religion (Marshall and Olson 2018). From this perspective, the criterion to define spirituality resides much more in certain historical and cultural transformations of Western religiosity, than in a presumed universal, a-historical and unique set of characteristics.

The Many Meanings of Spirituality

In the inglorious pursuit to find a coherent definition for spirituality in our secular world, some researchers wondered whether individuals who display no religious interests would still present some form of spirituality. Are atheists and agnostics spiritual in some sense? This question has raised much controversy because it seemed to attribute atheists a characteristic that they might not use to define themselves.

In a survey I have carried out with 1450 Brazilian respondents from more than 20 Brazilian states (Maraldi 2014), interesting commonalities (as well as differences) between religious and spiritual (but not religious) believers emerged from the findings. One of the aims of the study was to investigate the extent to which religious believers differed from spiritual participants and self-proclaimed atheists and agnostics in a series of psychological variables, including their self-reported levels of spirituality. As one could expect, spiritual individuals presented lower levels of church attendance when compared to religious believers (that is, individuals who defined themselves as members of a religion) but did not differ substantially in terms of frequency of spiritual practice (such as prayer, meditation or rituals): 29.2% of religious participants reported practicing on a daily basis against 29.5% of spiritual individuals.

A significant percentage (32.9%) of religious believers, as well as spiritual but not religious participants (21.2%) agreed with the statement 'I have a spirituality based on the search for an integration of different religions and philosophies. I believe there is some truth in all of them'. Interestingly, a non-negligible percentage of religious believers (19.8%) also agreed with the statement 'I have a spirituality independent of religion', although this item seemed much more appropriate to spiritual individuals (in fact, 28.2% of the latter chose this option). Atheists/agnostics, on the other hand, were more likely to choose the statements 'Life has no definite meaning' (43.6%) and 'I'm just not sure about my perspective on religious or philosophical issues' (3.8%) when compared to the other two groups.

The above results reflect some important cultural characteristics. The phenomenon of multiple religious belonging, which occurs when the same individual has more than one religion or attends different religious contexts is well known in Brazil. Based on this characteristic, it is not surprising to find that a significant percentage of religious believers agree that there is some truth in all religions and that they could be integrated into one and the same perspective. As an example, Umbanda (a Brazilian mediumistic religion) is based on the complex syncretism of Indigenous, Christian, African, Spiritualist and Esoteric beliefs. Similarly, it is also not surprising to find that some religious believers might have a 'spirituality independent of religion', since the fact that they are members of a religious group do not necessary imply that they believe only in the teachings of that particular group or religion.

What all these results seem to reveal is that spirituality might not be a monolithic, universal concept with which a person may or may not agree, may or may not hold. Individuals from different groups or cultures will probably interpret spirituality differently, which bears important implications for research on the relationship between spirituality and wellbeing. Indeed, after testing the universality of spirituality across eight different countries and languages, MacDonald et al. (2015) identified some similarities, but also significant measurement invariance. The authors thus concluded that:

> ... spirituality is not a concept that 'transcends' culture and holds a firm universality of meaning. Rather, it seems the opposite holds true; the specific meaning ascribed to spirituality appears to be intrinsically bound by culture and cannot be fully understood without consideration given to cultural factors. That is, while there are similarities, spirituality is not the same across cultures. (MacDonald et al. 2015, 32)

Based on this general conclusion, MacDonald et al. (2015) argued that the psychological benefits of spirituality might be best viewed in terms of how a person perceives and appraises his/her quality of life as manifested in subjective wellbeing, a process which might differ according to the cultural context and one's own functioning and psychological predispositions. More investigations employing a cross-cultural methodology are urgently needed to test this interesting assumption.

Our finding (Maraldi 2014) that more than one third of Brazilian atheists and agnostics see life as deprived of any particular meaning (and, consequently, of 'spirituality', at least according to some definitions based on meaning and purpose in life) raises an important question: is spirituality really a matter of wellbeing? If yes, would non-spiritual (or less spiritual) individuals report lower wellbeing?

Spirituality and its Discontents

Despite substantial evidence supporting a positive relationship between spirituality and wellbeing indicators, there are also divergent findings. Lindeman, Blomqvist and Takada (2012), for example, were unable to find an association of spirituality with mental or physical health, social relationships and satisfaction in marriage or work, although significant correlations emerged for purpose in life and feelings of inner peace during spiritual experiences. King et al. (2013), on their turn, found spiritual individuals to be more vulnerable to a series of psychopathological indicators and conditions, from drug dependence to anxiety disorders. These participants were more likely to take psychotropic medication and to present a neurotic disorder. More importantly, they significantly differed from both traditional religious believers and those who were neither religious nor spiritual. These findings contradict the more positive results from other studies and indicate that people with a spiritual understanding of life in the absence of a religious framework might evidence worse mental health.

King's study had an important methodological advantage: it included a group of neither religious nor spiritual participants. Indeed, a usual methodological gap in most psychological studies of spirituality is the absence of appropriate comparison groups. While much attention has been devoted in the last decades to the relationship between spirituality, religiousness and mental health, few studies have attempted to investigate the coping capacity and wellbeing of non-religious or non-spiritual people, such as atheists and agnostics. As we have seen, these individuals do not necessarily attribute a definite or special meaning to life events and do not usually define themselves as 'spiritual' (Maraldi 2014). To evaluate the extent to which spirituality is indicative of mental health, it is important to include individuals holding strong secular worldviews (Beit-Hallahmi 2007; Zuckerman, Galen and Pasquale 2016). Studies involving only spiritual or religious participants run the risk of providing a false image; they may suggest that believers are healthier when, in fact, they do not differ significantly from those who do not hold a spiritual understanding of life.

Measures of widespread use are characteristically biased toward certain types of beliefs—e.g., Christian—thus covering a very limited range of supernatural and religious worldviews. Individuals scoring low on such scales may not necessarily be irreligious, but simply non-Christians. Similarly, individuals with low religiosity (as measured by psychological scales) may not be irreligious in the sense of atheists or other individuals holding strong secular beliefs; quite the contrary, they could be non-affiliate religious believers, or even religious individuals facing a crisis of faith or other religious and spiritual problems (Lukoff, Lu and Turner 1992). In this scenario, their differences from other religious or spiritual participants could be misleadingly assumed to represent evidence of a direct influence of spirituality on health, when in fact they just highlight the importance of an individual being committed with his/her system of values or worldview, be it metaphysical or secular (Hwang, Hammer and Cragun 2011; Zuckerman, Galen and Pasquale 2016).

Zuckerman (2009) examined a series of studies investigating the psychological profile of atheists and agnostics and found large variation in the results. While some investigations showed that spiritual and religious people are better able to cope with adverse life situations, overcome depression, and report happiness or wellbeing, other studies showed atheists were equally likely to present such characteristics. In fact, in two experimental investigations, Farias et al. (2013) found that belief in science was as effective against stress and anxiety as spiritual beliefs.

Hwang (2009) carried out a qualitative investigation with 15 atheists presenting spinal cord injury (eight men and seven women) with the aim of investigating their coping strategies, that is, the ways through which they cope with their medical condition. Contrary to what was expected, participants generally reported no change in their notion of spirituality after the accident that caused the injury, and some even claimed that their atheism and disbelief had been strengthened by this situation. Some of the respondents have found meaning in their own secular conceptions, referring, for example, to evolutionism and to the survival of our species. Others have found meaning in their families and in the education of their children. But there were also some interviewees who simply attributed no meaning or purpose to their lives. Some other participants developed a very individual perspective, finding strength in their own internal resources.

Wilkinson and Coleman (2010) reported the results of interviews carried out with two groups of 60-year-old British participants. The first group consisted of 11 strongly atheistic people, while the second group was composed of 8 people with strong religious beliefs. The purpose was to investigate the role of both belief systems (religious and secular) in coping with difficulties and losses associated with the ageing process. The results revealed that, regardless of the belief system to which the interviewees subscribed, both groups had developed adequate coping strategies in face of the ageing process. The authors concluded that more important than the content or the type of belief is having a solid and coherent belief system to face different adverse life situations. In this sense, the subscription to a strong system of secular beliefs can be as beneficial as the assumption of a religious or spiritual belief system.

In the survey with Brazilian respondents mentioned earlier (Maraldi 2014), I have also compared the three groups (religious believers, spiritual individuals and atheists/agnostics) in a series of psychopathological indicators. What I found was that the groups did not significantly differ in terms of depressive symptoms and reports of childhood trauma. In the cases in which a difference was statistically significant, it was the religious and spiritual participants who presented the worse indicators: they scored significantly higher than atheists/agnostics in reports of dissociative symptoms (such as depersonalization episodes, auditory hallucinations and alterations in the sense of self) and psychosomatic and stress symptoms.

Although one might suspect that atheists purposefully reported fewer symptoms, perhaps with the aim of reflecting a positive image of themselves, the same pattern would be expected for the depressive symptoms and childhood trauma memories, which was not confirmed. Moreover, if this argument is valid, it should be equally applied to spiritual and religious believers in the case of studies in which a positive association between spirituality and health was observed. The tendency of some participants to provide socially expected responses is a methodological problem variously called 'response bias' or 'social desirability bias'—a topic about which I have written elsewhere (Maraldi 2018). However, the fact is that the existing research does not seem to support a strong influence of response bias on the relationship between spirituality and mental health, so this explanation would not be entirely feasible to explain our previous findings concerning atheists and agnostics (unless we had reasons to doubt atheists' sincerity in providing their responses to psychological scales). In any case, this remains a relevant issue for future studies, especially given the usual lack of control for such confounders (Maraldi 2018).

In a second study conducted two years later, in 2016, I compared three groups of participants: spiritual but not religious individuals, atheists and agnostics (Maraldi 2017). Instead of just combining atheists and agnostics in the same group, I decided to separate them, since many studies show that the nonreligious are not a homogenous group but tend to differ from each other in relation to a series of demographic and psychological characteristics (Zuckerman, Galen and Pasquale 2016). Some of the same psychopathological variables evaluated in the previous investigation were included (in order to check if the previous findings would hold true for a new sample of respondents), but two other measures were added: one evaluating existential anxiety toward death and the other assessing self-esteem. Given that spirituality is usually regarded as an important source of wellbeing and meaning in life, I hypothesized that spiritual participants would score higher on self-esteem while scoring lower on death anxiety and psychopathological symptoms when compared with atheists and agnostics. Finally, a measure of social desirability was added to the battery of questionnaires to check if participants would minimize or omit negative characteristics, such as psychopathological symptoms, as speculated above.

Atheists obtained the highest mean score on the Rosenberg Self-Esteem Scale (Rosenberg 1965) when compared to the other groups. No difference was found between the agnostics and the spiritual individuals in terms of self-esteem. Self-esteem evidenced a positive, small correlation with social desirability ($r = .23$, $p < .001$), but the statistical control of desirability did not eliminate the significant difference between groups ($p < .05$). The groups also did not differ in terms of social desirability. The group which most reported existential anxiety toward death was the group of agnostics. There was no significant difference between atheists and spirituals in death anxiety.

In relation to the psychopathological indicators, a curious gradation between groups was observed for dissociative symptoms (i.e., alterations in the sense of identity and in the perception of the environment): spiritual participants scored higher than both agnostics and atheists, but agnostics scored higher than atheists. No difference was found between groups in reports of childhood trauma. The statistical control of social desirability did not change the obtained findings.

Overall, our findings present a more complicated picture than the 'spirituality equals wellbeing' hypothesis implies. None of our initial expectations were confirmed: instead, the results evidenced some interesting nuances between the groups of spiritual and non-spiritual participants. First, irreligious individuals are not a homogeneous group, as other authors have correctly remarked, and they may differ from each other in terms of psychological characteristics, such as self-esteem. Secondly, spiritual individuals are not necessarily more protected against psychopathological symptoms (such as dissociative experiences). It must be stressed, however, that dissociative experiences are not always viewed as pathological, and may occur as part of cultural activities such as religious rituals (Maraldi et al. 2017). The discussion of whether certain experiences really deserve the label of 'pathological' is of fundamental importance to the study of the relationship between spirituality and wellbeing. The study of spiritual experiences could shed light on the nature of diverse psychological processes which psychiatrists and psychologists have hitherto investigated from an almost exclusively psychopathological perspective.

In any case, we must take into consideration not only our findings with Brazilian respondents, but also other investigations reviewed above, such as King's study, which clearly suggest that some spiritual individuals are indeed more vulnerable to a series of psychopathological indicators (see also Menezes-Júnior, Alminhana and Moreira-Almeida 2012). Could spiritual practices be part of the explanation? Could they induce negative experiences?

The Dark Side of Meditation

Meditation is a widely known and highly used spiritual practice in our contemporary society. While historically meditation only had spiritual applications, recently it has been applied in a more secular, self-realization or self-help form (Perez-De-Albeniz and Holmes 2000). A recent study estimated that 8% of the US adult population uses these techniques and the current popular climate is filled with reports and studies lauding meditation, particularly in terms of its perceived benefits for increasing health and wellbeing (Creswell et al. 2014). Even the famous atheist Sam Harris attested to the psychological benefits of meditation in his book *Waking Up: A Guide to Spirituality Without Religion* (Harris 2014).

Although meditation techniques have many adherents, and all have certain claims to health benefits, some questions still remain. Currently, the literature on the adverse effects of meditation is scarce, though some exists—and what exists is concerning. For example, studies have shown that different meditation techniques could result in hallucinations (Nakaya and Ohmori 2010), suicidal attempts (Lazarus 1976), visual or auditory aberrations and unusual somatic experiences (Kornfield 1979).

Probably the first systematic investigation of the prevalence, duration and intensity of adverse effects of meditation was the study by Otis (1984). This was the continuation of a paper published in *Psychology Today*, where Otis (1974) had already reported some of the complaints of mental and physical distressing he received from people practising Transcendental Meditation (TM). For his second study, he re-examined the data from a survey conducted with members of the Students International Meditation Society (SIMS), one of the major organizations at the time for spreading the Maharishi Mahesh Yogi's teachings. Additionally, he included data from another sample of novice and experienced meditators that were receiving training to become teachers. One of Otis's hypotheses was that dropouts would report more adverse effects than those who kept practising meditation, but what he found was that dropouts claimed significantly fewer complaints than more experienced meditators. This finding seemed to indicate that they were not just the result of difficulties or challenges faced during the initial practice of meditation.

The differences between beginners and experienced meditators were highly consistent and 'were suggestive of people who had become anxious, confused, frustrated, depressed, and/or withdrawn (or more so) since starting TM' (Otis 1984, 203). Another interesting finding was that, independently of years of practice, teacher trainees matched SIMS experienced meditators in their claimed adverse effects. For Otis, the data suggested not only that adverse reactions tend to increase the longer a person practises meditation, but also that 'the more committed a person becomes to TM as way of life (as indicated by the teacher trainee group), the greater the likelihood that he or she will experience adverse effects' (Otis 1984, 204).

Some years further, in a replication and extension of Otis' study, Shapiro (1992) was able to find similar results working with a small sample. But this time, adverse effects were assessed both retrospectively and prospectively. 62.9% of the subjects reported at least one adverse effect at one of the three assessment periods. Two subjects decided to stop meditating because of the symptoms. In a way very similar to Otis' findings, participants at time three reported the higher frequency of adverse effects (75%). The same relationship found by Otis between length of practice and report of adverse effects was observed. But Otis and Shapiro were not alone in their findings. In a sample of 1081 university students (of which 221 had undergone meditation training), Persinger (1993) also identified a 'dose-dependence' relationship: those who practised meditation more frequently and for a longer time were also more likely to report adverse events.

The studies summarized above usually comprised samples of TM adherents, but comparable results were obtained for other types of meditation. In his phenomenological investigation of vipassana meditation, Kornfield (1979) aimed to catalogue and map the frequency and patterns of the meditative experience among participants of intensive meditation retreats and a comparison group of non-retreat meditation students who practised only one or two hours per day. The results revealed a broad range of meditative experiences, such as strong emotional variations and mood swings, altered bodily sensations, fear and tension, agitation and anger, restlessness, nightmares and anxious thoughts. Although unusual, some of the reported experiences were apparently positive or neutral, such as colour perception changes across the visual field or visions of Buddha or Christ. Analyses of follow-up questionnaires showed that many of these effects had a short duration, and simply disappeared sometime after the retreats, but many participants reported having experienced difficulties integrating back to their daily lives. When compared with participants of intensive retreats, the comparison group reported fewer and less intense unusual experiences.

Although many individuals reporting adverse events related to meditation practice show no history of psychiatric complications, there were cases in which socioeconomic and family problems could partially account for the onset of symptoms and the search for meditation as a way to obtain relief or to find a solution for personal difficulties (Chan-Ob and Boonyanaruthee 1999; Kuijpers et al. 2007; VanderKooi 1997). Notwithstanding, Nakaya and Ohmori (2010) remind us that whereas psychosocial stressors may play an important role, the meditation could function as a 'trigger' by providing the absorptive state necessary for symptoms such as hallucinations and delusions to emerge.

The adverse effects of meditation were also revealed to be 'democratic' in what concerns gender and cultural background, affecting both men and women, Western and Eastern meditators (Chan-ob and Boonyanaruthee 1999; Nakaya and Ohmori 2010). In some of the studies (such as the ones by Otis and Shapiro), participants had to report the frequency of potential side effects of meditation using a questionnaire developed for that purpose. But in the studies by Kornfield (1979) and Lomas et al. (2015), participants commented on these experiences spontaneously, as the researchers did not ask them to recall either positive or negative events related to meditation.

It is unclear whether these events are always viewed by the meditators as negative or undesirable. Part of the unusual perceptions experienced by meditators are sometimes viewed as innocuous or inoffensive (Kornfield 1979). Lomas et al. (2015) noted that some of the interviewees in their study had quit meditation as a result of adverse effects, and one even turned to therapy in order to deal with the disturbing emotions provoked by meditative practice. On the other hand, participants also highlighted the positive effects of meditation and viewed negative emotions and experiences as challenges which are ultimately beneficial.

In the collection of cases presented by Castillo (1990) some individuals did not report any significant impairment, and some have indeed observed an improvement of performance in their social and occupational functioning after starting meditation. Their depersonalization experiences following meditation were not necessarily viewed as pathological or disturbing. For Castillo (1990) the negative or positive implications of such experiences depend to a great extent on the interpretations and meanings attributed to them:

> [...] the relative lack of reported anxiety in response to the depersonalization is a result of the ideational construction of the experiences in terms consistent with the mythic model of TM [Transcendental Meditation]. In other words, instead of "pathologizing" the experiences – that is, interpreting them as psychopathology according to the medical model of reality – they are "sacralizing" the experiences. (Castillo 1990, 167)

Castillo (1990) also mentions the fact that, for some meditators, what is initially a side effect of meditation may become a long-term or permanent characteristic of the individual. Over the years, some of his patients became so accustomed to the perceptual alterations and lack of emotionality that characterized their depersonalization episodes following meditation that they no longer found them uncomfortable or disturbing. Now, these experiences were a fundamental part of their psychological make-up, and they could feel confused if the depersonalization temporarily ceased.

There are also cases in which participants do not show any apparent sign of abnormality, nor complain of any adverse event, but their physiology seems to indicate otherwise. In the Creswell et al. (2014) study, the students exposed to the mindfulness training reported lower psychological stress compared to the control group, but their cortisol levels actually increased. Some of the studies reviewed were designed specifically to assess different adverse effects of meditation, but other investigators (such as Creswell et al.) identified them unintentionally. This suggests that evidence of adverse effects may sometimes be covert or mixed with the potential benefits of meditation.

The specific mechanisms by which meditation generates alterations in perception and other psychological and somatic negative events still deserve a detailed investigation. Despite substantial variation across studies, some authors have attempted to develop integrative hypotheses to explain adverse reactions. One of the first attempts can be defined here as the *amplification hypothesis*, according to which meditation amplifies underlying psychological or physiological vulnerabilities. This idea was defended by, among others, Walsh and Roche (1979) whose cases seemed to suggest that the side effects observed (e.g., psychotic symptoms) were more related to the intensity of meditation and other extraneous factors (such as a history of Schizophrenia) than to the meditative practice itself. This hypothesis may well account for part of the results obtained, but it is untenable when considered as a general explanation, given that many individuals claiming adverse reactions showed no psychiatric or psychological problems before practising meditation. The moderate to high prevalence of adverse effects among meditators (Cebolla et al. 2017; Kornfield, 1979; Lindahl et al. 2017; Otis 1984; Persinger 1993; Shapiro 1992) tends also to contradict the amplification hypothesis, as one would have to assume that *all* these individuals had prior vulnerabilities.

A second hypothesis suggested by the meditators themselves defines meditation as part of a *process of personal growth* (Kornfield 1979). Meditation would make a person more aware of his or her problems, and also more willing to report and confront them. This process would involve manifestations of 'unstressing', that is, an initial and transient condition during which non-resolved difficulties and repressed contents tend to emerge and are dealt with (Otis 1984). This hypothesis assumes that adverse effects are initial barriers or difficulties in the process of personal growth which will naturally disappear over time (Walsh 1984). But contrary to the prediction, the studies reviewed showed that adverse events could last for many years, have sometimes incorporated into an individual's personality and have increased (instead of decreased) over time, with experienced meditators and teachers reporting them more often and more intensely than beginners and dropouts.

A third hypothesis developed to explain the adverse effects of meditation is the *relaxation-induced anxiety hypothesis* (Heide and Borkovec 1983), according to which relaxation techniques (such as meditation) may paradoxically initiate or exacerbate anxiety in certain individuals. The mechanisms by which this adverse reaction occur are still poorly understood, but the evidence suggests that meditation indeed shares many of the characteristics of other relaxation techniques—that is why it is so difficult to come up with a placebo for meditation (Farias and Wikholm 2015). Anxiety responses could explain part of the adverse events reported by meditators, such as muscle tension, sleeplessness, and even certain physiological reactions indicative of stress, such as increases in heart rate and blood pressure. Anxiety could also have an indirect impact on episodes of depression and depersonalization. However, it is unclear whether other symptoms claimed by meditators could be explained away by anxiety, such as hallucinations, psychotic-like behaviour and interpersonal difficulties. While similar in terms of their outcomes, meditation and relaxation may differ in the mechanisms by which they promote relaxation responses (Jain et al. 2007) and, consequently, relaxation-induced anxiety. In this sense, part of the adverse events reported could derive from processes that are exclusive of meditation, requiring further investigation. Finally, it is unclear whether this theory could account for more than a minority of individuals with particular susceptibility to relaxation-induced anxiety.

The above hypotheses tend to emphasize one or more aspects of the reported adverse effects, ignoring factors of equal (or even more) importance. But a fourth hypothesis that can be advanced here is what I call the self-boundaries *hypothesis*. I argue that meditation promotes a modification of self-boundaries which can be appraised as negative. According to this view, meditation would be better defined as a technique of self-knowledge that does not necessarily strengthen the ego, but, on the contrary, tears it down. In a way similar to the *growth process hypothesis*, I maintain that the adverse effects of meditation are related to the self-knowledge it provides, but not in a linear fashion, as if such effects would necessarily extinguish over time. These symptoms should be considered as permanent challenges to be faced along the process, and may be reported at any moment, especially by those highly involved with meditation. That is why intensive retreats and unguided meditation tend to be hazardous for some individuals (Kennedy 1976). It follows from this that some level of psychological strength is a pre-requisite for practising meditation, and not exactly its main (or exclusive) goal.

Spirituality as Individuation: Toward a Critical Approach to Spirituality

All this discussion around the strength of the empirical evidence for the psychological benefits and harms of spirituality is necessary, but only if we manage to integrate scientific knowledge into everyday life. The excessive focus on the medical and psychological data might have actually contributed to lead us away from a deeper understanding of spirituality. The religious and philosophical traditions whereby meditation techniques have developed were more concerned with their potential to redefine our presuppositions and beliefs about the self and the world around us than with any therapeutic effect that could arise from their practice (Farias and Wikholm 2015). These techniques were initially developed with the purpose of dissolving and transcending the ego, and not 'normalizing' it. The psychotic symptoms and depersonalization experiences reported by some meditators are examples of this assertion. Individuals interested in contemplative and spiritual exercises should be informed about the risks involved in their practice, including long-term alterations in their sense of identity.

Rather than wellbeing, I suggest *individuation* as our reference category when discussing the beneficial implications of spirituality. The concept of individuation was proposed by the Swiss psychiatrist Carl Gustav Jung (1875–1961) to designate the developmental process by which we give access to our potentials, while, at the same time, strengthening our identities and establishing a mature relationship with others. Our main task in life, in Jung's view, is, on the one hand, to actualize our extensive common humanity, and, on the other, to become differentiated from everybody else. The goal of individuation is thus to expand the *ego* (our personal identity, the conscious personality) into what Jung calls the *self*, the personality in its wholeness, conscious and unconscious.

To Jung, the self is wider than the ego. In the 'self' reside many of our still undeveloped potentials, as well as other aspects we fear about ourselves or might want to avoid altogether. Individuation, however, is not just something we choose, it is not entirely under our control. It is a natural, imperative process we all must face, in one way or another. It is both satisfying and uncomfortable, enjoyable and annoying, blissful and terrifying, as life itself.

Although the individuation process is relatively unique to each person, Jung believed that the many religious and spiritual traditions offered some important shortcuts and tips of general value to help us along the way. Religious symbols and rituals represent some of the main challenges in the individuation process, while pointing, at the same time, to some possible solutions. According to Jung, the excessive development of the ego, however, uprooted us from the natural processes of the psyche that could assist us in the journey of self-knowledge. A diffuse, individualistic and utilitarian spirituality took place, an impoverished form of religiousness without religion, of ephemeral access to the transcendent without sacrifice, frustration or altruism (Carrette and King 2005). It was this change in the way we deal with individuation that made it possible to think of spirituality more in terms of its practical implications, rather than its wider philosophical or existential consequences. It also influenced the way we study spirituality, a research area marked by the focus on health issues rather than on the social, cognitive and emotional factors underlying the many types of religious or spiritual involvement in contemporary society.

An important factor implicated in what I call the 'health-centred' approach to spirituality is the eminently aphilosophical nature of most research carried out in contemporary psychology and psychiatry. Profound, sensible issues such as 'meaning and purpose in life', 'wellbeing', or 'transcendence' are reduced without ceremony to brief, impoverished statements to which a respondent should express his/her level of agreement or disagreement based on multiple choices or Likert-type scales. This does not mean that such methods should not be employed to study spirituality and other psychological constructs, but the findings obtained in this way would require a much more contextualized, critical and thorough discussion than usually observed in the literature. The fact is that the ethical and philosophical implications of research on spirituality are rarely or poorly addressed. Unlike many of the founding fathers of the mental health area, such as Sigmund Freud (1856–1939), William James (1842–1910) and Carl Jung, whose theories were sustained on sophisticated worldviews inspired by the contributions of eminent philosophers of the past (such as Schopenhauer and Nietzsche), contemporary psychologists, with a few exceptions, usually limit themselves to the empirical realm, showing little consideration for what philosophy or history have to say about the origins and functions of concepts such as spirituality and wellbeing. This led to the development of reductionist, 'all or nothing' definitions and hypotheses, more easily investigated from experimental and quantitative perspectives.

Jung's notion of individuation, in contrast, gives room for both the positive and the negative aspects of spirituality, thereby allowing for a more refined understanding of spirituality in research and clinical practice. When we accept that spirituality is not inherently beneficial, we might be better able to cope with adverse situations such as the side effects of contemplative practices and other pitfalls along our journey for self-knowledge. Individuation also puts spirituality in a broader perspective, within which it is not exclusively linked to religiousness, but encompasses it (and historically derives from it, in a certain way).

From a health-centred approach, the definition of spirituality in terms of individuation might help us to take a broader picture of spirituality. The implications for health, while still important, become secondary, giving rise to new forms of research, aimed at understanding spirituality in other areas of human life. If spirituality is no longer the locus of wellbeing, what can it teach us about who we are and about the world we live in? This question is actually very old, and the many answers to it are scattered throughout different spiritual traditions around the world, but a scientific, theoretically sound understanding on this regard is still lacking. This is a challenge for the future.

Conclusion

The many studies reviewed suggest that spirituality is not necessarily a matter of wellbeing and that its association with mental health and wellbeing is complex. The protective and therapeutic potential of spiritual practices must be reaffirmed, since the evidence available is now too large and reliable to be simply ignored (e.g., VanderWeele, Balboni and Koh 2017). However, it is also important to understand their limitations and the negative aspects involved.

To accomplish this, it is essential, first, to make clear what we understand by spirituality and to propose more specific definitions. Second, a more rigorous understanding of the relationship between spirituality and wellbeing should be searched for, including the investigation of possible confounders (such as response bias), mediators and moderators of this relationship (i.e., the factors that make it possible, increase or diminish it). And, finally, the lack of atheist, truly secular control groups should be addressed (Hwang, Hammer and Cragun 2011). Overall, we tend to agree with MacDonald et al. (2015) in that the psychological benefits of spirituality might be best viewed in terms of how a person perceives and appraises his/her quality of life as manifested in subjective wellbeing, a process which might differ according to the cultural context and one's own functioning and psychological predispositions.

Above all, we must recognize that the study of the relationship between spirituality and wellbeing is far from being a neutral, objective enterprise (as could be said, in effect, of many other topics of scientific interest) but invites us to critically reflect on our society and its values, our way of living and defining what is a life well-lived.

Biographical Note

Everton de Oliveira Maraldi is a professor at the Post-Graduate Program on Religious Studies of the Pontifical Catholic University of São Paulo, Brazil. He has a bachelor's degree in psychology from Guarulhos University, as well as master's and doctor's degrees in Social Psychology from the Institute of Psychology of the University of São Paulo, Brazil, where he also carried out postdoc research. Everton was a postdoctoral research fellow at Coventry University (Brain, Belief, and Behaviour Lab) and University of Oxford (SCIO—Scholarship and Christianity in Oxford), UK. He is a member of the Board of Directors of the Parapsychological Association (USA).

Acknowledgement

This work was funded by São Paulo Research Foundation (grant number #2015/05255-2).

Bibliography

Balboni, M. J. and J. R. Peteet. 2017. *Spirituality and Religion Within the Culture of Medicine: From Evidence to Practice*. New York: Oxford University Press. https://doi.org/10.1093/med/9780190272432.001.0001

Beit-Hallahmi, B. 2007. 'Atheists: A Psychological Profile'. In: *The Cambridge Companion to Atheism*, edited by M. Martin, 300–317. New York: Cambridge University Press. https://doi.org/10.1017/CCOL0521842700.019

Bonelli, R. M. and H. G. Koenig. 2013. 'Mental Disorders, Religion and Spirituality 1990 to 2010: A Systematic Evidence-Based Review'. *Journal of Religion and Health* 52 (2): 657–673. https://doi.org/10.1007/s10943-013-9691-4

Chan-Ob, T. and V. Boonyanaruthee. 1999. 'Meditation in Association with Psychosis'. *Journal of the Medical Association of Thailand* 82 (9): 925–930.

Cardeña, E., S. J. Lynn and S. Krippner (Eds.). 2014. *Varieties of Anomalous Experience: Examining the Scientific Evidence* (2nd edn). Washington, DC: American Psychological Association. https://doi.org/10.1037/14258-000

Carrette, J. and R. King. 2005. *Selling Spirituality: The Silent Takeover of Religion*. London: Routledge. https://doi.org/10.4324/9780203494875

Castillo, R. 1990. 'Depersonalization and Meditation'. *Psychiatry* 53: 158–168. https://doi.org/10.1080/00332747.1990.11024497

Cebolla, A., M. Demarzo, P. Martins, J. Soler and J. Garcia-Campayo. 2017. 'Unwanted Effects: Is There a Negative Side of Meditation? A Multicentre Survey'. *PLos One* 12 (9): e0183137. https://doi.org/10.1371/journal.pone.0183137

Creswell, J. D., L. E. Pacilio, E. K. Lindsay and K. W. Brown. 2014. 'Brief Mindfulness Meditation Training Alters Psychological and Neuroendocrine Responses to Social Evaluative Stress'. *Psychoneuroendocrinology* 44: 1–12. https://doi.org/10.1016/j.psyneuen.2014.02.007

Farias, M., G. Claridge, M. Lalljee. 2005. 'Personality and Cognitive Predictors of New Age Practices and Beliefs'. *Personality and Individual Differences* 39: 979–989. https://doi.org/10.1016/j.paid.2005.04.003

Farias, M., A. Newheiser, G. Kahane and Z. Toledo. 2013. 'Scientific Faith: Belief in Science Increases in the Face of Stress and Existential Anxiety'. *Journal of Experimental and Social Psychology* 49: 1210–1213. https://doi.org/10.1016/j.jesp.2013.05.008

Farias, M. and C. Wikholm. 2015. *The Buddha Pill: Can Meditation Change You?* London: Watkins Publishing Limited.

Flannely, K. J., H. G. Koenig, C. G. Ellison, K. Galek and N. Krause. 2006. 'Belief in Life after Death and Mental Health: Findings from a National Survey'. *The Journal of Nervous and Mental Disease* 194 (7): 524–529. https://doi.org/10.1097/01.nmd.0000224876.63035.23

Goode, E. (2000). *Paranormal Beliefs: A Sociological Introduction*. Long Grove, IL: Waveland Press.

Harris, S. 2014. *Waking Up: A Guide to Spirituality Without Religion*. New York: Simon and Schuster.

Heide, F. J. and T. D. Borkovec. 1983. 'Relaxation-Induced Anxiety: Paradoxical Anxiety Enhancement due to Relaxation Training'. *Journal of Consulting and Clinical Psychology* 51 (2), 171–182. https://doi.org/10.1037//0022-006X.51.2.171

Hwang, K. 2009. 'Experiences of Atheists with Spinal Cord Injury: Results of an Internet Based Exploratory Survey'. *SCI Psychosocial Processes* 20 (2): 4–17.

Hwang, K., J. H. Hammer and R. T. Cragun. 2011. 'Extending Religion-Health Research to Secular Minorities: Issues and Concerns'. *Journal of Religion and Health* 50 (3): 608–622. https://doi.org/10.1007/s10943-009-9296-0

Jain, S., S. L. Shapiro, S. Swanick, S. C. Roesch, P. J. Mills, I. Bell and G. E. Schwartz. 2007. 'A Randomized Controlled Trial of Mindfulness Meditation Versus Relaxation Training: Effects on Distress, Positive States of Mind, Rumination, and Distraction'. *Annals of Behavioural Medicine* 33 (1): 11–21. https://doi.org/10.1207/s15324796abm3301_2

James, W. [1902] 2002. *The Varieties of Religious Experience: A Study in Human Nature (Centenary Edition)*. London: Routledge.

Jung, C. G. 1933. *Modern Man in Search of a Soul*. London: Kegan Paul.

Jung, C. G. 1969. *Psychology and Religion*. Princeton, NJ: Princeton University Press.

Kennedy, R. B. 1976. 'Self-Induced Depersonalization Syndrome'. *American Journal of Psychiatry* 133 (11): 1326–1328. https://doi.org/10.1176/ajp.133.11.1326

King, M., L. Marston, S. McManus, T. Brugha, H. Meltzer and P. Bebbington. 2013. 'Religion, Spirituality and Mental Health: Results from a National Study of

English Households'. *The British Journal of Psychiatry* 202: 68–73. https://doi.org/10.1192/bjp.bp.112.112003

Koenig, H. G. 2011. *Spirituality and Health Research: Methods, Measurement, Statistics, and Resources.* West Conshohocken, PA: Templeton Press.

Kornfield, J. 1979. 'Intensive Insight Meditation: A Phenomenological Study'. *The Journal of Transpersonal Psychology* 11: 41–58.

Kuijpers, H. J. H., F. M. A. van der Heijden, S. Tuinier and W. M. A. Vorhoeven. 2007. 'Meditation-Induced Psychosis'. *Psychopathology* 40: 461–464. https://doi.org/10.1159/000108125

Lazarus, A. A. 1976. 'Psychiatric Problems Precipitated by Transcendental Meditation'. *Psychological Reports* 39: 601–602. https://doi.org/10.2466/pr0.1976.39.2.601

Lindahl J. R, N. E. Fisher, D. J. Cooper, R. K. Rosen and W. B. Britton. 2017. 'The Varieties of Contemplative Experience: A Mixed-Methods Study of Meditation-Related Challenges in Western Buddhists'. *PLoS ONE* 12 (5): e0176239. https://doi.org/10.1371/journal.pone.0176239

Lindeman, M. 2014. 'Spirituality Studies are in Need of Differentia: A Reply to Garssen and Visser'. *Journal of Nervous and Mental Disease* 202 (2): 178. https://doi.org/10.1097/NMD.0000000000000106

Lindeman, M., S. Blomqvist and M. Takada. 2012. 'Distinguishing Spirituality from Other Constructs: Not a Matter of Well-Being But of Belief in Supernatural Spirits'. *Journal of Nervous and Mental Disease* 200 (2): 167–173. https://doi.org/10.1097/NMD.0b013e3182439719

Lindeman, M. and A. M. Svedholm. 2012. 'What's In a Term? Paranormal, Superstitious, Magical and Supernatural Beliefs by Any Other Name Would Mean the Same'. *Review of General Psychology* 16 (3): 241–255. https://doi.org/10.1037/a0027158

Lomas, T., T. Cartwright. T. Edginton and D. Ridge. (2015). 'A Qualitative Analysis of Experiental Challenges Associated with Meditation Practice'. *Mindfulness* 6: 848–860. https://doi.org/10.1007/s12671-014-0329-8

Lukoff, D., F. Lu and R. Turner. 1992. 'Toward a More Culturally Sensitive *DSM-IV*: Psychoreligious and Psychospiritual Problems'. *Journal of Nervous and Mental Disease* 180: 673–682. https://doi.org/10.1097/00005053-199211000-00001

MacDonald, D. A. 2000. 'Spirituality: Description, Measurement, and Relation to the Five-Factor Model of Personality'. *Journal of Personality* 68: 153–197. https://doi.org/10.1111/1467-6494.t01-1-00094

MacDonald, D. A., H. L. Friedman, J. Brewczynski, D. Holland, K. K. K. Salagame, K. K. Mohan, Z. O. Gubrij and H. W. Cheong. 2015. 'Spirituality as a Scientific Construct: Testing its Universality Across Cultures and Languages. *PLoS ONE* 10 (3): e0117701. https://doi.org/10.1371/journal.pone.0117701

Maraldi, E. O. 2014. *Dissociação, crença e identidade: Uma perspectiva psicossocial (Dissociation, Belief and Identity: A Psychosocial Perspective).* Doctoral thesis (Social Psychology). São Paulo, Brazil: Institute of Psychology, University of São Paulo. https://doi.org/10.1097/NMD.0000000000000694

Maraldi, E. O. 2017. 'As muitas faces da irreligiosidade: dimensões cognitivas e psicossociais do ateísmo, do agnosticismo e da espiritualidade sem religião'

('The Many Faces of Irreligiosity: Cognitive and Psychosocial Dimensions of Atheism, Agnosticism and Spirituality Without Religion). In: *XI Seminário Internacional de Psicologia e Senso Religioso, 21 a 23 de novembro*. Pontifícia Universidade Católica do Rio Grande do Sul, Porto Alegre.

Maraldi, E. O. 2018. 'Response Bias in Research on Religion, Spirituality and Mental Health: A Critical Review of the Literature and Methodological Recommendations'. *Journal of Religion and Health*. https://doi.org/10.1007/s10943-018-0639-6

Maraldi, E. O., S. Krippner, M. C. Barros and A. Cunha. 2017. 'Dissociation from a Cross-Cultural Perspective: Implications of Studies in Brazil'. *Journal of Nervous and Mental Disease* 205: 558–567. https://doi.org/10.1097/NMD.0000000000000694

Marshall, J. and D. Olson. 2018. 'Is "Spiritual but Not Religious" a Replacement for Religion or Just One Step on the Path Between Religion and Nonreligion?'. *Review of Religious Research* 60 (4): 503–518. https://doi.org/10.1007/s13644-018-0342-9

Menezes-Júnior A., L. Alminhana and A. Moreira-Almeida. 2012. 'Sociodemographic and Anomalous Experiences Profile in Subjects with Psychotic and Dissociative Experiences in Religious Groups'. *Archives of Clinical Psychiatry* 39: 203–207. https://doi.org/10.1590/S0101-60832012000600005

Migdal, L. and D. A. MacDonald. 2013. 'Clarifying the Relation between Spirituality and Well-being'. *The Journal of Nervous and Mental Disease* 201 (4): 274–280. https://doi.org/10.1097/NMD.0b013e318288e26a

Moreira-Almeida, A., A. Sharma, B. J. van Rensburg, P. J. Verhagen and C. C. H. Cook. 2016. 'World Psychiatric Association Position Statement on Spirituality and Religion in Psychiatry'. *World Psychiatry* 15 (1): 87–88. https://doi.org/10.1002/wps.20304

Nakaya, M. and K. Ohmori. 2010. 'Psychosis Induced by Spiritual Practice and Resolution of Pre-Morbid Inner Conflicts'. *German Journal of Psychiatry* 13: 161–163.

Otis, L. S. 1974. 'The Facts on Transcendental Meditation: Part III. If Well-Integrated but Anxious, Try TM'. *Psychology Today* (April): 45–46. https://doi.org/10.1037/e400592009-004

Otis, L. S. 1984. 'Adverse Effects of Transcendental Meditation'. In: *Meditation: Classic and Contemporary Perspectives*, edited by D. H. Shapiro and R. N. Walsh, 201–208. New York: Aldine. https://doi.org/10.4324/9780203785843-26

Perez-De-Albeniz, A. and J. Holmes. 2000. 'Meditation: Concepts, Effects and Uses in Therapy'. *International Journal of Psychotherapy* 5 (1): 49–58. https://doi.org/10.1080/13569080050020263

Persinger, M. A. 1993. 'Transcendental Meditation™ and General Meditation are Associated with Enhanced Complex Partial Epileptic-Like Signs: Evidence of "Cognitive Kindling?"'. *Perceptual and Motor Skills* 76: 80–82. https://doi.org/10.2466/pms.1993.76.1.80

Persinger, M. A. and K. Makarec. 1990. 'Exotic Beliefs may be Substitutes for Religious Beliefs'. *Perceptual and Motor Skills* 71: 16–18. https://doi.org/10.2466/pms.1990.71.1.16

Rhine, J. B. and J. G. Pratt. 1957. *Parapsychology: Frontier Science of the Mind*. Evanston, IL: Charles C. Thomas Publisher.

Roof, W. C. 1999. *Spiritual Marketplace: Baby Boomers and the Remaking of American Religion*. Princeton, NJ: Princeton University Press.

Rosenberg, M. 1965. *Society and the Adolescent Self-Image*. Princeton, NJ: Princeton University Press. https://doi.org/10.1515/9781400876136

Schofield, M. B., I. S. Baker, P. Staples and D. Sheffield. 2016. 'Mental Representations of the Supernatural: A Cluster Analysis of Religiosity, Spirituality and Paranormal Belief'. *Personality and Individual Differences* 101: 419–424. https://doi.org/10.1016/j.paid.2016.06.020

Shapiro, D. H. 1992. 'Adverse Effects of Meditation: A Preliminary Investigation of Long-Term Meditators'. *International Journal of Psychosomatics* 39 (1–4): 62–67.

Sparks, G. G. (2001). 'The Relationship Between Paranormal Beliefs and Religious Beliefs'. *Skeptical Inquirer* 18: 386–395.

Steensland, B., X. Wang and L. C. Schmidt. 2018. 'Spirituality: What Does it Mean and To Whom? *Journal for the Scientific Study of Religion* 57 (3): 450–472. https://doi.org/10.1111/jssr.12534

Sutich, A. J. 1968. 'Transpersonal Psychology: An Emerging Force'. *Journal of Humanistic Psychology* 8(1):77–78. https://doi.org/10.1177/002216786800800108

Underwood, L. G. 2006. 'Ordinary Spiritual Experience: Qualitative Research, Interpretive Guidelines, and Population Distribution for the Daily Spiritual Experience Scale'. *Archives for the Psychology of Religion* 28 (1): 181–218. https://doi.org/10.1163/008467206777832562

Vanderkooi, L. 1997. 'Buddhist Teachers' Experience with Extreme Mental States in Western Meditators'. *The Journal of Transpersonal Psychology* 29 (1): 31–46.

VanderWeele, T. J., T. A. Balboni and H. K. Koh. 2017. 'Health and Spirituality'. *JAMA* 318 (6): 519–520. https://doi.org/10.1001/jama.2017.8136

Walach, H. 2015. *Secular Spirituality: The Next Step Towards Enlightenment*. New York: Springer. https://doi.org/10.1007/978-3-319-09345-1

Walsh, R. N. 1984. 'Initial Meditative Experiences'. In *Meditation: Classic and Contemporary Perspectives*, edited by D. H. Shapiro and R. N. Walsh, 265–271. New York: Aldine. https://doi.org/10.4324/9780203785843-34

Walsh, R. and L. Roche. 1979. 'Precipitation of Acute Psychotic Episodes by Intensive Meditation on Individuals with a History of Schizophrenia'. *American Journal of Psychiatry* 136: 1085–1086. https://doi.org/10.1176/ajp.136.8.1085

White, R. A. 1997. 'Dissociation, Narrative, and Exceptional Human Experience'. In *Broken Images, Broken Selves: Dissociative Narratives in Clinical Practice*, edited by S. Krippner and S. J. Powers, 88–121. Washington, DC: Brunner/Mazel.

Wilkinson, P. J. and P. G. Coleman. 2010. 'Strong Beliefs and Coping in Old Age: A Case-Based Comparison of Atheism and Religious Faith'. *Ageing and Society* 30 (02): 337–361. https://doi.org/10.1017/S0144686X09990353

Willard, A. K. and A. Norenzayan. 2017. '"Spiritual but Not Religious": Cognition, Schizotypy, and Conversion in Alternative Beliefs. *Cognition* 165: 137–146. https://doi.org/10.1016/j.cognition.2017.05.018

Wulff, D. 2014. 'Mystical Experiences'. In *Varieties of Anomalous Experience: Examining the Scientific Evidence* (2nd edn), edited by E. Cardeña, S. J. Lynn and

S. Krippner, 369–408. Washington, DC: American Psychological Association. https://doi.org/10.1037/14258-013

Zinnbauer, B. J., K. I. Pargament, B. Cole, M. S. Rye, E. M. Butter, T. G. Belavich, K. M. Hipp, A. B. Scott and J. L. Kadar. 1997. 'Religion and Spirituality: Unfuzzying the Fuzzy'. *Journal for the Scientific Study of Religion* 36 (4): 549–564. https://doi.org/10.2307/1387689

Zinnbauer, B. J. and K. I. Pargament. 2005. 'Religiousness and Spirituality'. In *Handbook of the Psychology of Religion and Spirituality*, edited by R. F. Paloutizian and C. L. Park, 21–42. New York: Guilford Press.

Zuckerman, P. 2009. 'Atheism, Secularity and Well-Being: How the Findings of Social Science Counter Negative Stereotypes and Assumptions'. *Sociology Compass* 10: 949–971. https://doi.org/10.1111/j.1751-9020.2009.00247.x

Zuckerman, P., L. W. Galen and F. L. Pasquale. 2016. *The Nonreligious: Understanding Secular People and Societies.* New York: Oxford University Press. https://doi.org/10.1093/acprof:oso/9780199924950.001.0001

Chapter 2

Clinical Parapsychology: The Interface Between Anomalous Experiences and Psychological Wellbeing

Chris Roe

Introduction

Parapsychology has been defined as 'The scientific study of experiences which, if they are as they seem to be, are in principle outside the realm of human capabilities as presently conceived by conventional scientists' (Irwin and Watt 2007, 1). This is a useful definition because it draws attention to two important features. Firstly, parapsychology is concerned with *understanding* such experiences rather than committing to a particular interpretation of them—while some commentators are deeply sceptical as to whether 'paranormal phenomena' are objectively real, none can take issue with the assertion that many people have experiences that they interpret as paranormal[1] and hold beliefs about those experiences. For example, Pechey and Halligan (2012) conducted a representative survey of UK residents using a market research company and found that 75% of the respondents had had one or more anomalous experience(s), with 13% reporting that these occurred 'often'. More specifically, 48% claimed to have sensed when a friend or family member was in trouble, 36% to have had premonitions of events that had yet to take place, and 20% to have seen or sensed a ghost. Castro, Burrows and Wooffitt (2014) similarly found that 24% of their sample claimed to have experienced a premonition, 13% extrasensory perception (ESP; where they became aware of information not previously known to them or available to them via their conventional senses of sight, hearing, etc.), and just over 10% believed they had interacted with people whom they knew at the time to be deceased. Such levels of belief and experience are not peculiar to the UK: Dein (2012) overviewed surveys conducted across the world and found that over half of respondents reported at least one anomalous experience. These kinds of experience are collectively termed 'psi', where psi is the Greek symbol used in the algebraic sense to stand for something that is, as yet, unknown. Because their focus is on understanding experiences, parapsychologists are comfortable with the possibility that at least some (perhaps all) instances of psi could in principle be explicable in conventional psychological terms, including deception, self-deception, misperception, errors of memory and so on—the experiences and their explanations would still be regarded as part of the subject matter for parapsychology.

Notwithstanding this, the second important feature of the definition given above is an acknowledgement that the phenomena as experienced might not be explicable in terms of current understanding and so may require our contemporary scientific models of reality to be revised or extended. To this end, parapsychologists undertake experiments to determine whether reported phenomena can be reproduced in the laboratory under circumstances that take into account and control for conventional psychological explanations such as those listed above. Should the effects persist under these tightened conditions, then this would argue against the plausibility of those conventional explanations and for some alternative explanation that better accounts for the observed effects. Research to date suggests that at least some lines of experimentation produce effect sizes and replication rates that compare favourably with other areas of psychological research and so deserve serious scientific consideration rather than the casual dismissal that is more characteristic of the mainstream (cf. Cardeña 2018; Roe 2016).

Nevertheless, there is a great taboo associated with paranormal phenomena. They are often regarded as obviously false because they are deemed to contravene fundamental principles that have been repeatedly demonstrated in other areas of science. C. D. Broad (1949, 291) described these as 'basic limiting principles' that:

> we unhesitatingly take for granted as the framework within which all our practical activities and our scientific theories are confined. Some of these seem to be self-evident. Others are so overwhelmingly supported by all the empirical facts which fall within the range of ordinary experience and the scientific elaborations of it ... that it hardly enters our heads to question them.

Among these principles, Broad included: (i) causes must temporally precede effects; (ii) an event in a person's brain can only effect a change in the material world via the body's motor systems; (iii) mental events are a product of brain activity, such that if the brain ceases to function then mental events will also cease; and (iv) we can only acquire information about the world around us via our sensory systems. These principles seem to be violated in reports of, respectively: premonitions or other kinds of apparently backward causation; psychokinetic effects such as noncontact mental healing or 'spoon bending' of the type that was popular in the 1970s and 1980s; any claims of survival of personality after bodily death such as mediumistic communications, apparitional experiences during bereavement, near-death experiences, or reports of reincarnation; and various forms of ESP experience such as telepathy and clairvoyance. As a consequence of this perceived incompatibility, there is an almost total lack of interest in such experiences among academics and policy makers (Eybrechts and Gerding 2012). In turn, this silence has encouraged members of the public to be reticent about sharing their experiences with others (especially members of the health professions) for fear of seeming, at best, naive or gullible (Evenden, Cooper and Mitchell 2013) or, at worst, as suffering from some underlying psychopathology (Roxburgh and Roe 2014). In this chapter I shall consider how such experiences and their disclosure to others can have consequences for the wellbeing of the experient,[2] particularly in terms of concerns the experient might have about being labelled as psychologically deficient or unwell by virtue of having had them, and especially because of the psychological distress that can be caused when trying to make sense of and come to terms with events for which no satisfactory explanatory framework is offered by the scientific community or psychological support services. Finally, I shall explore what can be done to improve things.

Reactions to Spontaneous Anomalous Experiences

People understandably vary in their reactions to an unexpected and unsolicited paranormal event. For example, Milton (1992) conducted a small-scale study with 22 people who had had paranormal experiences some time earlier. Their emotional reactions included amazement, surprise, curiosity, puzzlement, fear, joy and elation. Many reported that they needed someone to talk to them about their experience, to advise them, or explain it in ways that they could understand and come to terms with. Tellingly, some simply wanted someone who would believe them. The variety of life impacts found by Milton ranged from negligible to fundamentally life-changing (including respondents who believed they had been saved from suicide or had transformed their life plan so that it emphasized spiritual exploration or development). Typically, the experience(s) served to confirm, strengthen or create belief in a nonmaterial aspect to existence, or in a more complex and richer view of the nature of the mind, enhancing their spiritual or philosophical outlook, reducing fear of death and increasing belief in life after death. Similarly, Kennedy and Kanthamani (1995) surveyed a convenience sample of 120 people actively interested in parapsychology who reported having had at least one paranormal and/or transcendent experience. A majority of respondents reported positive impacts from their experiences, including increased belief in life after death, belief that their lives are guided or watched over by a higher force or being, interest in spiritual or religious matters, a sense of connection to others, feelings of happiness and wellbeing, confidence, optimism about the future, and a sense that life is imbued with meaning. They also claimed reductions in their fear of death, depression or anxiety, isolation and loneliness, and fears about the future. The magnitude of changes in wellbeing and spirituality were positively associated with the number of anomalous experiences (most of the sample had had multiple experiences). Although 45% of Kennedy and Kanthamani's respondents indicated that their paranormal experience had made them feel very afraid or confused at the time, this appeared to be temporary or mixed with positive feelings, with only 9% indicating in retrospect that their experiences were fearful and of no positive value. Of course, this low figure for negative reactions may reflect this sample's greater familiarity with the literature on parapsychology, which is likely to emphasize that such phenomena fall within the normal range of human experience.

Anomalous experiences seem to be particularly common in bereavement. Eybrechts and Gerding (2012), for example, report on a random telephone sample of 736 Dutch persons, of whom 63% felt that contact with the deceased was possible, with 40% of those claiming to have had such an experience. The majority (83%) of experiencers were not frightened by their post-mortem contact, and 70% believed it to have been supportive in the grief process. I recently explored this further with colleagues (Cooper, Roe and Mitchell 2015) in a project reviewing studies that used various methodologies to explore after death communications, including surveys, case collections and interviews. We concluded that anomalous experiences can occur as a natural part of the bereavement process, and typically are regarded by the experient as beneficial for coping and recovery, particularly in providing an opportunity to say goodbye, enabling closure and forgiveness concerning relationship difficulties, and emphasizing a continuing bond with the deceased.

In contrast, it has long been recognized that a significant minority of people are disturbed by paranormal experiences and may need counselling in order to come to terms with them (e.g., Hastings 1983; Siegel 1986). The experiences themselves can be 'unpleasant, frightening, or frankly hellish', and can produce a 'psychological impact [that] may be profound and long lasting' (Greyson and Bush 1996, 209). For some, subsequent reactions can include fear, anxiety, depression and distress (Parra 2012). In addition, individuals may have existential questions following 'out-of-the-ordinary' experiences (Eybrechts and Gerding 2012;

Heriot-Maitland, Knight and Peters 2012) and not know where to seek support, or worry that if they do, they will have the experience devalued, interpreted as 'not real' (Steffen and Coyle 2012), or that they will be labelled as 'mad' (Davis, Lockwood and Wright 1991). The reactions of others can reinforce the sense that there is something abnormal or even shameful about the experience. Tierney (2012), for example, describes the case of 'W', a 15-year-old girl who had demonstrated apparently psychokinetic phenomena (such as bending metal objects without touching them) to various witnesses. He notes (p. 21) that 'the family had become uneasy about these phenomena. The girl's mother had tried to discourage W from involving herself with the phenomena and had asked those that witnessed it to not talk about it to anyone else'. Soon afterwards the phenomena dwindled.

Counselling for Anomalous Experiences

A significant number of people who have anomalous experiences are sufficiently concerned that they feel motivated to seek counselling as a means of understanding and coping with them. Parra (2012) describes a survey of Argentinean undergraduate students in which a quarter of those who reported anomalous experiences went on to consult a physician, and a third confided in friends and family. Eybrechts and Gerding (2012) found that 16% of those among their telephone sample who reported an encounter with the deceased sought professional help, but note that among those who had been frightened by their experience, most (65%) did not consult a healthcare professional about it. They attribute this to the finding that 'many interviewees had low expectations of regular health-care advice, given the exotic nature—the "strangeness"—of the experiences' (p. 39).[3] Indeed, workers in the mental health and counselling professions do generally seem ill-prepared to deal with clients who disclose anomalous experiences. Of those in Eybrechts and Gerding's (2012) sample that sought support after experiencing contact with a deceased person, 53% considered the help they received to be inadequate. Similarly, more than half of a sample of 84 individuals reporting near-death experiences were keen to seek support from a counsellor so that they could make sense of their experience, but almost half of those that did so reported a worsening of problems (Corbeau 2004, cited in Eybrechts and Gerding 2012, 41). Perhaps not surprisingly, satisfaction with their therapist was related to 'the authenticity of being taken seriously', 'the feeling of being accepted', and 'the perceived time and opportunity dedicated to discussing the [anomalous experience] during counselling' (Eybrechts and Gerding 2012, 41).

In the United Kingdom the picture is even less promising. A recent study by Taylor (2005) investigated the counselling experiences of 10 bereaved people who had reported instances in which they sensed the presence of the deceased. Participants had suffered their loss at least 30 months previously and had received counselling. The deaths they reported were of four children, three partners, one friend, four parents, two siblings, and one niece. The mode of death ranged from long-term illness, old age and heart attack, to sudden deaths, including murder, suicide, termination and still birth. Taylor interviewed each participant, and found that the majority of them felt their counsellors were not accepting of their experiences or neglected to explore their cultural and spiritual aspects—one counsellor 'very much pooh poohed this idea [of the continued existence of spirit] and said I was in an unreal world, and that I had to come to terms with reality and pull myself together' (p. 55). Others reported more positive outcomes, which involved feelings of being accepted and of having their story normalized. Roxburgh and Evenden (2016a) similarly recruited clients who had at least one anomalous experience that they had discussed in counselling. Clients had seen counsellors from a range of therapeutic orientations for at least six sessions following their experience. Semi-structured interviews were conducted with a sample of eight clients during which they described their experiences, the impacts these had had on them and the response of their therapist to them. Thematic analysis of the material identified that participants were initially circumspect about disclosing their anomalous experiences with counsellors because of the negative reactions of others in wider society, such as friends and family members. This was exacerbated by feeling dismissed or silenced by the therapist when they did tentatively broach the subject during a session. Of particular concern were attempts by the therapist to reframe the account as symbolic rather than literal or otherwise indicate that the experience was not authentic or a legitimate focus for therapeutic interaction—one participant described it as like 'banging your head against a brick wall'. Clients explained that their goal in revealing anomalous experiences was to have someone acknowledge and normalize them (without necessarily endorsing any paranormal interpretation), and to provide an open-minded and non-judgemental space in which their meaning could be explored. There was a feeling that these needs were generally not being met because the counsellors lacked training in or experience of the topic. One respondent summarized this as follows:

> It's not mainstream and you know I think my experience with the early counsellors really hit that home that they didn't have a clue what I was

on about, and it made me feel that the world of counselling was a little narrower than I had expected. (Roxburgh and Evenden 2016a, 216).

The researchers followed up by exploring the therapist's perspective (Roxburgh and Evenden 2016b). They conducted semi-structured face-to-face interviews with eight therapists who had worked with at least one client who had reported an anomalous experience in therapy. Therapists came from a range of orientations and had been practising for between 4 and 27 years (mean = 12 years). Participants noticed that clients would 'test the waters' before disclosing anomalous experiences and needed assurance that it was okay to talk about them without being seen as 'crazy'. Disclosure might begin with framing that pre-empted this kind of negative attribution ('You're gonna think I'm crazy when I tell you this ...'), which is a strategy that has been described by others as a means of revealing anomalous experiences in a way that fields against attributions of gullibility or delusion (e.g., Wooffitt 1992). It was clear to therapists that clients regarded their experiences as stigmatizing and potentially something to be ashamed of or embarrassed about. This could be overcome, therapists found, by exploring the meaning of the experience from the client's perspective, rather than offering their own interpretation or analysis—whatever its ultimate ontological status, the phenomenon could have real consequences for the client if it was psychologically real for them. They could also help normalize the experience by letting clients know that many otherwise normal and healthy people have had similar experiences and that this is a legitimate subject to discuss within the safe confines of therapeutic interaction. However, therapists identified that such an outcome may only be possible when fellow professionals were better educated about the incidence and effects of anomalous experiences and felt sufficiently informed to be able to encourage clients to disclose them.

Eybrechts and Gerding (2012) reported on a survey of 129 health professionals in the Netherlands, of whom 59% had been consulted by a client who claimed contact with a deceased person, 55% had experienced ESP, and 51% psychic healing of some form. Few of these healthcare professionals felt that they had sufficient knowledge to support clients with these experiences (20% for ESP, 23% for spirit contact, 15% for near-death experiences); a 'vast majority' (83%) had received no specific training on anomalous experiences and a significant minority (35%) expressed a need for additional education. They were particularly concerned that 'traditional medical and psychological help services essentially and persistently fail to address the existential questions that ... turn up in the wake of exceptional experiences' (p. 36).

Roxburgh, Ridgway and Roe (2015, 2016) conducted similar research with therapists and clients that focused on the prevalence and phenomenology of synchronicity experiences; that is, the co-occurrence of events that contain elements that to the experient seem meaningfully related, but which do not share a common cause and are not regarded as attributable to bare coincidence.[4] Roxburgh, Ridgway and Roe (2016) surveyed a sample of 226 therapists, and found that 44% had experienced synchronicities in the therapeutic setting, with psychotherapists significantly more likely to report them than counsellors or psychologists. Notwithstanding whether they had had these experiences, 67% of the sample felt that they could be therapeutically valuable. Roxburgh, Ridgway and Roe (2015) conducted semi-structured face-to-face interviews with nine therapists who reported that they had experienced synchronicity in the therapeutic setting. The sample comprised three counsellors registered with the British Association for Counselling and Psychotherapy (BACP), three psychologists registered with the British Psychological Society (BPS), and three psychotherapists registered with the UK Council for Psychotherapy (UKCP), so as to reflect the range of orientations of respondents in the survey study. Interview material suggested that synchronicity experiences were seen as inherently meaningful, an expression of an underlying sense of deeper interconnection between client and therapist, and that they facilitated communication of something that was difficult to express (or to hear). However, therapists also found that it took time to make sense of their experiences, often involving an initial stage of shock and a search for a conceptual model to explain something that challenged their concept of reality. This might lead to a recognition that there was no ready explanation they were happy to adopt so that they instead learned to feel comfortable with that uncertainty.

Clinical Parapsychology

In order to address this identified discrepancy between the needs of clients and the provision offered by therapists, specialist counselling services have been set up in a number of countries (including the UK, France, Germany, the Netherlands and Argentina) for the specific purpose of counselling clients who report anomalous or spiritual experiences (Roxburgh and Evenden 2016b). Workers at these institutions specialize in clinical parapsychology, which is described as 'a new kind of profession with dual training in counselling, psychotherapy and clinical professional psychology to the point of licensure on the one hand, and training in the paranormal, including parapsychology, on the other' (Klimo, 1998). As Roxburgh and Evenden (2016a, 212) note, it is not necessarily the anomalous experience itself that has an impact on whether or not the person experiences psychological distress, but rather how they appraise such experiences, their perceived levels of social support, and whether or not there are opportunities to reduce stigma in a context that normalises and validates the experience.

Thus, much of the focus is on creating a non-judgemental space in which to hold the experience and explore the meaning of it, particularly with respect to existential issues that might have been raised. Tierney (2012) similarly advises that counselling for anomalous experiences is concerned with 'encouraging the client to tolerate uncertainty, come to terms with the experience in a way that fits with their world view, in a non-directive, non-judgmental manner' (p. 28). It is also paramount to be able to discriminate between those experiences that might relate to some underlying pathology and those that do not, especially where clients are primarily motivated by a need to find ways to have the experiences cease, to resolve confusion or unease about the experience, and particularly to be assured (where appropriate) that they were not indicative of pathology (Kramer 2012).

It has been argued that successful integration of such experiences might not only ameliorate distress, but could enhance wellbeing. For example, Braud (2012) argued that if exceptional experiences are not dismissed or bracketed as anomalous, deviant or irregular, but rather are worked with sufficiently, they can foster beneficial and transformative changes in the experiencer, including shifts in one's sense of self and one's connection with others. Indeed, Braud argues that the value of self disclosure about personally significant experiences and of confiding in others underpins counselling and therapeutic traditions that can lead to personal growth and acceptance.

One striking example of this benefit occurred during data collection for a project I led that explored near death experiences (NDEs). We interviewed Emily,[5] who described an NDE that occurred approximately 15 years earlier after complications following childbirth. Her NDE contained classic features, including an out-of-body element, an encounter with a loving light, and meeting deceased relatives. After the interview, my research assistant was able to explain that these were typical of many NDE cases, and the experient's relief in having her experience (but not necessarily her interpretation of that experience) accepted was palpable. She disclosed that although the experience had happened so long ago, she had not shared it with anyone—not her husband or other family members, and certainly not any medical staff—for fear that she would be 'packed off to the looney bin'. She felt like she had been carrying a burden that had finally been lifted from her. It was clear from this encounter that people working in clinical parapsychology have an obligation to support people like Emily in their attempts to come to terms with their anomalous experiences, by providing reassurance (where appropriate) that many so-called paranormal experiences need not be regarded as abnormal, but can occur to otherwise healthy and functional people.

Managing Anomalous Experiences: The Case of Mental Mediumship

Clinical parapsychology has the potential to identify strategies that could help people come to terms with experiences that sometimes are regarded as nonvolitional, intrusive and distressing. Parapsychologists work with individuals such as self-identified mediums or psychics who have regular or persistent experiences that might, in other circumstances, be interpreted as symptoms of a 'mental disorder'. For example, we interviewed one medium who described her experience as follows:

> sometimes I do see pictures on the screens in my mind, sometimes I do hear voices objectively ... I hear my name called ... but mostly I hear thoughts in my head that I know aren't mine ... and then the one that really works the best, which I feel brings the best evidence when I'm demonstrating on the rostrum is the clairsentience because I feel the personality of the person, I feel the changes in my own personality, I feel as if I've lost a leg, you know, or if I've got heart pains, chest pain, back pain, eye pain, I feel that personality as different to mine. (Mary, in Roxburgh and Roe 2013, 33)

Claims that one sees things that others cannot see, hears things others cannot hear, has internal experiences that one attributes to external agencies are all susceptible to a psychiatric diagnosis (Kerns et al. 2014), and could potentially be very distressing to the experient. Perhaps surprisingly, these experiences do not seem to be associated with psychological distress and social dysfunction among mediums in the way that they are among other populations (Taylor and Murray 2012). If clinical parapsychologists can develop an understanding of how mediums and psychics come to understand and manage their challenging experiences then this could offer ways to ameliorate distress for other groups who have similar experiences.

We explored this in a survey study that compared the wellbeing of Spiritualist mediums (who regularly had such experiences) and Spiritualists who were not mediums (so shared the same belief system but did not have such experiences). A total of 80 Spiritualist mediums participated.

All met pre-specified criteria in being accredited certificate holders affiliated with a recognized national Spiritualist organization active in the UK. A further 79 non-mediums who self-identified as Spiritualists and attended services run by the same organization constituted our comparison group. All participants completed a questionnaire pack that included measures of dissociation, fantasy-proneness and mental health. The last named is divided into two components that focus on psychological wellbeing (happiness, feeling valued by others, calm and contented) and psychological distress (anxiety, depression, loss of behavioural or emotional control). Mediums scored significantly higher than non-mediums on psychological wellbeing and lower on psychological distress, but no significant differences were found between the groups on dissociation or fantasy proneness. These findings suggest that mediumistic experience is not associated with a greater risk of dissociative experiences or pathology; indeed, for wellbeing and distress the medium group scored significantly better than patient and student samples for which norms are available. This begs the question, if other groups within society find such experiences have an adverse effect on their wellbeing, what is it that mediums are doing that enables them to assimilate and make sense of them in such a way as to remain healthy and functional?

We addressed this by conducting interviews with mediums from the same sampling pool as the survey study (Roxburgh and Roe 2013, 2014). We recruited ten Spiritualist mediums who were all award holders for demonstrating mediumship (five males and five females, aged 46–76 years). They had practised as mediums for between 9 and 55 years, so varied somewhat in experience. Interviews focused on their understanding of mediumship, including how they perceive their abilities to have originated and developed, how the phenomena are experienced and managed, and what purpose the phenomena play in their lives and the lives of their sitters.

Analysis of interview transcripts used interpretative phenomenological analysis, a qualitative method that privileges the experient's worldview and focuses on the process of meaning making through which participants make sense of their experiences (Smith, Flowers and Larkin 2009). Findings from this analysis indicated that anomalous experiences that participants had during childhood were regarded as influential in their later becoming a medium. The experiences themselves could be pleasurable or frightening, but it was the reaction of others (particularly family members) to accounts of the experience that seemed to determine their impact. Where there was a climate of openness to spiritual matters, the experiences were treated as legitimate topics for conversation and the child might be described as 'sensitive' or 'gifted', and the occurrence (or even cultivation) of further experiences was condoned. Where the experiences were dismissed as nonsense or treated as sinister, and not suitable for discussion, the child typically learned to hide or suppress them in a manner that typically proved to be unsuccessful, even damaging. These outcomes are illustrated in the contrast between Melissa's and Sarah's recollections:

> I grew up in a home where Spiritualism and self-awareness was normal. My mother's mother was a Spiritualist medium and a famous medium and my father's mother was also a Spiritualist, so both my mum and dad had spiritualist mediums in the family. My mother was a natural healer, her sister was a healer in the Christian Scientist Church, I have various relatives who are involved with Spiritualism and allied religions, so when I was a kid seeing spirit people was normal and I was very lucky that it wasn't just me, I had spirit friends that my parents acknowledged as being real ... so actually I can't really say when I became a medium because I have always been one. (Melissa)

> The first memory that I actually have was hearing voices after my father died ... one night I went to bed and I woke up and I'd had these voices talking to me saying that my dad was fine, he was living, there wasn't a problem, he wouldn't want me to be upset and I thought I was dreaming, so I thought 'pull yourself together' and as I turned over to go back to sleep the voices were still there ... so I thought 'I'm losing it, I'll go down and make a cup of tea' so I went down and all the while I was making this cup of tea these voices were still talking to me ... so I went to the Doctor's and I told him what had happened, I said 'I must be having a nervous breakdown', so he gave me some pills, as they do, told me to go away for a few days and just try and chill and relax ... never took the pills because I don't take tablets, I don't believe in that sort of thing ... I thought 'Right this is me and now I need to cure myself to get better' so I just pulled myself together, blocked absolutely everything out, thought I've just really got to get back on track and I did that probably for about 6–7 years. (...) I started to talk to ... [a medium] ... and we sat just chatting about things and that is when my interest started because they were explaining things to me because that was my first real knowledge that somebody was talking to me (...) Steph and her sister were starting to explain all these things to me and all the little things that had happened over the years which you just put down as 'Oh that must be that and that must be that' so you know, things just started making sense. (Sarah)

In our sample, participants who grew up in a home where Spiritualism was normal found themselves able to come to terms with their experiences much more quickly, while those who encountered resistance or concern reported extended periods of distress during which they attempted to shut out or medicate away their experiences, which were commonly interpreted as indicators of mental illness. These accounts are consistent with Heriot-Maitland, Knight and Peter's (2012) findings that a more positive outcome after an 'out-of-the-ordinary' experience was related to the ability to incorporate them into the experient's personal and social worlds in a way that gave them meaning and value, while more negative outcomes were associated with exposure to others who treated the experiences as invalid and potentially pathological.

The process of providing a framework within which mediumistic experience is normalized gives the phenomena a clear purpose that can also be rewarding and socially valued. For example, participants talked about the service they provide to others by giving them messages that reassure them of the continued existence of loved ones who had died:

> It gives a lot of comfort to people if they know that their mothers, fathers, aunties, uncles are alive and well in the spirit realm, and that they are also looking out for them while they are here on the Earth plane. (Graham)

One participant expressed her belief that supporting people through bereavement is an important aspect of mediumship and mentioned that she had studied counselling to help her become a better medium: 'A little bit of, if you like, bereavement counselling is involved in it, which is why I studied that'.

A spiritual explanatory framework also provided mediums with psychological resources that enabled them to manage their experiences, particularly in having some control over when they occurred and what direction the communications took. Our participants described it as follows:

> For me I am working or I am not, you know, so it would be absolutely no point spirit talking to me unless I'm working ... so I am not aware of spirit unless I want to be ... and that depends on the person, if you are an open book all of the time then you are going to feel spirit because our families are around us, so you are going to feel them but for me that feels unhealthy. (Sarah)

> Although I do believe I'm receptive to spirit communication all the time you can't really let it interfere with your life, so there is like a barrier that says don't communicate now. (Graham)

The use of preparatory practices before a mediumistic demonstration or private sitting—such as cleansing or meditation practices, or activities intended to 'open up' the psyche or set back the ego self in ways that are believed to make one receptive to spirit—also serve as boundary markers to signal when one is (and thus also when one is *not*) available for this kind of anomalous experience. Indeed, some of our participants more overtly negotiated with their spirit agents about when they would or would not be able to work, and who could and could not 'come through'. Our interviewees attributed a protective role to their 'spirit guides'. For example, Tom explained:

> We've got supervisors, we've got staff up there, it's like a conveyor belt, and then we've got the supervisor at the end of the line saying 'Yes, right, you're on now' or they might say 'Yes, right, hang on a minute, you're on in a minute' I become aware of the communicator, but the helper might say 'Right Tom, the next one is going to be difficult', 'you're going to have trouble with them' or you know, and they only give me the nod if it's going to be like that.

Temple and Harper (2009) also found that in order to manage negative or overwhelming experiences, neophyte mediums attended development circles at which they learnt techniques for controlling communication with spirits, such as invoking protection from spirit guides. Research with voice hearers who do not identify as mediums similarly indicates that directly engaging with voices (rather than attempting to suppress them) can promote a more positive relationship between voice hearers and their voices (Corstens, Longden and May 2012). Some voice hearers have reported a sense of companionship with their voices (Romme and Escher 2000) or have sought guidance from them (Nayani and David 1996), and Sorrell, Hayward and Meddings (2010) found that clinical and non-clinical voice hearers could be distinguished in terms of the latter being more likely to perceive their voices as benevolent, and being less likely to distance themselves from them. Chin, Hayward and Drinnan (2009) conducted interviews with ten service users and performed an interpretative phenomenological analysis (IPA) on transcripts to explore how voice hearers relate to their voice. They found that whilst some participants believed their voices maintained a position of power over them, others described the relationship with their voice(s) in terms of an intimate engagement or alliance. Some participants had developed strategies for coping with the voices, such as setting boundaries as to when the voice would be listened to and communicated with, which had some success. In this way they were able to exercise control over their environment, a factor that has been found to be associated with life satisfaction (Roe and Bell 2016; Windle and Woods 2004).

Conclusion

In this chapter we have considered a wide range of experiences that are variously described as anomalous, paranormal, spiritual and so on, because their occurrence seems to be contrary to some basic materialistic understandings of how the world should work; for example, that thoughts cannot be transferred from one person to another without the mediation of the conventional senses, or that a person's centre of consciousness dies when their brain dies. Such experiences are also unusual in that, for the most part, they are quite unexpected and often are difficult for the experient to make sense of. Nevertheless, they are relatively common occurrences across cultures and have been reported throughout history by people who are otherwise normal and healthy. However, the tendency of the scientific mainstream to ignore or ridicule 'the paranormal' has left people wary of disclosing such experiences to others for fear of being regarded as gullible or as suffering from some underlying pathology. This taboo has consequences for experients' wellbeing; first because, as we have seen, the experience itself can be distressing and can provoke existential questions that themselves can be troubling; and secondly because the lack of opportunity to share and reflect on experiences in a supportive space makes it difficult for them to be appropriately processed and integrated, leaving the experient to adopt less healthy strategies such as denial and repression.

Unfortunately, where people are sufficiently troubled by these experiences that they have sought support from psychotherapists and counsellors, they have generally been disappointed to discover that these professionals are unable to deal with such disclosures in a way that is satisfactory to them. Clients' accounts of the therapeutic interaction often involve the recasting or diminution of their anomalous experiences and their interpretation of them in ways that leave them feeling unheard or misunderstood. Therapists also report that their training has left them ill-prepared to deal with this kind of material. Clinical parapsychology offers a response to this mismatch by arguing for therapeutic practice that is founded on an evidence-based understanding of the nature and causes of the phenomena. Such an approach emphasizes the need to normalize the experience, discriminating between phenomena that may be associated with pathology and those that do not have such an association (cf. Cardeña, Lynn and Krippner 2014), and providing the means for clients to assimilate or manage them by finding a personal experiential framework or explanatory model that allows them to come to terms with their experiences.

Research focusing on the experiences of mediums could provide the basis for a more general model for how to work with challenging countercultural 'spiritual' experiences. Mediums have a history of spontaneous experiences (often beginning in childhood) and illustrate how the reactions of others can have significant consequences for the degree to which the experiences are seen as inexplicable, uncontrollable and distressing. When reframed using a spiritual model that gives them meaning and purpose, the experiences become much less challenging and more amenable to control using psychological devices such as negotiation and protection. Whether or not these explanations have a solid ontological basis is moot—the fact that they are psychologically real seems to be sufficient for them to have real psychological effects.

The experiences related in this review also speak to the importance of connecting with a community that shares a belief system that is respectful of the phenomena. Unfortunately, we have seen that this is not a common response among the helping professions, and there is a clear need for the education of psychologists, psychotherapists and counsellors so that they appreciate that the experiences are rarely indicative of pathology and are often deeply meaningful to the experient.

Biographical Note

Chris Roe is Professor of Psychology at the University of Northampton, UK, and Director of the Centre for the Psychology and Social Sciences that is based there. Chris is the Perrott-Warrick Senior Researcher (Trinity College, Cambridge) and Visiting Professor at Bucks New University. He is President of the Society for Psychical Research and the International Affiliate for England of the Parapsychology Foundation. He has served as Chair of the British Psychological Society Transpersonal Psychology Section, and as President of the Parapsychological Association. He is an Associate Editor for the *Journal of Parapsychology* and is on the editorial board for the *Journal of the Society for Psychical Research* and the *Transpersonal Psychology Review*. His research interests are around understanding the nature of anomalous experiences and includes research on the phenomenology of paranormal experience, particularly as it affects wellbeing, the psychology of paranormal belief and of deception, as well as experimental approaches to test claims for extrasensory perception and psychokinesis, particularly where they involve psychological factors. Recent research has been concerned with the relationship between altered states of consciousness and psychic experience. He has published over 100 journal papers and book chapters and given over 150 invited and conference presentations.

Notes

1. Such experiences are variously labelled, *inter alia*, 'paranormal', 'anomalous', 'transpersonal', 'exceptional', and 'spiritual', depending on the orientation of the experient and/or the academic discussing them. For the purposes of this chapter, these terms are treated as synonymous.

2. In this chapter I take 'wellbeing' to refer to 'how people feel and how they function, both on a personal and a social level, and how they evaluate their lives as a whole' (New Economics Foundation 2012, 6). In this vein, mental ill health is characterized here in terms of beliefs, perceptions and behaviours that are inconsistent with the person's prevailing culture, are regarded as outside of the person's volition and control, are a source of distress to them or to those close to them, and/or make it difficult for them to maintain productive social and vocational relationships (cf. Kerns et al. 2014).
3. Another factor that might serve to reduce the number who seek counselling is suggested by Greyson and Bush (1996, 211), who note that 'people who have distressing experiences may resist talking about them to avoid reliving a personal horror, or from a sense that others must be spared a knowledge too dreadful to bear'.
4 For example, a client might report a series of dreams in which the number '909' features prominently, and this turns out to be the unpublished house number of the therapist they are working with (Hopcke 2009, cited in Roxburgh, Ridgway and Roe 2016, 45). This event is interpreted by Hopcke in terms of the deepening connection between the two individuals that form the therapeutic dyad, and its role in facilitating a breakthrough for a socially phobic client.
5. All respondent names are pseudonyms so as to preserve anonymity.

Bibliography

Braud, W. 2012. 'Health and Well-Being Benefits of Exceptional Human Experiences'. In *Mental Health and Anomalous Experience*, edited by C. Murray, 107–124. New York: Nova Science Publishers.

Broad, C. D. 1949. 'The Relevance of Psychical Research to Philosophy'. *The Journal of The Royal Institute of Philosophy* 24 (91): 291–309. https://doi.org/10.1017/S0031819100007452

Cardeña, E. 2018. 'The Experimental Evidence for Parapsychological Phenomena: A Review'. *American Psychologist* 73 (5): 663–677. https://doi.org/10.1037/amp0000236

Cardeña, E., S. J. Lynn and S. Krippner (Eds.). 2014. *Varieties of Anomalous Experience: Examining the Scientific Evidence* (2nd edn). Washington, DC: American Psychological Association. https://doi.org/10.1037/14258-000

Castro, M., R. Burrows and R. Wooffitt. 2014. 'The Paranormal is (Still) Normal: The Sociological Implications of a Survey of Paranormal Experiences in Great Britain'. *Sociological Research Online* 19 (3): 1–15. https://doi.org/10.5153/sro.3355

Chin, J. T., M. Hayward and A. Drinnan. 2009. '"Relating" to Voices: Exploring the Relevance of this Concept to People who Hear Voices'. *Psychology and Psychotherapy: Theory, Research and Practice* 82: 1–17. https://doi.org/10.1348/147608308X320116

Cooper, C. E., C. A. Roe and G. Mitchell. 2015. 'Anomalous Experiences and the Bereavement Process'. In *The Ecstasy of the End: Death and Dying Across Traditions*, edited by T. Cattoi and C. Moreman, 117–131. New York: Palgrave MacMillan. https://doi.org/10.1057/9781137472083_8

Corbeau, I. (2004). *Verlangen naar het licht. Ein onderzoek naar psychische problematiek en hulpverlengening nabijnadoodervaringen.* Utrecht, The Netherlands: University of Utrecht.

Corstens, D., E. Longden and R. May. 2012. 'Talking with Voices: Exploring What is Expressed by the Voices People Hear'. *Psychosis: Psychological, Social and Integrative Approaches* 4: 95–104. https://doi.org/10.1080/17522439.2011.571705

Davis, J., L. Lockwood and C. Wright. 1991. 'Reasons for Not Reporting Peak Experiences'. *Journal of Humanistic Psychology* 31: 86–94. https://doi.org/10.1177/0022167891311008

Dein, S. 2012. 'Mental Health and the Paranormal'. *International Journal of Transpersonal Studies* 3: 61–74. https://doi.org/10.24972/ijts.2012.31.1.61

Evenden, R. E., C. E. Cooper and G. Mitchell. 2013. 'A Counseling Approach to Mediumship: Adaptive Outcomes of Grief Following an Exceptional Experience'. *Journal of Exceptional Experiences and Psychology* 1 (2): 14–23.

Eybrechts, M. V. and J. L. F. Gerding. 2012. 'Explorations in Clinical Parapsychology'. In *Perspectives of Clinical Parapsychology: An Introductory Reader*, edited by W. H. Kramer, E. Bauer, and G. H. Hövelmann, 35–48. Bunnik, The Netherlands: Stichting Het Johan Borgman Fonds.

Greyson, B. and N. E. Bush. 1996. 'Distressing Near-Death Experiences'. In *The Near-Death Experience: A Reader*, edited by L. W. Bailey and J. Yates, 207–230. New York: Routledge.

Hastings, A. 1983. 'A Counseling Approach to Parapsychological Experience'. *Journal of Transpersonal Psychology* 15: 143–167.

Heriot-Maitland, C., M. Knight and E. Peters. 2012. 'A Qualitative Comparison of Psychotic-Like Phenomena in Clinical and Non-Clinical Populations'. *British Journal of Clinical Psychology* 51: 37–53. https://doi.org/10.1111/j.2044-8260.2011.02011.x

Irwin, H. J. and C. A. Watt. 2007. *An Introduction to Parapsychology* (5th edn). Jefferson, NC: McFarland.

Kennedy, J. and H. Kanthamani. 1995. 'An Exploratory Study of the Effects of Paranormal and Spiritual Experiences on Peoples' Lives and Well-Being'. *Journal of the American Society for Psychical Research* 89: 249–265.

Kerns, J. G., N. Karcher, C. Raghavan and H. Berenbaum. 2014. 'Anomalous Experiences, Peculiarity, and Psychopathology'. In *Varieties of Anomalous Experience: Examining the Scientific Evidence* (2nd edn), edited by E. Cardeña, S. J. Lynn, and S. Krippner, 57–76. Washington, DC: American Psychological Association. https://doi.org/10.1037/14258-003

Klimo, J. 1998. 'Clinical Parapsychology and the Nature of Reality'. Retrieved from http://www.jonklimo.com/papers/clinpara-uspa.pdf

Kramer, W. H. 2012. 'Experiences with PSI Counselling in Holland'. In *Perspectives of Clinical Parapsychology: An Introductory Reader*, edited by W. H. Kramer, E. Bauer and G. H. Hövelmann, 7–19. Bunnik, The Netherlands: Stichting Het Johan Borgman Fonds.

Milton, J. 1992. 'Effects of "Paranormal" Experiences on People's Lives: An Unusual Survey of Spontaneous Cases'. *Journal of the Society for Psychical Research* 58: 314–323.

Nayani, T. H. and A. S. David. 1996. 'The Auditory Hallucination: A Phenomenological Survey'. *Psychological Medicine* 26: 177–189. https://doi.org/10.1017/S003329170003381X

New Economics Foundation. 2012. *Measuring Wellbeing: A Guide for Practitioners*. London: New Economics Foundation.

Parra, A. 2012. 'Group Therapy Approach to Exceptional Human Experiences: An Argentinean Experience'. In *Perspectives of Clinical Parapsychology: An Introductory Reader*, edited by W. H. Kramer, E. Bauer and G. H. Hövelmann, 88–102. Bunnik, The Netherlands: Stichting Het Johan Borgman Fonds.

Pechey, R. and P. Halligan. 2012. 'Prevalence and Correlates of Anomalous Experiences in a Large Non-Clinical Sample'. *Psychology and Psychotherapy: Theory, Research and Practice* 85: 150–162. https://doi.org/10.1111/j.2044-8341.2011.02024.x

Roe, C. A. 2016. 'Is Inconsistency Our Only Consistent Outcome?' *Mindfield* 8 (2): 70–75.

Roe, C. A. and C. Bell. 2016. 'Paranormal Belief and Perceived Control Over Life Events'. *Journal of the Society for Psychical Research* 80 (2): 65–76.

Romme, M. and S. Escher. 2000. *Making Sense of Voices: A Guide for Mental Health Professionals Working with Voice-Hearers*. London: MIND.

Roxburgh, E. C. and R. E. Evenden. 2016a. 'Most People Think You're a Fruit Loop: Clients' Experiences of Seeking Support for Anomalous Experiences'. *Counselling and Psychotherapy Research* 16 (3): 211–221. https://doi.org/10.1002/capr.12077

Roxburgh, E. C. and R. E. Evenden. 2016b. '"They Daren't Tell People": Therapists' Experiences of Working with Clients who Report Anomalous Experiences'. *European Journal of Psychotherapy & Counselling* 18 (2): 123–141. https://doi.org/10.1080/13642537.2016.1170059

Roxburgh, E. C., S. Ridgway and C. A. Roe. 2015. 'Exploring the Meaning in Meaningful Coincidences: An Interpretative Phenomenological Analysis of Synchronicity in Therapy. *European Journal of Psychotherapy & Counselling* 17 (2): 144–161. https://doi.org/10.1080/13642537.2015.1027784

Roxburgh, E. C., S. Ridgway and C. A. Roe. 2016. 'Synchronicity in the Therapeutic Setting: A Survey of Mental Health Professionals'. *Counselling and Psychotherapy Research* 16 (1): 44–53. https://doi.org/10.1002/capr.12057

Roxburgh, E. C. and C. A. Roe. 2013. '"Say From Whence You Owe This Strange Intelligence": Investigating Explanatory Systems of Spiritualist Mental Mediumship Using Interpretative Phenomenological Analysis'. *International Journal of Transpersonal Studies* 32 (1): 27–42. https://doi.org/10.24972/ijts.2013.32.1.27

Roxburgh, E. C. and C. A. Roe. 2014. 'Reframing Voices and Visions Using a Spiritual Model: An Interpretative Phenomenological Analysis of Anomalous Experiences in Mediumship'. *Mental Health, Religion, & Culture* 17 (6): 641–653. https://doi.org/10.1080/13674676.2014.894007

Siegel, C. 1986. 'Parapsychological Counselling: Six Patterns of Response to Spontaneous Psychic Experiences'. In *Research in Parapsychology 1985*, edited by W. G. Roll, 172–174. Metuchen, NJ: Scarecrow Press.

Smith, J. A., P. Flowers and M. Larkin. 2009. *Interpretative Phenomenological Analysis*. London: Sage.

Sorrell, E., M. Hayward and S. Meddings. 2010. 'Interpersonal Processes and Hearing Voices: A Study of the Association Between Relating to Voices and Distress in Clinical and Non-Clinical Hearers'. *Behavioural and Cognitive Psychotherapy* 38: 127–140. https://doi.org/10.1017/S1352465809990506

Steffen, E. and A. Coyle. 2012. '"Sense of Presence" Experiences in Bereavement and Their Relationship to Mental Health: A Critical Examination of a Continuing Controversy'. In *Mental Health and Anomalous Experience*, edited by C. D. Murray, 33–56. New York: Nova Science Publishers.

Taylor, S. F. 2005. 'Between the Idea and the Reality: A Study of the Counselling Experiences of Bereaved People who Sense the Presence of the Deceased'. *Counselling and Psychotherapy Research* 5: 53–61. https://doi.org/10.1080/14733140512331343921

Taylor, G. and C. Murray. 2012. 'A Qualitative Investigation into Non-Clinical Voice Hearing: What Factors May Protect Against Distress?'. *Mental Health, Religion, & Culture* 15: 373–388. https://doi.org/10.1080/13674676.2011.577411

Temple, J. and D. Harper. 2009. 'Clairaudience in the Spiritualist Church: When Hearing Spirits is a Culturally Sanctioned Experience'. Paper presented at the First World Hearing Voices Congress, Maastricht, September 17–18.

Tierney, I. 2012. 'Lessons from a Case Study: An Annotated Narrative'. In *Perspectives of Clinical Parapsychology: An Introductory Reader*, edited by W. H. Kramer, E. Bauer and G. H. Hövelmann, 20–29. Bunnik, The Netherlands: Stichting Het Johan Borgman Fonds.

Windle, G. and R. Woods. 2004. 'Variations in Subjective Wellbeing: The Mediating Role of a Psychological Resource'. *Ageing and Society* 24 (4): 583–602. https://doi.org/10.1017/S0144686X04002107

Wooffitt, R. 1992. *Telling Tales of the Unexpected: Organization of Factual Discourse*. Hemel Hempstead: Harvester Wheatsheaf.

Section Two:
The Body in Focus

Chapter 3

Made in the Image: The Christian Understanding of the Body

Jeff Leonardi

And the Word was made flesh and dwelt among us. (John 1:14)

Introduction

In the Western world we inhabit something of a battleground with regard to our relationship with our bodies: our own and those of others. Standards of 'the body beautiful' emanate from the media whilst obesity and anorexia are matters for public health concern. There is much evidence that both genders are beset by anxieties about their body image, which can also become a psychological health issue and cause or symptom of anxiety, depression and even suicidal tendencies. The battle to stay slim and healthy is conducted in the face of junk food industries, sedentary leisure activities and burgeoning (sedentary) electronic media use. Sexuality is also a battleground, with pornography websites having the highest online usage of all. There are questions about whether there is such a thing as addiction to pornography, but at a time of great sexual freedom, the extremely high rates of access to pornography suggest that perhaps overall interpersonal sexual satisfaction as such is no greater than in the past, and possibly less so, given the unrealistic and possibly unhealthy expectations that heterosexual young men especially have for themselves and their partners, derived from a web pornography-based education in sexual matters.

In this chapter I should like to explore the cultural background or underpinning of Western attitudes to the human body, to try to explain why our behaviour seems beset by such conflictual attitudes and desires, and to suggest ways in which progress might be made towards physical, psychological and, indeed, spiritual wellbeing. Since focussing on this theme I have conducted a number of 'straw polls' of audiences in various educational contexts, asking for a show of hands as to whether they thought Christianity exhibits a positive or negative attitude towards

(a) the human body and (b) sexuality. The results have been consistent and for question (a) roughly 50% positive/negative; and for (b) around 70% negative. These results seem consistent with a more generally held perception in British society that Christianity is at least ambivalent, and often negative, towards the physical body and human sexuality. This is paradoxical, to say the least, given that Jewish literature has a positive take on sexuality and sensuality, for example The Song Of Solomon in the Jewish Bible/Old Testament, and Jesus' own behaviour and relationships are frequently celebratory of life and love, for example Luke 5:34, 7:34.

My own perspective is based in a psycho-spiritual approach, bringing together Christian and other spiritual understandings of the significance of the body with those of humanistic psychology and, in particular, the Person-centred Approach. Humanistic psychology has a primary goal of integration of the whole person—physical, mental and spiritual. Person-centred theory has at its core the concept of the actualizing tendency towards greater integration and effectiveness of the organism, human and otherwise, and caters for a concept of the person which recognizes that the human organism as a totality contains far greater wisdom and awareness than the conscious mind or intellect alone, thus placing a greater emphasis upon bodily awareness too. This can include 'gut feelings' and intuitions, as well as significant emotional responses. We shall return to these considerations later in our account.

In the Beginning

Christianity evolved out of Judaism and incorporates the Jewish Bible as the first part of the Christian Bible. The first book of both Bibles, Genesis, deals with the origin of the cosmos, the earth and its creatures, and humankind. Most will be familiar with the story of the 'Fall' of the proto-human beings, Adam and Eve, in the Garden of Eden (Genesis 3). This is usually presented as a moral teaching about obedience to God, and the consequences of disobedience. But we can also view it in terms of an early depiction of a conflict between external authority (God) and human desire, a conflict which is also located within the human beings themselves. As soon as they partake of the forbidden fruit they realize that they are naked, feel shame and cover their bodies. It seems that their naked bodies, which had hitherto been experienced unselfconsciously and unproblematically, became a source of discomfort once they had engaged with the 'knowledge of good and evil'. In Jungian psychology the story is interpreted as the first stage of the (positive but costly) journey from innocent pre-consciousness to experienced mature consciousness (Wickes 1977, 12).

Whatever the status of this story as myth, psychology or prehistory, it has become a foundation of Christian theology, (cf. also 'Original Sin', St Augustine) and generates a substantial body of doctrine around the concept of human nature, sinfulness, redemption and atonement: 'Christianity uses the Genesis myth to express the fact that man's basic malady is sin …. Original sin is the world's condition of faithlessness to God' (Halverson and Cohen 1960, 136–7). We will attend to this cultural legacy only in so far as it contributes to the present predicament surrounding bodily relationships. It may well be true that in terms of contemporary culture and practice the West is largely post-Christian, but the themes and tropes of Christianity continue to exert a powerful influence, whether acknowledged as such or not. Unfortunately that legacy and influence has often been less than helpful in many ways, and even directly harmful, in so far as it has been interpreted in ways that encourage a negative or hostile approach to the relationship with our bodies and the physical world to which we belong and in which we participate. We shall also hope to recognize the paradox, and perhaps tragedy, that a faith tradition which can be justly claimed to be essentially life- and body-affirming, should have become misappropriated by the opposing tendency, with life- and self-punitive consequences.

Not Just Religious

We have spoken thus far in terms of the Judaeo-Christian heritage of our culture. The Enlightenment is taken to be the stage at which the religious worldview was challenged and gradually replaced by the rationalist and secular one. But rationalism as it developed can be seen to embrace a view of the body which can contribute to the same negative developments we are suggesting. When Descartes invoked the primary existential statement *cogito ergo sum:* 'I think therefore I am' ('Discourse on Method', 1637), he elevated thought above other components of human existence such as the physical. By separating mind and body ('Cartesian dualism') rationalism diminishes the status of the physical and contributes to a model of the human in which mind is the controller and the body is reduced to the status of a dependent mechanism or slave. This therefore re-establishes the ground for conflict between body and mind, and so many of the frustrations to which the human being is prone. Many of the most dangerous issues of our times—the environment and ecology, farming and pollution, technology and genetics, etc. can be seen to derive from an inaccurate and harmful emphasis on humanity as 'master' or controller and not as celebratory and respectful participant in a physical existence and universe.

It should be noted that there are other models of consciousness and existence in the Western tradition, e.g., the *Phenomenology* originating with Hegel ('Phenomenology of Mind', 1807) but developed as a school by Husserl ('Logical Investigations, 1900–1) and Heidegger ('Being and Time', 1927) and, before them, Berkeley's *Esse est percipi*: 'to be is to be perceived' ('Principles of Human Knowledge, 1710). But Cartesian dualism exerts a strong continuing influence in the general intellectual culture, almost perhaps at an unconscious level.

But however much the secular culture has added to these difficulties, Christianity certainly laid a substantial foundation of dualism, and discomfort with the body. To return to Genesis, the first humans are given 'mastery' of the earth for their benefit (Genesis 1: 28). The original term was probably closer to 'stewardship'—which conveys a much more co-participative and responsible attitude—but there is no doubt that the 'mastery' concept held sway in Christendom, and still does in those streams of Western Protestantism which emphasize individual responsibility and achievement, and can be seen to be particularly expressed in American culture (see for example Fletcher 2006). Human beings need no excuses, it seems, for ruthlessly exploiting the natural world, but if they are Christians they do seem to find a ready permission and justification in the 'mastery' ordinance in Genesis.

A Wider Perspective

We have so far introduced two early perspectives on the body: the Judaeo-Christian and the rationalist, but there is an even earlier, and wider, tradition of which both of these can be seen to partake: *Asceticism*. Most if not all religious traditions contain this practice in various forms: the belief that depriving the body of food and comfort will encourage the spiritual life of the adherent (see for example Brown 2008; Wimbush and Valantasis 2003). In Christianity, the 40 days of Lent in particular are taken to be a time to renounce worldly comforts and practise asceticism as a personal tribute to Christ's time in the wilderness at the start of his public ministry, and more importantly as a preparation for the profound events of Holy Week, Good Friday and Easter Day, i.e., the Crucifixion and Resurrection of Christ. In these present times this can be as superficial as renouncing chocolate or alcohol, or take more determined forms of disciplined fasting, service to others and prayer. In Islam there is Ramadan and abstaining from food and drink during the hours of daylight. This is again a spiritual discipline and a reminder and act of solidarity with the poor who have no food.

In the Hindu tradition many determined spiritual seekers have for millennia committed themselves to a discipline of prayer, poverty and renunciation as holy men and women, both within monastic settings and also itinerant in the world. Buddhism has a ready language of renunciation for escaping the snares of desire and attachment to seek release and enlightenment. In that sense, Buddhism encapsulates the essential doctrine of asceticism, that attachment to physical, carnal desires and their satisfaction inhibits spiritual development, and that the converse, renunciation of such pleasures and dependencies, can enable the seeker to progress on the spiritual path. (see Wimbush and Valantasis 2003).

A Further Stage

Beyond renunciation lies *mortification*. Asceticism can consist in a passive reduction in self care by fasting and other reductions in physical comforts; mortification takes things a stage further by actively treating the body as an enemy to be mistreated or punished in the same cause of spiritual liberation. In the Hindu tradition the 'bed of nails' and extreme disciplines leading to the atrophy of bodily members might convey this approach but we find plentiful examples in the Christian tradition, such as wearing 'hair shirts' or 'sackcloth and ashes', self-flagellation, and at the extreme, temporary crucifixion on Good Friday. In all these cases the body has become the place of punishment for the 'sins of the flesh' or out of devotional identification with the sufferings of Christ. In the former case it can be argued that there is a profound self-deception (which may not be deliberate, but simply a logical outcome of a certain theology of sin) about that which chooses to sin—the person—and that which performs the sin—the person's body. But there is no doubt that the underlying cultural dualism about mind and body contributes to this deception. We can find texts in scripture which encourage this way of thinking, e.g., Jesus in Matthew 5:30: 'If your hand leads you to sin, chop it off, or your eye similarly, pluck it out, for it is better to do this than suffer in hell' (for your sins). This is an extreme teaching which can be understood as hyperbole, but it illustrates the perspective and the dangers of too literal an interpretation. The Inquisition was another example of the prioritizing of the soul over the body, where it was considered worthwhile to subject a heretic's body to extreme suffering, torture and death in the cause of 'saving' their souls from eternal damnation if they repented of their heresy (see for example Glucklich 2003).

Purity

There is another perspective on spirituality and the body, and that is the concept of ritual or other *purity*. In ordinary terms purity signifies freedom from anything that debases, contaminates or pollutes. We can readily see what this means in terms of, for example, drinking water or food. But moral or spiritual purity introduces another dimension, of behaviour, attitude and relationship. In Hindu culture the lowest caste, Dalits or 'outcastes', are also called 'Untouchables' because for a Hindu of higher caste to touch them would pollute them and require ritual cleansing and (re-)purifying. This was, importantly, to do with the activities for which Dalits were employed, for example slaughtering and butchery of animals, tanning of hides, disposal of excrement etc., and the corresponding impure substances with which they thereby came into contact.

In the Jewish Bible and Christian Old Testament there are similar prohibitions on contact with certain foods and substances, and with those who were 'impure' by being outside the Jewish faith, i.e., Gentiles, with again corresponding rituals for cleansing and purification in the event of accidental or deliberate pollution. Ritual sacrifice of animals played an important part in Jewish temple worship, and such animals also had to be pure, 'without blemish' (e.g., Numbers 28:3).

A related and probably more profound level of purity is that of *moral purity*. This concept is again to be found in the Jewish Bible/Old Testament and speaks in terms of purity of *heart, faith* and *motives* e.g., Psalm 24:3 and 4: 'Who may ascend the mountain of the Lord? Who may stand in his holy place? The one who has clean hands and a pure heart, who does not trust in an idol or swear by a false god'. In the Christian New Testament, as Christianity expands to include Gentiles (who are progressively not required to keep Jewish dietary and other religious rules of purity), the emphasis shifts squarely on to purity of belief and behaviour e.g., James 1:27: 'Religion that God our Father accepts as pure and faultless is this: to look after orphans and widows in their distress and to keep oneself from being polluted by the world'. The phrase 'polluted by the world' (or 'the world, the flesh and the devil' from the Litany of the Book of Common Prayer; cf. Ephesians 2:1–3) echoes the tendency to separate soul (pure) from body (impure) which will later be recognized as a heresy, as we shall see when we refer to Gnosticism below. Jesus' own statements were very clear about the error of thinking in terms of bodily pollution, as we can see in, for example, Matthew 15:10–20: '(it is) not what goes into the mouth (that) defiles a person, but what comes out of the mouth ... whatever goes into the mouth goes into the stomach and so passes on. But what comes out of the mouth proceeds from the heart, and this defiles a person. For out of the heart comes evil thoughts, murder, adultery, fornication, theft, false witness, slander. These are what defile a person, but to eat with unwashed hands does not defile a person'. Indeed, in his personal contacts and relationships Jesus personifies a person liberated from the concerns of ritual purity (e.g., 'The woman at the well', John 4:1–42).

Sexuality

We have recently noted that Jesus included in the list of immoral behaviours which 'defile' a person some that refer to sexual activity, namely adultery and fornication. Most if not all of the world religions include prescriptions and proscriptions for sexual behaviour. Most of these permit sexual relationships only within accepted relationships, namely marriage. Historically of course there has been the social regulation of relationships in the name of social order and legitimacy of offspring, and usually the 'ownership' of women as wives who are constrained only to produce their husband's offspring. Religion extends this biological and social ordering into the moral and spiritual spheres. The Jewish Bible/Old Testament includes polygamous relationships but by New Testament times monogamy is the rule and Jesus can refer to a son and a daughter leaving their respective parents and 'becoming one flesh' (Mark 10:7–8a), and then proceeds to a proscription of divorce: 'So they are no longer two, but one flesh. That which God has joined together, let no-one put asunder' (Mark 10:8b–9; also incorporated into the Anglican marriage vows). In our times Christianity has been seen more as a bastion of tradition than as a liberal influence, but biblical scholars suggest that Jesus' teaching here was in reaction to the ease with which a man could dispense with his wife, leaving her destitute (Nineham 1969, 259–263; Barclay 1975, 237–240), but also as affirming the *covenantal* and therefore sacred nature of marriage as such. But where marriage vows are taken seriously there is no doubt that Christian teaching supports lifelong monogamy and condemns adultery.

In terms of our exploration of Christian attitudes to the body, perhaps the more important consideration is whether the teachings about relationships and sexuality convey a positive or negative attitude. In the Jewish Bible/Old Testament. the Mosaic Ten Commandments contain one forbidding adultery, and so uphold the sanctity of marriage as above, but the book entitled the Song of Solomon is a lyrical celebration of the joys of heterosexual love. In the Christian New Testament there is every encouragement towards chastity and responsible monogamy, and strong condemnation of 'fornication and adultery' as we have seen, but very little by way of positive celebration of erotic love. On the other hand there are accounts of Jesus behaving with relaxed attitudes to physical intimacy (e.g., Luke 7:36–50; John 13:23), but with no suggestion of impropriety or sexual activity beyond that which is implicit in physical and sensuous contact. The expression used by Jesus, 'one flesh', of course implies sexual union at the heart of marriage, and Jesus was operating in the Jewish culture of his times, which was not prudish or a- or anti-sexual except at its ascetical extremes. (St Paul does write—albeit in the expectation that the end of the world was imminent—that chastity is preferable to marriage (1 Corinthians 7:25–end) but allows that those with physical (sexual) needs would be better to marry.)

Homosexual relations are of course a battleground for the contemporary church. If there is little by way of instruction, celebration or edification on sexual matters in the New Testament, there is even less about homosexuality. Many of the world's cultures contain negative attitudes in this area. Minorities are vulnerable, especially when identifiable. The Churches have upheld traditional forms of relationship as described and have struggled to accept variations from the perceived norm. The only texts which can be claimed to explicitly condemn homosexual relations are to be found in the Jewish Bible/Old Testament, and scholars dispute whether they are specific to promiscuous and/or coercive relationships, as opposed to loving and faithful ones. The Christian churches took something of a lead in the emancipation of slavery, but sexual territory has been more problematic and retrogressive. The problem arises, paradoxically, from the fear of departing from fidelity to scriptural authority, and this affects a wider range of issues than sexuality. Despite this fear, many parts of the Churches worldwide are now beginning to question what is the most loving attitude to homosexuality, and some have moved to full acceptance and the liturgical blessing of homosexual relations and administration of the sacrament of marriage (see, for example, Groves 2008).

Intermediate Summary

We have seen that there is definitely a theological struggle, historically and into the present, between the affirmation and celebration of physical bodies and a cautious and negative view of 'bodily appetites'. There is in so much of this behaviour and belief an underlying tension between a loving dedication to spiritual development, which can include disciplines of renunciation, but with the focus always on the goal of a closer walk with God, on the one hand, and a kind of self hatred and discomfort with carnal existence which would prefer to achieve the release from the physical flesh which can only occur at death. This dichotomy and preference for the discarnate life of the soul was in fact identified as a heresy in itself by the early church in its rejection of *Gnosticism*. But this judgement has not prevented the heresy from living on in many forms. *The Christian*

Neurosis by the French psychiatrist Pierre Solignac is a good collection of case studies of the shadow side of Christian belief and practice, where fear, guilt, shame and self-denigration lead to very many aberrations and psychological damage and ill health (Solignac 1982).

I have been a counsellor/psychotherapist for 40 years (the terms are interchangeable). For a major part of that time I was employed by the Church of England as a 'Bishop's Adviser for Pastoral care and Counselling', and most of my counselling clients were Anglican ministers, ordained and lay, and their spouses or family members. Much of the counselling derived from aspects of the human condition which are common to all people, believers or not. But a regular and significant proportion was derived from particular aspects of holding Christian faith, and being Christian ministers, or related to them. Often these concerns had to do with self-care and self-giving, and setting boundaries to expectations, internal and external. One instance was of a Christian woman in her sixties, the wife of a Free Church minister, who had suffered from depression over time. When I saw her she told me that in her youth she had enjoyed both dancing and painting, but from the time she had made a serious Christian commitment she had relinquished these activities because they were frivolous and not properly Christian uses of her time and energy. I could only think that her depression was caused, to some degree, by her choosing to cut herself off from major sources of expression and wellbeing. If a believer allies themselves with negative views of simple pleasures and self-expression this must inevitably have negative implications for their wellbeing and even health, by curtailing their engagement with activities and impulses which are nourishing and re-creational. For this person, both dancing and painting had been sources of life-giving joy, but she no longer allowed herself to experience these satisfactions, and it did not seem that her particular form of holding faith was providing adequate compensation for this loss. There is also, of course, the likelihood that such attitudes are themselves a source of internal tensions which can also impact on the person's health and wellbeing.

We should not exaggerate the prevalence of these unhappy examples of Christianity distorted and taken to extremes, but neither should we pretend that they are so rare as to be unrepresentative. Christians can find real theological support in some of the teachings of the Christian churches for such views. There are other approaches which are more conducive to psychological and spiritual wellbeing. To these latter approaches we shall now turn.

Incarnation as a Virtue

It is indeed a great paradox that the very Christian tradition which claims that God become incarnate—embodied, carnal, fleshly—in Jesus Christ should have developed strands of such disdain for human flesh. In the majestic prologue to St John's Gospel we read: 'and the Word became flesh and dwelt among us, full of grace and truth' (John 1:14). This is the 'Word' (Greek: *Logos*) which (who) 'was with God from the beginning' and 'was God' (John 1:1), without whom 'nothing was made that was made' by God. In other words, the audacious claim is being made that Jesus Christ, the man who lived and died, was present with and participated in the being of God, and was active in Creation, from the outset. This 'cosmic Christ', to use the language of Teilhard de Chardin (Teilhard de Chardin 1970, 121) was also capable of being incarnated in a human body of flesh and blood, needs and desires.

The Orthodox Churches have perhaps developed the theology of Incarnation to a greater extent than the Western Churches, recognizing that in the birth of Christ as a human being, divinity inhabited humanity and materiality, and thereby (re-) infused the whole Creation with the Spirit of God. In Genesis, God had created Adam and Eve from inanimate matter 'in the image and likeness of God, male and female he created them' (Genesis 1:26). In Christian theology the Incarnation takes a further step of declaring that in Christ, God was capable of full human participation and expression without ontological barriers. In John's Gospel Jesus declared that his followers might attain to the same unity with God that he had, 'that they might be one as he and God are One, and that God might dwell in them' (John 17:21-23). The further Orthodox doctrine of *Theosis* or *Divinization* declares that the goal of human development is the fullest realization of this divine nature in human form: 'until all of us come to the unity of the faith and of the knowledge of the Son of God, to maturity, to the measure of the full stature of Christ' (St Paul, Ephesians 4:13).

The three terms: divinization, deification and theosis, are all equivalent, signifying 'likeness to and union with God' (Staniloe 2002, 64). Alfeyev makes clear the scope and significance of Orthodox Christian faith in this way:

> The concept of deification is central to the Eastern Orthodox theological and mystical tradition. To confess the true faith, to be a church member, to observe God's commandments, to pray, to participate in sacraments: all these are necessary primarily because they lead to deification, the ultimate goal of everyone's existence ... God made us so that we might become partakers of the divine nature and sharers in his

eternity, so that we might come to be like him through deification by Grace. (Alfeyev 2002, 191)

Divinization is not to be understood as assimilation of the person into the divine, where the separate personhood of the individual no longer exists, neither does the individual come to participate in the otherness or transcendence of God, rather the person is said to participate in God's *energies* (Ware 1979, 168). This is not the place for an elaborate theological statement of these ideas. The purpose in exploring them is simply to demonstrate how these foundational Christian perspectives are very far from conveying a denigratory attitude to human embodiment. Nelson makes a forthright declaration of what he sees to be an utterly orthodox position in these matters, whilst acknowledging the need for this view to be expressed more widely: 'Through its Old Testament rootage in the goodness of creation and through the New Testament's central focus on divine incarnation, Christian theology ought to have an immensely positive bias towards embodiment' (Nelson 1979, 19).

The use of 'ought' in this statement inevitably reveals that Nelson is arguing for something different from the prevailing situation, but in this seminal work he makes an eloquent case for the revision of the Christian perspective on the body, sexuality and spirituality in keeping with these sentiments. There have been an increasing number of voices, both from within and outside the Churches, arguing for these changes, for example Matthew Fox (Fox 1983), Rob Bell (Bell 2012), Richard Rohr (Rohr 2012) etc. In so far as theology can be seen to have struggled with the issues of the status of bodily existence, it is of interest that, in modern times, humanistic psychology has provided a serious articulation of the quest for wholeness which includes a full integration and respect for the human body, and to these developments we must now turn, with a view to discerning their relevance to the Christian understanding of the body.

The Contribution of Psychology

Humanistic psychology and psychotherapy embrace a holistic understanding of the human being: physical, emotional, psychological, intellectual and spiritual (Maslow 1962; Rogers 1961). The words *whole, holy* and *heal* all share a common root (Old English *halig;* Greek *holos).* In psychological terms the goal of growth and healing is *wholeness* or integration of all these aspects of being a person, including, importantly, the physical body. There are specific therapeutic approaches to *body work,* but all humanistic therapeutic approaches include a healthy respect for the importance of the physical body and its organs and systems. In particular the Person-centred approach, which is the psychotherapeutic approach with which I am most acquainted, emphasizes the importance of the human *organism*, and of *organismic* awareness. (Rogers 1959, 210; Seeman 1984, 146; Barrett-Lennard 1998, 487–8).

One of the axioms or *core conditions* of the Person-centred approach is that the 'client' is in a state of *incongruence*, while the therapist is in a state of *congruence*. Congruence and incongruence refer to the extent to which a person's self-concept and presentation of self accurately match their inner state of being. We could describe this in terms of honesty and sincerity, or *genuineness*, but in this case we need to allow for the possibility of an unconscious discrepancy between actual and expressed self-image and presentation. Indeed, it is such discrepancy, manifesting as tension or other psychological unease, which can lead a person to seek therapeutic help.

Rogers (1959) describes the *human organism* as having two essential aspects: the capacity to experience, and to distinguish between experience which is in accord or discrepant from the subject's *self-concept*; and the drive or tendency towards greater integration between experience and self-concept, expressed in the concept of *the actualizing tendency*.

In all of the material universe Rogers (1980) suggests there is a *formative tendency* towards increased order and complexity: a *syntropy* as opposed to *entropy*. This applies to inorganic matter as well as organic life. In organic life forms this becomes *the actualizing* tendency, which includes the drive towards the fulfilment of potential (Rogers 1959, 196). When organic life reaches the human form, the actualizing tendency includes the actualization of the *self* 'in ways which serve to maintain or enhance the *Organism*' (ibid.). A distinction needs to be expressed between the *self* (which includes all dimensions of the person: physical, psychological, intellectual etc., in other words the whole person) and the *self-concept*, which is the story a person tells themselves about who they are. The self-concept may bear all the consequences of *introjected* values, beliefs and behaviours which have become assimilated in the person and function as a given, almost beneath the conscious awareness. (*Introjection* is the process whereby a person, especially in childhood, absorbs and accepts instructions, values and behaviour from significant others—parents, etc.—who have the authority or power to impose them; these values etc. may be at variance with the individual's instinctive or organismic awareness, but because of the power and/or dependence relationship s/he comes to accept them and eventually assimilate them *as if they were their own*). It is in the potential discrepancies between the self-concept with its introjected values and beliefs, ('*conditions of worth*') and the *organismic self* of the person, that psychological tension arises. The actualizing tendency is the continuing urge within the person to heal this division and bring greater psychological integration and wholeness.

It will be clear from all this that Rogers' approach places a great emphasis upon 'the wisdom of the organism' (including biochemical, physiological and perceptual systems) over and against the purely intellectual self-understanding. His extensive clinical experience had provided ample evidence of the capacity of the conscious mind of the individual to deny and distort the messages of the person's total organism in favour of those which fitted their self-understanding and conditions of worth. A simple illustration might be a child who is brought up in a home where the expression of anger is disapproved of or forbidden. Such a child learns that anger is 'bad' according to his parents, and has in theory two choices: to consciously accept that it is inadvisable to display anger in their presence and to choose to avoid doing so to escape disapproval and punishment, in which case the child's self-awareness can still include these feelings and impulses, even if largely or entirely unexpressed (at least in their presence). The second, and more likely 'choice' will be to acquiesce with the parents' view of anger, to adopt (introject) their view of it and to disapprove of its occurrences to their self-awareness. Eventually this attitude can become assimilated as 'I am not an angry person' because 'angry persons are bad'. Eruptions of anger within the person can then be suppressed and denied to awareness, manifesting perhaps as bodily discomforts, physical tensions, headaches, digestive issues etc, and also as the corresponding psychological tensions: anxiety, sleep disturbances and nightmares, obsessive behaviours and thinking etc. This is one illustration of such a process and consequences, but there are very many other examples, not limited to anger, but of any felt response and behaviour in the child which is suppressed in order to conform to conditions of worth and thereby to avoid the disapproval of significant others. For example, a boy child may be disapproved of by a 'strong' father if he displays sensitive or vulnerable feelings. A girl child may be encouraged, often by her mother, to always put others' needs before her own, and disapproved of if she displays any self-assertiveness.

Having outlined the ways in which human beings can be led to a condition where there is an extent of alienation between their organismic awareness and their self-concept and conscious awareness of self, with corresponding harms to their sense of integration and wellbeing, it may be helpful to outline the beneficial outcomes of successful therapy and reintegration of the parts of the person towards a wholeness of being. Person-centred therapy takes place when the therapist offers the *core conditions* of the Person-centred approach, namely *empathy, genuineness* and *unconditional positive regard* (Rogers 1959, 213). If these conditions are present consistently and in good measure and experienced as such by the person seeking help, then growth towards wholeness can occur. It may be observed that, rather than the therapist inducing such growth in the client, the therapist is providing the conditions of relationship where the actualizing tendency in the client can be accessed and activated and induce such growth.

In a chapter entitled A Process Conception of Psychotherapy (Rogers 1961, 125–158), Rogers offers a summary of the outcomes of successful therapy, in which a person moves away from fixity—of feelings, conceptions and behaviour—and towards openness and fluidity; from incongruence to congruence; from self-concealment to self-disclosure; from the avoidance of intimacy in relationships to its embracing: 'the person becomes a unity of flow, of motion ... he has become an integrated process of changingness' (Rogers 1961, 158). The person so described is clearly not only to be viewed in terms of the successful outcome of therapy, but also as a well-adjusted and 'fully functioning' human being in every sense.

Frick offers a comparable list of the ways in which such therapeutic development may occur for the client:

1. Away from the facades and the constant preoccupation with keeping up appearances.
2. Away from 'oughts' and an internalized sense of duty springing from externally imposed obligations.
3. Away from living up to the expectations of others.
4. Towards valuing honesty and realness in oneself and others.
5. Towards valuing the capacity to direct one's own life.
6. Towards accepting and valuing one's self and one's feelings whether they are positive or negative.
7. Towards valuing the experience of the moment and the process of growth, rather than continually striving for objectives.
8. Towards a greater respect for and the understanding of others.
9. Towards cherishing of close relationships and a longing for more intimacy.
10. Towards a valuing of all forms of experience and a willingness to risk being open to all inner and outer experiences, however uncongenial or unexpected.

(Frick 1971, 179)

In many of these cases we can see an indication of what the integration of organismic awareness implies, both within the individual and between the individual and other persons in the relationship. In his final major work (Rogers 1980), Rogers describes his hypothesis of 'The Person of Tomorrow' in ways which reflect these depictions of the direction of therapy towards 'fully functioning'. He names twelve qualities or traits that he claims to perceive already in such people in his present experience: (1) openness, (2) desire for authenticity, (3) scepticism regarding science and technology, (4) desire for wholeness, (5) the wish for intimacy, (6) process persons, (7) caring, (8) attitude toward nature, (9) anti-institutional, (10) the authority within, (11) the unimportance of material things, (12) a yearning for the spiritual (Rogers 1980, 350-2). It will be noted that the final, twelfth quality listed is 'spiritual yearning'. I have elsewhere developed the spiritual aspects of the Person-centred approach (Leonardi 2008, 2016) but here it can be noted that there are profound implications of Rogers' account of human wellbeing in therapeutic terms, the importance of the body in organismic awareness, and the spiritual implications of what it means to be human in a fully integrated sense. At this point we can return to the Christian focus of our argument.

The Christian Understanding Further Developed

This exploration into the insights and perspectives of Person-centred psychology may seem to have taken us a long way from the initial focus on the Christian understanding of the body, but on further reflection I believe this will be seen quite differently, and as highly relevant. Jesus' teaching that the person who would find his self must paradoxically lose their self (Matthew 10:39) and that 'gaining the whole world' at the price of losing their self is a price too far (Luke 9:25) are two texts among many which can be read as indicating a choice, not just between overt temptations to sin and material aggrandizement, but as a deeper temptation to overlook and overrule the promptings of the deeper self (and conscience) in favour of these external accomplishments. If we look at an extended quote on these lines it may be even more clear how a psychological interpretation about the move from conditions of worth to an integrated self can be made credible:

> For I have come to set a man against his father, and a daughter against her mother, and a daughter-in-law against her mother-in-law, and a person's foes will be members of their own household. Whoever loves father or mother more than me is not worthy of me; and whoever loves son or daughter more than me is not worthy of me, and whoever does not take up the cross and follow me is not worthy of me. Those who find their life will lose it, and those who lose their life for my sake will find it. (Jesus in Matthew 10:35-39)

If we define Christ as 'our true self in God' then such a passage straddles the meanings of 'life' and 'self'. Richard Rohr is one of many contemporary spiritual writers who emphasize the inner and psychological significance of a great deal of the Christian scriptures. Always the direction of travel is towards greater integration and self honesty:

> I learned the terms 'True Self' and 'false self' from Thomas Merton – words he used to clarify what Jesus surely means when he said we must die to ourselves or we must 'lose ourselves to find ourselves'. Merton rightly recognised that it was not the body that had to 'die' but the 'false self' that we do not need anyway. The false self is simply a substitute for our deeper and deepest truth. It is a useful and even needful part of ourselves, but it is not all; the danger is when we think we are only our false, separate, small self. Our attachment to false self must die to allow True Self – our basic and unchangeable identity in God – to live fully and freely. (Richard Rohr, Centre for Action and Contemplation website posting, 18.9.2018, http://cacradicalgrace.org)

Mearns and Thorne, two leading Person-centred psychologists, could be illustrating the above quoted passage from Matthew when they write of the tensions evoked in the journey into Self, and of the need for the therapist to keep mindful of the importance of the client's family and social networks for the client's wellbeing, and of the need to support the client in satisfactorily negotiating the relationship between their emerging sense of authentic self and these relationships with significant others who, while they may well have investments in retaining the previous forms of relationship with and definitions of the client's self, are nonetheless significant for them:

> [...] there will be times when the pressure of the actualising tendency (towards congruence) will inspire a resistance. Such resistance is intimately related both to the actualising tendency and to the person's current existence as a social being. The effect of the resistance serves to maintain a balance which allows for a degree of expression for the actualising tendency while taking care to preserve the viability of the social context within the person's 'life space' … The forces of social mediation form a coherent and functional part of our existence as social beings, allowing us expression of the actualising tendency but exerting an imperative which cautions against the endangering of the social life space. (Mearns and Thorne 2000, 182–3)

These writers allow for more moderation and dialogue between the person's therapeutic process and their social context, between their emerging sense of self and their significant others, than does the gospel passage quoted above. But at their extremes, the search for authentic selfhood can seem like a life or death struggle, and certain significant others can seem like the 'enemy', at which point a person may face very painful and difficult choices, not unlike those in Jesus' teaching.

True Self

We have seen that in both humanistic psychology and Christian spirituality there are significant references to the self. In Christianity we have seen a distinction made between the self which needs to be 'lost', and that which must then be 'found', i.e., our 'false', egotistic selves, and our 'true', God-centred and -inspired selves. Person-centred psychology describes the self-concept which, through introjection and the distortion of the organismic valuing system, may be at variance with the organismic or 'true' self. There needs to be a further clarification made here, however. If we ask of Person-centred psychology, whether there is a concept of a 'true self', we find a subtle change in perspective, from self-concept as, if you like, a (selective) aggregate of life history, dispositions and experience, to organismic awareness as a process and not an object or outcome. In other words, the 'true self' in Person-centred psychology is a moment by moment process of changingness of awareness. In this sense the self is not material content but phenomenological process. Such a view is of course consistent with the current popularity of Mindfulness-based approaches to health and wellbeing.

So much psychological discomfort and tension arises from experiences, both from within and outer, which injure the individual's self-esteem. Mindfulness, consistent with its origins in Buddhist mindfulness, addresses such suffering by encouraging a movement away from self as 'image' or concept—which can indeed be challenged or 'injured'—to self as moment by moment process of awareness, and in the Buddhist case at least, ultimately 'no self' as such. If there is no self, there is no self to be injured or diminished. Again we can find parallels with the Christian teaching of losing the self to find the self, and there are indeed schools of Christian Mindfulness.

Conclusion

In this brief exploration of Christian understandings of the body we have seen that there are a number of different perspectives within the tradition, from a denigratory to a more celebratory attitude. It is perhaps not surprising that a tradition which has its heart an image of a human being dying a painful death by crucifixion, and which esteems this image as an icon of self-giving love, both human and divine, should have at the least an ambivalent attitude to the human body. If torture and death can be seen as potential gateways to resurrection and eternal life, then the body may not be the most important consideration. On the other hand, the Judaeo-Christian tradition affirms the created world and its creatures, including human beings as 'very good' in the Creator's eyes

(Genesis 1:33), and says of human beings in particular that they are made in the image and likeness of the Creator (Genesis 1:26). It would be hard on such grounds to disparage the physical bodies thus affirmed. In the Incarnation of Jesus Christ this divine inheritance is made even more explicit, and in Jesus, humanity is declared to be capable of divine inheritance: 'You are my Son, my beloved; with you I am well pleased' (Mark 1:11). We have seen how this tension or ambivalence, between affirmative and denigratory attitudes to the body emerges in the tradition through history. We have also examined this tendency in a wider context of cultures, faiths and philosophy, expressed variously in terms of asceticism, mortification of the flesh, and the pursuit of various notions of purity, including the sexual. Returning to the affirmative Christian doctrines of Incarnation and Divinization, we have introduced the psychology of the actualizing tendency and organismic awareness and integration, and found these to be highly relevant to both spirituality and the pursuit of health and wellbeing. The affirmation of the body as a wider locus of awareness and understanding than that provided by the intellect alone has profound implications for the study of spirituality. The Western emphasis upon conceptual understanding can neglect this broader territory and its riches. Indeed, it can be suggested that it is only when the study of spirituality and religion embraces such an integrative approach that real understanding of these matters can develop.

It is suggested also that an approach which respects both body and mind, and also emotion, intuition and intellect, can yield a highly beneficial psychology and spirituality of health and wellbeing, and that these latter suggest that religion teaching should recognize the danger of self- and bodily-denigration and enter a more affirmative vision of these matters. Finally we have suggested that contemporary spiritual and psychological approaches to bodily and sensory mindfulness may well be a meeting place and further starting point for self-understanding by the individual and thereby integration of mind and body, health and wellbeing.

Biographical Note

Jeff Leonardi is a Person-centred Counsellor, Supervisor, Trainer and Spiritual Companion, and a retired Anglican priest who was for 17 years Bishop's Adviser for Pastoral Care and Counselling in the Lichfield Diocese of the Church of England. He has been a Person-centred Counsellor for the past 40 years and has a PhD in the spirituality of Person-centred Counselling in relation to Christian spirituality, and the implications for Christian ministry and pastoral practice. He is currently undertaking research into Relational Spirituality and is an Honorary

Research Fellow of the Religious Experience Research Centre at the University of Wales Trinity Saint David at Lampeter.

Bibliography

All biblical quotations are taken from The Bible, New Revised Standard Version.

Alfeyev, H. 2002. *The Mystery of Faith.* London: Darton, Longman & Todd.
Barclay, William. 1975. *The Gospel of Mark.* Edinburgh, UK: St Andrew Press.
Barrett-Lennard, G.T. 1998. *Carl Rogers Helping System: Journey & Substance.* London: Sage.
Bell, R. 2012. *Love Wins.* London: Collins.
Brown, P. 2008. *The Body and Society*, 2nd revised edn. New York: Columbia University Press.
Fletcher, D. A. 2006. *One Nation Over God: The Americanisation of Christianity.* lulu.com.
Fox, M., 1983. *Original Blessing: A Primer in Creation Spirituality.* Santa Fe, NM: Bear & Co.
Frick, W. B. 1971. *Humanistic Psychology: Interviews with Maslow, Murphy and Rogers.* Columbus, OH: Charles F. Merrill.
Glucklich, A. 2003. *Sacred Pain: Hurting the Body for the Sake of the Soul.* Oxford, UK: Oxford University Press.
Groves, Philip. 2008. *The Anglican Communion and Homosexuality.* London: SPCK.
Halverson, M. and A. Cohen (Eds.). 1960. *A Handbook of Christian Theology.* London: Collins.
Leonardi, J. 2008. 'What We are Meant to Be: Evolution as the Transformation of Consciousness'. In *The Human Being Fully Alive: Writings in Celebration of Brian Thorne*, edited by J. Leonardi, 58–75. Ross on Wye, UK: PCCS Books.
Leonardi, J. 2016. 'Tenderness in Person-Centred Therapy: A Spiritual Dimension?'. In *The Person-Centred Counselling and Psychotherapy Handbook: Origins, Developments and Current Applications*, edited by C. Lago and D. Charura, 34–44. Maidenhead, UK: Open University Press/McGraw Hill.
Maslow, A. 1962. *Towards a Psychology of Being.* Princeton, NJ: D. Van Nostrand. https://doi.org/10.1037/10793-000
Mearns, D. and B. J. Thorne. 2000. *Person-Centred Therapy Today: New Frontiers in Theory and Practice.* London: Sage.
Nelson, James B. 1979. *Embodiment: An Approach to Sexuality and Christian Theology.* Minneapolis, MN: Augsburg Books.
Nineham, D. E. 1969. *Saint Mark.* Harmondsworth, UK: Penguin Books.
Rogers, C. R. 1959. 'A Theory of Therapy, Personality and Personal Relationships as Developed in the Client-Centred Framework'. In *Psychology: A Study of a Science*, vol 3: Formulation of the Person and the Social Context, edited by S. Koch, 184–256. New York: McGraw-Hill.
Rogers, C. R. 1961. *On Becoming a Person.* London: Constable.
Rogers, C. R. 1980. *A Way of Being.* London: Constable.

Rohr, R. 2012. *Falling Upwards.* London: SPCK. Centre for Action and Contemplation website posting, 18.9.2018. http://cacradicalgrace.org.

Seeman, J. 1984. 'The Fully Functioning Person: Theory and Research'. In *Client-Centred Therapy and the Person-Centred Approach: New Directions in Theory, Research and Practice*, edited by R. F. Levant and J. M. Shlien. New York: Praeger.

Solignac, Pierre. 1982. *The Christian Neurosis.* London: SCM Press.

Staniloe, D. 2002. *Orthodox Spirituality.* South Canaan, PA: St. Tikhon's Seminary Press.

Teilhard de Chardin, Pierre. 1970. *Hymn of the Universe.* London: Collins.

Ware, Bishop K. 1979. *The Orthodox Way.* Oxford, UK: Mowbray.

Wickes, Frances G. 1977. *The Inner World of Choice.* London: Couventure.

Wimbush, V. L. and Valantasis, R. 2003. *Asceticism.* Oxford, UK: Oxford University Press.

Chapter 4

Spirituality and Wellbeing in Traditional China: Food, Self-Sacrifice, and Spiritual Practice in a Chinese Buddhist Legend

Thomas Jansen

Introduction

China's search for happiness, to use a synonym for wellbeing employed in two landmark studies of Chinese discourses of happiness (Bauer 1976; Wielander and Hird 2018), always involved both material and spiritual aspects. The triad of folk popular deities displayed in many Chinese homes and during religious festivals comprises the gods of longevity, prosperity and posterity. They represent the aspiration for a long life, material wealth and (male) descendants. The spiritual life and values of many Chinese are thus inextricably linked to and expressed in material goals: the values of the spiritual sphere and the material sphere are seen as complementary and mutually dependent on each other, rather than as being in opposition to each other or even as mutually exclusive. Leading a long life secured by wealth and the affectionate care of one's children is as much a prerequisite for individual happiness as it is its perfect expression. The idea that material wealth constitutes in itself an impediment to spiritual advancement has not entered Chinese religious thinking, at least not its mainstream.

The symbiosis between the material and the spiritual in Chinese religious life is replicated in the role the human body can play in the process of spiritual growth. The relationship is most clearly shown by the significance attached to food both as a means of sustaining the body and as an agent of spiritual transformation. What we eat and how we prepare food has an immediate effect on the physiology of our bodies and therefore how we experience the world around us. The consumption of certain foodstuffs, or, conversely, the refusal to consume food, enables us to induce altered states of consciousness—think of the effects of chocolate or prolonged fasting—as a result of physiological transformations within the body. Food symbolizes the materiality of our earthly existence (Steel and Zinn 2017), but also the potential, in analogy to the cooking process, to transform our bodies and minds into something more spiritual and ethereal.

In this chapter I will explore the interrelationship between bodily nourishment, spirituality and wellbeing in Chinese religions, using the well-known Chinese Buddhist tale of the Princess Miaoshan as an example.[1] The *Legend of Miaoshan* touches upon several interrelated broader themes that are relevant for mapping out the relationship between spirituality and wellbeing in Chinese religions: filial piety, spiritual cultivation, body, gender and sexuality, and female empowerment.[2] My aim is to draw out the links between these various themes and to explain their significance with reference to concepts of individual and social wellbeing in China.

The *Legend of Miaoshan* is a tale about one of the most popular deities in the Chinese world, Guanyin, the Bodhisattva of Compassion or 'Goddess of Mercy'. Guanyin is the Chinese name for Avalokiteśvara, who is worshipped across the Buddhist world. However, the deity's manifestation as a female figure seems to be unique to China. In India, Sri Lanka, Southeast Asia and Tibet, Avalokiteśvara is worshipped as a male deity. In Tibet, the Dalai Lama is considered to be the reincarnation of this bodhisattva (Hedges 2012; Huang, Valussi and Palmer 2011, 107; Wu 2013, 149–151). Avalokiteśvara's transformation into a female deity in China is inseparably connected to the tale of Princess Miaoshan.

The story of Miaoshan is important and illuminating for a discussion of Chinese approaches to wellbeing because through her behaviour the story's main protagonist poses a fundamental challenge to the values centred on leading a long life, enjoying material wealth and having (male) descendants. The fact that this challenge of commonly accepted values also involved a challenge to patriarchal authority by a young woman raises interesting questions regarding gender and the status of female deities, particularly the relationship between religious social practices, on the one hand, and the symbolic constructs of gender relationships in religious texts on the other. This issue, which has been addressed by several scholars with varying results (Wing 2011; Jansen 2017a; Sangren 1983; Huang, Valussi and Palmer 2011), can be condensed into the questions: Did the story of Miaoshan contribute to the social empowerment of women in traditional China? And if it is so, how exactly did this happen? What does the story tell us about the respective approaches of women and men to spirituality and the pursuit of wellbeing? If we concede that gender identities, asymmetrical power relationships or the conceptualizations of our bodies, emotions and cognitive faculties influence how we define and experience wellbeing, then it makes sense to look at the above themes through the lens of a twelfth century religious tale.

However, before we can proceed in our discussion of these themes and how they are related to ideas of wellbeing, it is necessary to provide the gist of the story.

Princess Miaoshan (Marvelous Goodness) is the youngest daughter of King Miaozhuang, who cured her ailing father by cutting out her eyes and severing her arms from the body so that they could be made into medicine. Because of her compassion, Miaoshan is also worshipped as a manifestation of the Bodhisattva of Compassion, Guanyin in Chinese or Avalokiteśvara in Sanskrit. The core of the legend can be traced back to a stele inscription entitled *Dabei Pusa zhuan* (Biography of the Bodhisattva of Great Compassion). It was composed by a local prefect named Jiang Zhiqi (1031–1104) and inscribed on a stele in 1100 (Dudbridge [1978] 2004, 12; Chen 2012).

Princess Miaoshan defies her father's plans to marry her off in order to pursue a religious vocation instead. Angered by her resoluteness and concerned about the influence Miaoshan's piety might have on the female members of his court, the king casts her out into the flower garden at the rear of the palace. He cuts off her food and drink and sends Miaoshan's mother and two elder sisters to persuade her to change her mind and take a husband. When this does not work he sends Miaoshan to a Buddhist nunnery, suspecting that it is the nuns who are behind Miaoshan's religious zeal. The king promises to completely decorate the monastery should the nuns be able to persuade Miaoshan to follow his instructions. Otherwise the nunnery is to be burned down and its inhabitants killed. Miaoshan counters the nuns' entreaties to return to the palace with the argument that as followers of the Buddha they should have an insight into the illusory nature of the body and hence not fear death. The nuns are speechless after this reprimand and decide to make her life hard. Miaoshan has to toil in the kitchen garden, being charged with providing vegetables for the convent. She is able to discharge her duties with divine assistance in the form of the dragon spirit. The king, upon hearing that the nuns were unable to effect a change in his daughter, orders troops to surround the monastery, behead the nuns and burn down their quarters. Miaoshan, however, is taken by a spirit and thus is able to escape unscathed. She finds refuge at Mount Xiangshan where she lives the life of a hermit. Meanwhile, as a result of his bad actions, the king has contracted jaundice that no doctor can heal. A monk tells him that there is a cure, but that he needs the arms and eyes of one free of anger to blend into a medicine and take it. When the king suspects this medicine to be hard to find, the monk reassures him by saying:

> In the southwest of your dominion is a mountain named Fragrant Mountain. On its summit is a hermit practicing religious cultivation with signal merit, though none knows of it. This person has no anger [...]. In the past this hermit had a close affinity with you. By obtaining the hands and eyes this sickness of yours can be cured instantly, without any doubts. (Dudbridge [1978] 2004, 31)

When a royal envoy arrives at Miaoshan's thatched hut to relate the story of the king's illness, she willingly gouges out her two eyes and severs both arms with a knife, handing them over to the envoy. Back in the capital the monk presents the cure to the king who recovers from his sickness. Later, when the royal couple visit Fragrant Mountain to convey their gratitude to the hermit, they recognize their own daughter who just at this moment reveals herself as the All-Merciful Bodhisattva Guanyin of the Thousand Arms and Thousand Eyes. The king thereupon builds a shrine and a precious stūpa on the summit of Fragrant Mountain where he later also erects a thirteen-storeyed pagoda to house the 'true body' of the Bodhisattva.

My aim is to first examine the tale of Miaoshan with regard to the aspects linking the materiality of the body, its nourishment and healing with Miaoshan's spiritual path leading up to her transformation into a deity. In a second step I will then extend the discussion to include the themes of gender and filial piety. I will demonstrate how Miaoshan's life story had the potential to benefit the wellbeing of both men and women by lessening the tensions between the roles of filial daughter, nurturing mother and religious leader.

Spirituality, Food and Healing

The conflict between Miaoshan and her father plays itself out in the realm of eating (Jansen 2017a). From the vegetarianism imposed by her Buddhist beliefs to the sacrifice of her own flesh to nourish her ailing father, Miaoshan's food consumption forms a constant thread running through the story. Food as a catalyst in the transformation towards transcendence was at the heart of the Chinese religious experience since at least the Bronze Age (the first two millennia BCE). Especially prepared food offered in sacrificial bronze vessels during the various stages of the mortuary ritual 'symbolized the flesh that transmutes in and out of the unseen world through birth and death' (Cook 2005, 11). Both the bronze vessel and its culinary content had pivotal roles in securing the safe passage of the deceased human soul to Heaven where it would assume the position of an ancestor. Food production, as well as fecundity, were seen as gifts from Heaven—gifts that obliged the living to enter into a reciprocal nurturing relationship with their deceased ancestors. The ancestors received sacrifices and would in return confer their blessing upon their descendants in the form of food and progeny. The hierarchical structure of the ancient sacrificial system, which flourished during the late Shang (1200–1046 BCE) and Western Zhou (1046–771 BCE) periods, mirrored and thereby reaffirmed the hierarchical lineage system of the Shang and Western Zhou with the royal lineage at the top of the hierarchy. Food production and sacrifices thus provided an important cornerstone of the (male centred) political order of ancient China.

The political role of food for maintaining social and political order survived the gradual decline of the Zhou feudal order from the mid-eighth century onwards. Sacrifices and feasts continued to be used as tools for forging social bonds and political alliances. In the philosophical discourse of the Warring States and the early empire, the step towards agriculture was seen as the hallmark of civilization. Consider the following passage from *Huainanzi* (Master Huainan; second century BCE):

> In ancient times people ate vegetation and drank from streams; they picked fruit from trees and ate the flesh of shellfish and insects. In those times there was much illness and suffering, as well as injury from poisons. Thereupon the Divine Farmer (Shennong) for the first time taught the people to sow the five grains and diagnose the quality of soils—which were arid or wet, fertile or barren, highland or lowland. He tasted the flavors of the hundred plants and the sweetness and brackishness of streams and springs, causing the people to know which were to be avoided and which used. In the process he himself would suffer poisonings seventy times a day. (Campany 2005, 99–100, with minor modifications)

The Divine Farmer, one of the mythical culture heroes of antiquity, led people into farming, upon which other cultural achievements such as the 'invention' of writing, flood control, silkworm raising were to follow.

Meat

The ritual efficacy of meat (and alcohol, for that matter) is acknowledged in the earliest Chinese writings (Sterckx 2011). Both the Shang oracle bones and Zhou bronze inscriptions are replete with references to meat and alcohol that are shared among ritual participants, spirits and humans. However, meat had an ambivalent status in the value system of ancient and traditional China. The nutritional value of meat and the fact that it was practically out of reach for all but nobles and high officials, made meat a luxury product and symbol of high status. As Roel Sterckx has noted,

[t]he sacrificial meat exchange in early China operated at the heart of social and political relationship. The acceptance or refusal to accept sacrificial meats functioned as a symbolical reaffirmation or rejection of interpersonal and interstate allegiances. In the ritual gift economy of early China, the symbolical stature of meat superseded its relative economic value. (Sterckx 2011, 28)

On the other hand, the temptation of overindulgence and wastefulness through using food as entertainment were never far off, as in the hymn 'Summoning Back the Soul' (Zhao hun) from the anthology *Chuci* (Verses of Chu). 'Summoning Back the Soul' was originally a shamanistic ritual to resuscitate a dying or recently deceased person by catching his/her soul before it had gone too far away, and restore it to the body. The literary reworking contained in the *Chuci*, however, was written for the entertainment and cure of the ailing King Xiang of Chu (Hawkes [1959] 1985, 223). To achieve this goal, beautiful women are presented alongside a range of delicacies, including 'ribs of the fatted ox, tender and succulent; sour and bitter blended in the soup of Wu; stewed turtle and roast kid, served up with yam sauce; geese cooked in sour sauce, casseroled duck, fried flesh of the great crane' (Hawkes [1959] 1985, 227-28) —and the list goes on. In other words, the soul of the unwell king is lured back into the body with the promise of food and sex.

The association between meat consumption and pleasure was the main reason for abstinence from eating meat during periods of mourning or grave loss. The ruler of the ancient state of Qi is said to have adopted a vegetarian diet after he had been defeated in battle by another state and lost some of his territory (Pu 2014, 63).

The tension in culinary matters between moral behaviour on the one hand, and entertainment, eroticism and personal indulgence on the other, is also highlighted through the food symbolism employed in the sixteenth century novel *The Plum in the Golden Vase* (*Jin ping mei*) —to give another, much later example. The title of the novel itself is highly suggestive of sexuality. The way the food motif is charged with sexual connotations and used to characterize the different female characters in the novel both mirrors and reinforces the male discourse on the subjugation of women, creating a striking 'tension between eroticism and religious moralism' (Yue 2013, 97).

The central role of food production and consumption for maintaining the political, social and religious order in China calls for an answer to the question: what does it mean when individuals or groups of people shun certain types of food or refuse to eat altogether? More specifically, what is the cultural significance of vegetarianism, the abstinence from meat and alcohol, both of which were considered essential ingredients in ancestor worship, mortuary feasts and banquets alike?

(Male) Buddhist Arguments in Favour of Vegetarianism in China

China is an exception with regard to Buddhist food practices insofar as it is one of the few countries (including Vietnam and Korea) where Buddhist monks observe a vegetarian diet. In many parts of the world Buddhist monks and nuns are not vegetarians. The standard narrative of vegetarian practices in China would start with the observation of the tension that existed between the prohibition of meat in the sutras and the monastic regulations which allowed the consumption of meat under certain circumstances. According to the monastic regulations of the Sarvāstivāda vinaya and the Dharmaguptaka Vinaya—these two were most influential in China—the Buddha had allowed the consumption of meat under three conditions:

> There are three types of unclean meat that should not be eaten. What are these three? If one has seen, heard or suspected. What is meant by "seen?" This means that one has seen that a life has been taken for one's sake. This is what is meant by "seen". What is meant by "heard?" This means that one has heard from a reliable person that the animal has been killed for one's sake. This is what is meant by "heard". What is meant by "suspected?" This means that one has cause for suspicion. If there is no butcher in the area and the animal has not died of itself, it must be that the donor has carried out the evil deed and taken life for one's sake. This is what is meant by "suspected". These three types of unclean meat are not to be eaten. (Kieschnick 2005, 188; Ruegg 1980)

The key rationale behind the formula of the 'three types of pure meat' is to avoid any association with the killing of an animal or knowledge thereof prior to the actual meal. What was important was the consciousness of the eater (was it pure or impure), not the context in which the meat was prepared (was the kitchen clean or not) and not the properties of the meat itself (was it fresh or not). Two ideas are of particular relevance here: the first is the idea of karma, according to which all actions performed by a person leave a 'footprint' in the world, an attachment which prevents a person from leaving the world of attachments and desires and condemns them to be part of the continuous cycle of birth, decay and death. The second is the capacity for compassion and selflessness which is destroyed by the consumption of meat. This externalist argument, which associated eaters with certain social values, is further illustrated by the reasons that are given for the proscription of certain types of flesh: elephant flesh, horse, serpent, dog, or human flesh. Elephant and horse flesh are forbidden because both come from animals used by rulers while the consumption of snake meat would offend the powerful *naga* gods. These were semi-divine serpent creatures, the females of which are called *nagis* or *naginis*. The idea lingers in the name of Lord Voldemort's snake Nagini! Monks avoid dog meat because it is associated with people of lower standing. For the same reasons—to show compassion with one's fellow beings and in order not to jeopardize one's own spiritual cultivation, the eating of human flesh is taboo despite the acknowledged medicinal value meat eating, including eating human meat, can have as a cure for illness. I will come back to this point later.

Let us also make a note here that the main reason for abstaining from meat is the eater, not the suffering of the animal. The focus of the argument against meat remains firmly on the negative effects on the eater, his or her ability to be compassionate. John Kieschnick notes that '[c]oncern for animal welfare – not to mention other modern motivations for vegetarianism such as environmental impact and health – is for the most part absent from discussion of vegetarianism in Indian Buddhism' (Kieschnick 2005, 192–93).

A meat rich diet was a sign of high social status, in China as elsewhere (Sterckx 2011, 28 and 51). The spread of vegetarianism among the Chinese ruling elite and aristocracy during the early medieval period—roughly between AD 300 and 600—largely followed the arguments presented before—one should not add to the suffering in the world by engaging in the killing of living beings, but instead cultivate compassion. In a 'Statement of Confession and Repentance' (*Chanhui wen*), written around 485 CE, the literatus and fervent Buddhist Shen Yue (441–513) reflects on his past dietary preferences:

> From early youth my heart has been given to excessive desire. I never knew the meaning of compassion nor discerned the retribution of my wrongdoing. I consigned the furry, finny and feathered tribes to my kitchen, and. since their previous incarnations were not directly confronting me, they were not subject to my pity. Chopping them up every morning and cooking them every night, month after month, year after year. I stuffed my belly to satisfy my appetite. It was all I ever did.
> (Mather 1981, 422)

The rejection of meat is embedded within a self-cultivational discourse driven by political interests of the imperial house and the aristocracy to distinguish themselves from commoners. A second important factor was the desire of the emperors to keep tight control over the wealthy and powerful Buddhist monasteries by setting strict standards for monks and nuns. The idea of religious merit takes hold at this time, the idea that high social status and political power would have to be based on religious merit—*gongde*, literally 'virtue through works'—and the ability to transfer religious merit to those who cannot save themselves. The most religious Chinese emperors at that time saw themselves as imperial bodhisattvas, enlightened beings who postpone their entry into paradise in order to lead the suffering beings in this world to salvation. Vegetarianism was one practice through which one could generate such merit. The release of animals from captivity into liberty was another. The practice shows that genuine concern for the animal had entered the discussion. In a letter to his friend, the official Zhou Yong (d.488) writes to his friend: '[For the animal] it is its life at stake, and it holds to it dearly; for us it is a flavour, something we can do without' (Kieschnick 2005, 196).

Female Renunciations of Meat/Flesh

The discourse on vegetarianism that I have examined so far provides but one perspective on the relationship between body and food in the Miaoshan legend. The story also inserts itself into an older medical-meritorious discourse, in which the eating of human flesh serves both as an effective cure for diseases and meritorious religious act of a Bodhisattva. Chinese medical compendia promoted the eating of human flesh as an effective cure for diseases as early as the eighth century (Yu 2012, 66), while the gift of flesh (eyes, head, or body) to succour ailing parents is a standard theme in stories of the previous lives of the Buddha (jātaka). The figure of the Bodhisattva as a universal healer who sacrifices his/her body to save another human being is an established figure prior to the composition of the Miaoshan story (Dudbridge [1978] 2004, 90–91).

    The significance of food and body in the Christian religious tradition of medieval Europe has been treated most extensively by Caroline Bynum in her 1987 landmark study *Holy Feast and Holy Fast: The Significance of Food to Medieval Women* (Bynum 1987). Bynum, who focuses on female spirituality, outlines the connections that one strain in medieval moral teaching saw between female food consumption and sexual pleasure, laziness, loquacity, scurrility and boldness, all of which had to be controlled by the opposite of culinary indulgence, namely asceticism and abstention. Bynum confirms that food practices of medieval women 'sometimes appear to be efforts not just to control but even to attack or punish the body' (Bynum 1987, 216). Underlying such a negative sense of the female body was a practical and symbolical (rather than philosophical) dualism which juxtaposed the weak and inferior female flesh and the superior male spirit or reason. However, while one cannot deny that misogyny was an influencing factor in women's self-perception to some extent, perhaps even a strong one, Bynum's key argument is that medieval asceticism and female ways of dealing with food do not represent, at the most basic level, a dualistic perception of female flesh versus male reason, of female corporeal indulgence versus male rational control; nor is female spirituality and women's role within religion characterized by an internalized negation of the body. Radical asceticism is emphatically not embodied misogyny or self-torture. Female food behaviour, Bynum argues, was, first, an effective way for women to manipulate their environment in a world where food was an important economic and symbolic resource. For example, wives and daughters used fasting as a means to escape the role of food preparer or provider (breastfeeding) or to avoid the sexual advances by men. Second, women's asceticism was an expression of their rejection of the medieval church and its increasingly positive view of the body; a church, in which their female role was defined as inferior. Female refusal to eat can, third, be interpreted as preparation for the ultimate fusion with the body of Christ (*imitatio Christi*). Thus, through ways of dealing with food women created new forms of spirituality which allowed them to bypass the male dominated ecclesiastical hierarchies and to forge a new type of charismatic spirituality in which a woman could enjoy union with Christ beyond the constraints of the church.

We find a very similar creative use of food consumption, abstinence and even bodily sacrifice in the story of Miaoshan. It shares with its European counterparts the main topics of marriage resistance, the questioning of patriarchal hierarchy, the challenge to the Buddhist monastic ideal (remember the reprimand of the nuns in the convent) and the religious ideal of bodily fusion with a deity. In its twelfth century recension, Miaoshan's story is that of a girl who follows her predestined path towards bodhisattva-hood with unshakable conviction. Throughout the story she remains completely unfazed by the trials and attempts of persuasion she is subjected to by her family (especially her father), showing no signs of wavering or self-doubt. Her birth is accompanied by unmistakable signs that something wonderful is happening: At the time of conception, the queen dreamed about 'swallowing the moon' (*tun yue*), a reference to a lunar eclipse announcing the birth of a great person (Yang and An 2005: 138). At birth, signs on her body mark her out as a bodhisattva, a saviour who delays his/her own entry into nirvana in order to save other sentient beings.

Already at the start of the story Miaoshan observes a vegetarian diet, limited to one meal after noon, in line with her Buddhist beliefs. As the story unfolds her diet becomes the more restricted the greater the distance between Miaoshan and her family gets. After her first altercation with her father regarding her refusal to marry, Miaoshan is sent to work in the garden, while her food and drink are reduced (Dudbridge [1978] 2004, 137). However, the word used for 'food' in this particular passage (*shan*, 'delicacy', 'meat') refers to food suitable for a member of the royal family. When Miaoshan has to leave the palace after an unsuccessful attempt at persuasion by her mother and sisters, she runs the kitchen garden of the nunnery to which she is confined. The implication is that she still has access to food (vegetables) but of an inferior variety. Her diet finally reaches a low-point at Fragrant Mountain to where she retires as a hermit after her father burned the nunnery down to the ground: 'Miaoshan dwelt there, eating from the trees, drinking from the streams' (Dudbridge [1978] 2004, 138). The simplicity of her diet stands in a directly reciprocal relationship with her spiritual growth, which is soon to reach its first culmination point: the gift of her eyes and arms turns Miaoshan from a consumer of food into a food provider. Miaoshan's apotheosis, her transformation from a daughter into a deity reaches its climax when her parents recognize in the crippled hermit their own daughter, and the king (in another version the queen) is about 'to lick her eyes with his tongue'. This intimate gesture of care, offered by the father, was normally performed by children on their aged and ailing parents to restore eyesight. The use of this gesture by Miaoshan's father indicates a complete reversal of roles. Furthermore, the act remains unfulfilled, because 'before his mouth had touched her eyes, Miaoshan was suddenly not to be found' (Yü 2001, 502). The expected reconciliation and propitiation between father and daughter does not take place. Her symbolic re-integration into the family, even with reversed roles, remains incomplete, because:

> At that moment heaven and earth shook, radiance blazed forth, auspicious clouds enclosed all around, divine musicians began to play. [And then] the All-Compassionate Guanyin of the Thousand Arms and Thousand Eyes appeared, solemn and majestic in form, radiant with dazzling light, lofty and magnificent, like the moon amid the stars. (Yü 2001, 503)

Miaoshan's apotheosis was complete.

The acknowledgement and acceptance of Miaoshan's gift of her body, the fact that she successfully transformed her body into 'sacrificial meat', completes her spiritual journey towards self-divinization and realization of her own true nature. She has successfully elevated herself above all worldly familial ties. In her new light, holy body, which the king is unable to burn, Miaoshan is able to become the recipient of sacrifice and worship herself. This is acknowledged by the royal couple who erect both a shrine and a stūpa housing Miaoshan's 'true body' (*zhen shen*) on the spot of her apotheosis.

The various expressions used to refer to Miaoshan's body or rather bodies—in the final passages of the story are significant. After Miaoshan reveals herself as a Bodhisattva, her parents address her saying: '"We pray you, Bodhisattva, in your compassion, to return your original body (*ben ti*) and permit us to make offerings." In a moment the hermit returned to her original person (*ben shen*), with her hands and eyes quite intact'. Terms used to designate Miaoshan's (mutilated?) body are 'holy body' (*sheng ti*) and 'numinous body' (*ling qu*) (Dudbridge [1978] 2004, 33). The holy body is indestructible, for when the parents try to burn the holy body of the hermit on a funeral pyre, surrounded by all kinds of pure incense, something unexpected happens: 'The fragrant fuel was consumed, but the numinous body towered there still and could not be moved' (Dudbridge [1978] 2004, 33).

Miaoshan's deification manifests itself in two types of presence: a mediated presence (holy body; numinous body) which highlights the transcendental qualities of its owner, and an unmediated, real presence (true body, original body) which can be worshipped and serves 'as the tangible and reliable agent through which the divine becomes more perceivable' (Lin 2014, 191).

'Kuan-yin is Said to Manifest as a Man in Order to Save Men and a Woman in Order to Save Women'—Male and Female Approaches to Conversion and Renunciation

The quote in the heading of this section (Yü 2000, 475) makes two assumptions: first, that there is a difference in how men and women approach salvation; and second, that male deities predominantly appeal to men as female deities do to women. On the basis of these assumptions we would expect clearly drawn boundaries between female and male approaches to spirituality, even though the different paths are ultimately unified by the fact that they represent different manifestations of a single deity, Guanyin. The question therefore is, do we have a clear dichotomy between male and female forms of spirituality, and by extension to wellbeing, in twelfth century China? Does the tale of Miaoshan primarily address a female audience? Statements such as 'female deities, unlike their male counterparts, do not favour the wealthy and influential over the poor, insiders over outsiders, or men over women' re-inforce the idea of a clear division of labour and responsibilities regarding the securing of wellbeing between male and female deities. While male deities are 'associated with hierarchy, authority, and legitimacy', their female counterparts, invested with motherly characteristics and aspirations, represent the ultimate wholeness and inclusivity of the community. A corresponding idea is that female deities are symbolic of and for women, while male deities overwhelmingly represent male concerns and aspirations.

Sherin Wing has presented strong arguments against such a reading of the Miaoshan tale, which in her view results from an unexamined androcentrism that has shaped the scholarly discourse on Chinese Buddhism, especially the role of women in Buddhism, and the interpretation of Buddhist texts. According to Wing, the Miaoshan tale is a male-gendered story, as its core secular theme focuses on marriage and the particular significance of this institution to the patrilinear family of the Song and hence to men. 'Marriage was [...] an arena in which men could create mutually beneficial ties economically, politically, and socially' (Wing 2011, 18). Thus, Miaoshan's refusal to marry impacted directly on the King's financial situation—in the likely case of an uxorilocal arrangement the King would have retained the large dowry as well as received the bride-price—and also his ability to forge beneficial social and political alliances through marrying his daughter. In terms of secular values, Miaoshan's actions are described as defiant, disobedient and subversive of the Confucian value system and social order; in short, she is a veritable nightmare for every male lineage head, gentry member or scholar-official. The tale thus serves as a public warning addressed to men about the dangers of female wilfulness and subversiveness, justifying the severe measures that may be needed in dealing with such a threat (Wing 2011, 24–25).

As much as Miaoshan appears as the antithesis of the Confucian ideal of femininity, her apotheosis at the end of the story vindicates her rejection of conventional Confucian values in favour of her Buddhist faith. More than that, it provides a resolution to the tensions between Confucian and Buddhist commitments by demonstrating the superiority of the Buddhist interpretation of filial piety and thus of Buddhism's superiority vis-à-vis the Confucian order. Miaoshan's deification does not, however, entail a victory of the female over the male; rather, through her apotheosis, she leaves the realm of human gender distinctions and dichotomies behind, which signals a "shift away from women and their agency" (Wing 2011, 27). The dominant use of 'male protocols'—for example the sharp separation of the monastic lifestyle Miaoshan is drawn to from conventional Confucian lifestyles; the emphasis of the superiority of Buddhist notions of filial piety over Confucian ones; the practices of renunciation, solitary cultivation and extreme self-sacrifice displayed by the protagonist, or the public display of the story in form of a stele inscriptions—provides strong indications that the story is part of a predominantly male religious discourse. In other words, Miaoshan's renunciation of conventional values, her Buddhist piety and subsequent transformation into a deity appealed, according to Wing, even more to men than they did to women, making Miaoshan into a role model and patroness for men. What appealed to Song men was how the story captured the hierarchical and dichotomic structure of Song gender relations, on the one hand, and how these hierarchies could be radically renounced through an inversion of gender, on the other hand. The mechanism of inversion of gender symbols is central here and involves two separate instances. In the first instance, it is Princess Miaoshan herself who 'rejected her mortal, female gender by enacting *male* protocols. She behaved like an aristocratic man pursuing Buddhism through social inversion' (Wing 2011, 26). She then inverted her gendered position again into that of a male ascetic, which then allowed her to produce the Buddhist piety of a male renunciant.

Wing's interpretation has a lot in its favour. Caroline Bynum, on whose work on later medieval religious imagery Wing's argument is largely based, has demonstrated convincingly that medieval men and women used religious symbols differently, with women 'say[ing] less about gender, [making] less use of dichotomous gender images, speak[ing] less of gender reversal, and [placing] more emphasis on interior motivation and continuity of self'. By contrast, men 'use more dichotomous images, are more concerned to define "the female" as both positive and negative, and speak more often of reversal and conversion' (Bynum 1992, 156).

The fact that the tale of Miaoshan was written by a male and consequently reveals strong male concerns does not mean that the story caters exclusively for male audiences. In fact, it held equally great significance for female audiences, as I will show next. At this point it is worth noting that every time we speak about wellbeing or happiness—I use both words synonymously—we operate within a 'shared discursive terrain' (Wielander and Hird 2018) of symbolic and narrative constructs to characterize and define what we mean by these terms. Narratives of wellbeing speak of the world as it *could* or *ought* to be, not as it really is. These narratives are shaped by gender, power relations, and social hierarchies in complicated and often inconspicuous ways. Though these different symbolic constructs do not directly translate into reality, they do influence what is deemed to be socially and morally acceptable. A thorough understanding of previous symbolic constructs of wellbeing is therefore a prerequisite to any future project of creating greater happiness through laws, social and political action or spiritual cultivation.

The Wellbeing Benefits of Spiritual Practice

The difficulties the Miaoshan tale presents to the modern interpreter can be partially circumvented once we put aside the question of symbolic constructions of wellbeing at the textual level and focus instead on how the Miaoshan story might have been used by people in real life. It is one thing to assume that a literary text caters primarily to a male or female audience based on the interpretation of the text's imagery, the ways in which it constructs gender and so forth. It is another to have evidence, textual or other, about how a particular text was used, by whom and for what purpose. In this last section I will thus shift the focus to the *practices* connected to the Miaoshan story and similar texts. My question is what people are actually *doing* with religious texts, and I aim to demonstrate that engagement with material such as the Miaoshan story through recitation, reading, copying and so forth was in itself seen as a way to improve wellbeing, independent from the question of how certain readers might understand the complex religious symbolism of a religious tale. I will also suggest that while a religious symbol like the Princess Miaoshan might be male-gendered in certain textual contexts, this does not preclude its being used by female religious practitioners in other, more practical contexts. To make my point, I will extend the investigation to later periods to include examples that may or may not be directly related to the Miaoshan tale. Let us look at the evidence that helps place the story in a real-life context.

In her study of everyday lives of women in Fujian province during the Song dynasty, Xu Man provides a comprehensive overview of the religious life of women during the Song period. Xu's description of women's real lives, although she too has to heavily rely on male-authored writings, i.e., epitaphs, in her analysis of female activities, comes to quite different conclusions than what we might expect on the basis of our interpretation of the Miaoshan legend. Xu demonstrates that involvement in Buddhist practices was not only widespread among elite women—Mark Halperin (2006, 6164), based on an empire wide survey of epitaphs, has calculated that 22 percent of elite women practised Buddhism—but that it was also widely accepted by male upholders of Confucian ideals. '[E]lite men's anti-Buddhist approach did not lead to widespread resentment over women's engagement in Buddhist practice, although they viewed Buddhism men [Sic!] as a different and more serious problem' (Xu 2016, 166). To be sure, it is not difficult to find male voices who condemned the religious interests of their wives and other female members of the household. Zhu Xi (1130–1200), the prominent Confucian revivalist, issued an official admonition as Prefect of Zhangzhou calling for Buddhist temples to refrain from 'gathering men and women day and night with the excuse of respecting Buddha and preaching sutras' (Xu 2016, 203). He also castigated monks for maintaining close ties with female believers and talking to them on every possible occasion. Zhu Xi's admonition suggests that women played an active part in Buddhist monastic affairs as visitors and patrons, who at times generously contributed money, time or other skills (e.g., their own skills in handicraft) to the different good causes centred around a monastery or temple. In many cases they did this together with their husbands. It is also worth noting that Zhu Xi's admonition addressed the religious providers, the clerics, not the women whose personal spiritual pursuits he seems to have approved of or at least tacitly accepted. Confucian revivalists such as Zhu Xi were concerned with upholding the public image of the Confucian order and maintaining the separation between the 'inner' (domestic affairs) versus the 'outer' (public affairs) spheres of social responsibilities. Spirituality was one area of life that cut across these gendered boundaries by allowing women to extend their personal spirituality into the public realm through participation in networks based in temples and other local organizations. Female spirituality blurred the boundary between secularity and spirituality, between personal belief and public engagement. 'Although physically practiced in the inner chambers, the "domestic religion" exposed women to the highly fluid society characterised by extensive networking and intensive communication between inner and outer' (Xu 2016, 194). Xu (2016, 202) further notes that 'Song literati were not bothered by women's external religious pursuits as much as Ming-Qing authors; very likely they had more flexible and diverse views of the matter'.

The reasons that prompted male tolerance towards female religious practices despite their own philosophical convictions—and here we return to the main theme of this essay—was the view that female spiritual endeavours contributed to the wellbeing of both family and community. Buddhist spirituality was credited with being able to reduce female anxiety and to ease domestic tensions. Sources summarizing the lives of Buddhist laywomen frequently mention 'tranquillity', 'calmness', 'harmonious relationships', 'compassion', 'patience' or 'composure' in difficult situations to characterize the exemplary behaviour displayed by these women and praised by men. The sense of tranquillity and calmness attributed to religious practice was further supported by the fact that many elite women created a separate space in their homes devoted to daily meditation and consumption of religious texts or images. Xu states:

> A Buddhist image, an incense burner and flowers are typical props that facilitated Buddhists' communication with deities in a temple. By furnishing an unoccupied room in the inner quarter with these religious objects, a laywoman created a ritual space greatly resembling a monastery. By shutting the door and blocking the relatives' inquiry, she created herself an isolated space, for the sake of spiritual independence instead of gender segregation. Enclosure did not necessarily indicate

women's subordination, but on the contrary may exemplify their agency, depending on the context. (Xu 2016, 179–180)

Note the monastic quality of the spaces created by pious women. This and the extensiveness of laywomen's involvement in monastic affairs is a powerful counterargument against the notion that the Miaoshan tale merely projects 'a series of androcentric monkish behaviors onto Miaoshan' (Wing 2011, 21). The evidence suggests that many Song women were attracted to monastic lifestyles of their own accord and independent from male projections.

A Buddhist manual associated with the worship of Miaoshan/Guanyin, the 'Methods of Worshipping the Water-moon Master Perceiver' (*Shuiyue guanzizai gongyangfa*), provides an insight into the practices associated with such private religious spaces:

> Recite the mantra facing the image. All your desires will be fulfilled in a short time. If you want to have food and clothing, stay in an uninhabited place, choose either a pure place or an ordinary place, burn incense and prepare flowers to worship the Great Compassionate Worthy One (Dabei zunzhe). All your sins will be dissolved. Your worldly and otherworldly desires will be accomplished. (Quoted from Xu 2016, 179)

The beneficial effects of reciting a Buddhist scripture (*sutra*) or mantra were well established by the Song dynasty and informed religious practice during the later imperial period. Given the centrality of procreation in Chinese conceptions of wellbeing and gender it is not surprising to find strong links between spiritual practices and childbirth (Chuu 2001). A very good example for the practical benefits sought through common religious activity is provided by a Ms You who put her eclectic taste in books to good use during her pregnancy:

> [Ms. You] chanted the *Admonitions for Women* and other [Confucian] classics every day to keep herself alert. She also believed in and respected Buddhism quite a lot. Whenever she got pregnant, she sat upright in a quiet room, burned incense and read Confucian and Buddhist books. She did not shout loudly or state angrily, and said, 'This is the way ancient people did prenatal education'. (Xu 2016, 182)

Scholars researching the use of religious texts sometimes state that religious scriptures were used to help in handling daily life affairs (e.g., Xu 2016, 183; Jansen 2017b, 224). This is an area where more research is required, but the issue of childbirth is certainly one area where women turned to religious writings for help. The following two examples from different time periods but both related to the worship of Miaoshan/Guanyin show how one and the same story could be used to opposite ends. In the first case, the supplicant addresses Miaoshan/Guanyin with a prayer for children, while in the second example the same or a very similar text is used to justify marriage refusal. The following quote is a short excerpt from a Precious Scroll entitled *Explanatory Precious Scroll of White-robed Kuan-yin Who Comes into the World Bringing Children* (Xiaoshi Baiyi Guanyin Pusa song yinger xiasheng baojuan), a sectarian scripture printed between 1572–1620:

> Turn your heart to goodness, keep a vegetarian diet, and call the name of the Buddha. When you chant the precious scroll once yourself, your blessing will be increased many times. Your sons and daughters will live long. When you ask someone else to chant it, you will be protected from disasters and your sins will be reduced. Members of your present household will be safe and sound, and your dead ancestors will be delivered from suffering and go to heaven. If you do not have any children, then you ought to get the White-robed Bodhisattva. You may build temples for her, or cast images of her, or chant the precious scroll. As long as you are sincere in your prayer, the Bodhisattva will show her compassion and send you a child and maiden. They will continue your line and bring glory to you. In case people may have doubts, there will be the evidence of the white caul. Everyone will then know for sure that it is true that the child is indeed sent to you by the Venerable Mother. Merciful, merciful, truly merciful! (Yü 2001, 468)

Anthropological research conducted by Marjorie Topley in Hong Kong, Singapore and rural Guangdong province during the 1950s has provided evidence of the undiminished importance of the Miaoshan/Guanyin cult in sectarian and folk Buddhist milieus centred around 'vegetarian halls' (*zhaitang*). These halls, which are part of the organization of several Chinese religions, provide 'members of the connected faith with a place where they can meet and engage in common worship and also practice certain individual religious tasks, especially in the sect. They are usually residential today'. The halls were popular as retirement homes for female workers or servants who would make regular payments to the hall during their working lives, thus securing a place for later on (Topley 2011, 406). While sectarian halls were normally open to men and women—sectarian groups stressed sexual equality and allowed men and women to pray together, hence the negative views of officialdom—certain aspects of their practice especially appealed to women looking for inspiration and moral support for refusing to marry.

> Aimed expressly at women was the "precious volume" (pao-chuan [baojuan]), which contained biographies of model women, usually recounted in ballad form. One such story, about Kuan Yin [Guanyin], the

> Goddess of Mercy, who is popularly believed to have been a princess who became a nun over her parents' objections, points out that she had no husband to claim her devotion, no mother-in-law to control her, and no children to hamper her movements. Many of my informants had "precious volumes" they acquired in their homeland which further emphasize that refusing to marry is not morally wrong and even that religion can help those brave enough to resist; that men cannot be trusted; and that suicide is a virtue when committed to preserve one's purity. (Topley 2011, 431)

The above case of women reading religious scriptures in support of their life choices leads us back to the question of the relationship between religious symbols and the real lives of practitioners, both male and female, of spirituality. Huang, Valussi and Palmer (2011, 112), writing about conceptions of the role of women and the female body and sexuality in Daoism, have argued that:

> it is certainly true that Chinese religion, and Daoism with it, is populated by a large number of female goddesses and that these goddesses have a large number of female followers, often these goddesses [...] circumvented the need for expected duties as wives and mothers by performing exceptional deeds in exchange for their unwillingness to marry. They are viewed and accepted as 'exceptional.' The women who worship them, however, are still expected to act according to the tenets of a highly patriarchal Confucian society: thus, neither the concept of 'the feminine' in Daoism nor the exceptionality of the female goddesses has an impact on the balancing of gender power in society. Therefore, when we look at the reality of Daoist women's lives, in historical as well as contemporary terms, we need to recognize that it is influenced much more by social, political, and cultural concerns than by Daoist ideology. (Huang, Valussi and Palmer 2011, 112)

According to these authors there is a clear dichotomy 'between the idealized female goddess and the real woman' (Huang, Valussi and Palmer 2011, 113). However, field studies like the ones conducted by Topley (2011) in the 1950s or more recently by DeVido (2010), Guggenmoos (2014) or Huang and Weller (1998) suggest a more nuanced interpretation of the interaction between symbolic constructions and individual or social practices. The Taiwanese Buddhist Compassion Relief Tzu Chi Foundation (Ciji Gongdehui), for example, has successfully exploited the symbolism of the Guanyin/Miaoshan cult to build an international charitable organization based on 'feminine' and 'maternal' virtues. The life story of its founder, the Ven. Zhengyan, mirrors key elements in the stories of goddesses who left home and remained unmarried. Zhengyan took an oath to Guanyin that she would become a Buddhist nun. While religious symbols may not have the power to influence the balance of gender power in society directly, they can be interpreted in ways that lead to a change in self-conception with real life impact. Guggenmoos writes about one of her interviewees, a Ms. Xu:

> As she grew up, her increasing involvement in Buddhism brought her into conflict with her father and society, who did not understand her desire to lead a monastic life. She does not bring this confrontation to a head, but instead finds a compromise that fits her circumstances, defining herself as an intellectual lay Buddhist who engages actively in society and envisions herself as a translator of Buddhist texts in the future. She also offers courses in Buddhist English, which is in line with her aim of supporting the international spread of Buddhism. She has lost sight of the monastic order during this process. (Guggenmoos 2014, 172)

Two things are worth noting here: the first is the fact that Ms Xu's self-perception contains elements reminiscent of the Miaoshan story, as was the case with the Ven. Zhengyan mentioned before. It would be worth examining in more detail to what extent the narrative self-constructions of Buddhist laywomen and laymen are shaped by tales of Miaoshan or other deities. While I would not go as far as to argue that Miaoshan necessarily provided an example which women would normally choose to follow, it is evident that some, such as the founder of the Ciji-Foundation, did precisely that. The other interesting point is that Ms. Xu is very conscious of both the personal 'conflict' as well as the potential 'confrontation' with her father and society as a result of her individual religious choice. The solution to this conflict/confrontation, however, is not a radical choice between two ends of a scale of possibilities, but a personal development which translates—her work as translator of Buddhist texts is perhaps no coincidence—the tensions into a transformed self-perception and action. 'Ciji succeeds in combining a very traditional idea of womanhood with a very modern sphere of action in the world" (Huang and Weller 1998, 390). The stark contrasts between religious ideology and peoples' social reality postulated by the exceptionality of the female goddesses are conspicuously absent from the self-portrayals of real people, as is in many cases the vocabulary of 'rejection', 'suppression or renunciation of gender roles', 'role reversal' and so forth. As DeVido (2010, 69) with reference to Qin (2000) has argued, 'Contradictory identities are not necessarily problematic, nuns in China "make use of their feminine, masculine, and 'neutral' characteristics according to necessity and circumstance."' The same is true for laypeople. Instead of using sharply defined conceptual dichotomies to highlight gender differences, the spiritual practices of laypeople, at least as far as women are concerned, are characterized by fluidity, adaptation and transformation rather than suppression and renunciation. It is worth quoting Caroline Bynum's remarks on gender-related imagery in the religious writings of the later middle ages in Europe. While male writers conceptualized the genders as dichotomous, '[w]omen writers used imagery more fluidly. Personal and social characteristics were more often shared by the two genders in women's writings' (Bynum 1992: 175). A second prominent symbol in male-authored narratives is equally absent in women's spiritual writings due to the male–female power differential; this is the female as a symbol of renunciation or reversal.

> Because women were women, they could not embrace the female as a symbol of renunciation. Because society was male-dominated, they could not embrace the male as a symbol of renunciation. To become male was elevation, not renunciation, and elevation was a less significant reversal given the values at the core of medieval Christianity. Thus, women did not in their writings play with male and female oppositions; they did not tell their own stories or the stories of other women as reversals or conversions. They did, however, explore and play in very complicated ways with what femaleness meant in the theological tradition—that is, physicality. (Bynum 1992, 171)

More research is needed on how women and men in China in the past conceptualized gender roles in religious writings, an endeavour made more difficult by the lower number of female-authored spiritual autobiographies compared to the abundance of male-authored writings about men and women. However, field studies in contemporary China and the comparative information provided by Bynum and others strongly points into a direction that forces us to reconsider approaches to gender and spirituality in Chinese history that rely heavily on dichotomous conceptualizations.

I would like to conclude this section with some brief reflections about how the Chinese material which I introduced above could be brought into a dialogue with more recent Western approaches to spiritual development. A fundamental question that shines through several of the sources quoted above is that of personal and, more generally, human development. What are we meant to be as human beings, caught up in a world of conflicting material and spiritual interests? Where do we go from here? How do we overcome the dichotomies and tensions of the here-and-now and move towards a stage characterized by greater inclusivity, interrelatedness, authenticity, and spirituality? An evolutionary perspective, a strong sense of the possibility of 'growing towards further stages of development' (Leonardi 2010, 60) is discernible both in the Miaoshan tale and, for example, the accounts of female Buddhist practitioners. This evolutionary vision, which is characterized by a strong spiritual dimension, provides the common ground between Miaoshan's life story and Carl Roger's view of 'the Person of Tomorrow' (Leonardi 2010, 60-63). The following characterization of the spiritual yearning of 'the Person of Tomorrow' is equally applicable to Miaoshan:

> These persons of tomorrow are seekers. They wish to find a meaning and purpose in life that is greater than the individual. Some are led into cults, but more are examining all the ways by which humankind has found values and forces that extend beyond the individual. They wish to live a life of inner peace. Their heroes are spiritual persons – Mahatma Gandhi, Martin Luther King, Teilhard de Chardin. Sometimes, in altered states of consciousness, they experience the unity and harmony of the universe.(Rogers 1980, 352; quoted from Leonardi 2010, 62)

Of the twelve key qualities a fully realized person displays, Princess Miaoshan displays all bar scepticism regarding science and technology: openness, a desire for authenticity and for wholeness, the wish for intimacy, a view of personhood as a process, a caring attitude, attitude toward nature, authority within, unimportance of material things, and a yearning for the spiritual (Rogers 1980, 350-52). The evolutionary vision culminates in the 'relinquishing and transcending of the self as the ultimate reference point' (Leonardi 2010, 62), by way of which the person does not give herself up but, on the contrary, becomes a fully functioning person in both Rogers's Person-centred approach and religious terms (Leonardi 2010, 63). A core idea shared by Chinese thinkers, Carl Rogers and a Christian philosopher like Teilhard de Chardin (1881–1955) is the notion that 'there exists a dialectical relationship between growing personalisation and increasing socialisation, the centring of the human person and the strengthening of bonds between persons in the human community' (King 1997, 45; Leonardi 2010, 65). Spirituality is a key ingredient that enables us to bond with other human beings and thus realize our own true self.

Conclusion

What is the significance of the Miaoshan tale for approaches to wellbeing? Through the examples discussed in this essay I have tried to demonstrate that the Miaoshan legend engages themes that lie at the heart of Chinese ideas of both wellbeing and spirituality. Guanyin/Miaoshan symbolizes cultural characteristics—motherhood, spiritual aspirations, physicality, social engagement—that go beyond conventional gender-related images but embrace general human concerns. By absorbing all these 'nested cultural characteristics' into one, Miaoshan/Guanyin and other deities, such as the Lady of Linshui (Baptandier 1996) or the Eternal Venerable Mother (Wusheng laomu), became the 'mediator for spiritual enlightenment but also for worldly happiness' (Yü 2001, 486).

The fact that women and men engaged with the tensions exemplified by Miaoshan's story in diverse and sometimes contradictory ways has wider ramifications for how we conceptualize wellbeing. The *Oxford English Dictionary* defines 'well-being' as 'the state of being comfortable, healthy, or happy'. The formation of the English word 'well-*being*' is revealing. It refers to a condition that exists at a specific time rather than to a process directed towards a future goal. The Chinese material discussed in this essay suggests a different approach to wellbeing. Wellbeing could be conceived not as a *state of being* defined by certain objectively measurable indicators such as income, life expectancy, social status and so forth, but rather as a fluid *process of becoming* in which the different actors constantly negotiate the meaning of wellbeing from personal, inter-personal or societal perspectives (Rogers 1961). There are two, probably more, reasons why it is better to conceptualize wellbeing not as a *state of being* but as a *process of becoming* instead. The first reason is that any state of being is of only limited duration whereas a process can more easily be conceived as a recurrent or open-ended movement towards a future goal. Second, as long as we live in an imperfect world, the unavoidable gap between normative concepts of wellbeing (the world as it ought to be) and the realities of human lives (the world as it is) will undoubtedly persist, creating tensions that present obstacles to the creation of wellbeing. In view of these tensions, wellbeing goals will become more achievable if those in pursuit of these goals are guided by concepts that are non-static, non-dichotomous and open to constant adaptation. The implications of this conceptual shift are significant. It means, for instance, that government-imposed wellbeing targets are impossible to reach unless achieving these targets allows for the possibility to negotiate, subvert or resist them through a variety of social and cultural practices and discourses, thus avoiding reification and those hard boundaries that undermine individual and social wellbeing in the first place. The value of religious narratives, spiritual biographies of individuals or groups, or stories of gods and deities, lies in their unlimited power to create discursive spaces and practices that constantly challenge what we define as 'wellbeing'.

Biographical Note

Thomas Jansen is Associate Professor in Chinese Studies at the University of Wales Trinity Saint David, Lampeter. He has published *Höfische Öffentlichkeit im frühmittelalterlichen China. Debatten im Salon des Prinzen Xiao Ziliang* (2000) and several articles on early medieval China. He co-edited *Globalization and the Making of Religious Modernity in China Transnational Religions, Local Agents, and the Study of Religion, 1800-Present* (2014). His current project is entitled *Religious Text Production in Late Imperial China: Social, Religious, and Performative Aspects of Chinese Sectarian Scriptures from the 16th to 19th Centuries* and will explore the manifold interactions between religious texts and their users.

Notes

1. I use Pinyin transliteration throughout this essay. When quoting from the work of other scholars I have tacitly adjusted transliterations in Wade-Giles to Pinyin for the sake of consistency.
2. I rely mostly on Dudbridge's textual reconstructions and translations of the various versions of the Miaoshan legend. However, I use different versions of the legend to support my argument rather than rely exclusively on the composite version of the original story which Dudbridge presents ([1978] 2004, 24-34).

Bibliography

Bauer, W. 1976. *China and the Search for Happiness: Recurring Themes in Four Thousand Years of Chinese Cultural History*. New York: Seabury Press. Originally published in German as *China und die Hoffnung auf Glück. Paradiese Utopien Idealvorstellungen in der Geistesgeschichte Chinas* (Munich: Hanser, 1971).

Baptandier, B. 1996. 'The Lady Linshui: How a Woman Became a Goddess'. In *Unruly Gods: Divinity and Society in China*, edited by M. Shahar and R. P. Weller, 105-149. Honolulu: University of Hawai'i Press. https://doi.org/10.1515/9780824865429-005

Bynum, C. W. 1987. *Holy Feast and Holy Fast: The Religious Significance of Food to Medieval Women*. Berkeley, CA: University of California Press.

Bynum, C. 1992. *Fragmentation and Redemption: Essays on Gender and the Human Body in Medieval Religion*. New York: Zone Books.

Campany, R. F. 2005. 'The Meanings of Cuisines of Transcendence in Late Classical and Early Medieval China'. *T'oung Pao* 91: 126-182. https://doi.org/10.1163/1568532054905124

Chen, J. 2012. 'Jiang Zhiqi and the Miaoshan Legend: A Case Study of the Roles Played by Laymen in Constructing Buddhist Sacred Sites in Medieval China'. In *Images, Relics, and Legends: The Formation and Transformation of Buddhist Sacred Sites*, edited by K. Shinohara, J. Chen, J. A. Benn and J. Robson, 195-212. Oakville, ON: Mosaic Press.

Chuu, L. L. 2001. *The Cult of Guanyin Who Brings Sons in China*. Unpublished MA thesis, University of British Columbia.

Cook, C. A. 2005. 'Moonshine and Millet: Feasting and Purification Rituals in Ancient China'. In *Of Tripod and Palate: Food, Politics, and Religion in Traditional China*, edited by R. Sterckx, 9–33. New York: Palgrave. https://doi.org/10.1057/9781403979278_2

DeVido, E. A. 2010. *Taiwan's Buddhist Nuns*. Albany, NY: State University of New York Press.

Dudbridge, G. [1978] 2004. *The Legend of Miao-shan*, 2nd edn. Oxford, UK: Oxford University Press.

Guggenmoos, E. 2014. '"Mrs. Ma" and "Ms. Xu" – On the Attractiveness of Denoting Oneself a "Buddhist" in the Increasingly Transnational Milieu of Urban Taiwan'. In *Globalization and the Making of Religious Modernity in China*, edited by T. Jansen, T. Klein and C. Meyer, 156–181. Leiden, The Netherlands: Brill. https://doi.org/10.1163/9789004271517_008

Halperin, M. 2006. 'Domesticity and the Dharma: Portraits of Buddhist Laywomen in Sung China'. *T'oung Pao* 92 (1): 50–100. https://doi.org/10.1163/156853206778553199

Hawkes, D. [1959] 1985. *The Songs of the South: An Ancient Chinese Anthology of Poems by Qu Yuan and Other Poets*. Hamondsworth, UK: Penguin.

Hedges, P. 2012. 'The Identity of Guanyin: Religion, Convention and Subversion'. *Culture and Religion* 13 (1): 91–106. https://doi.org/10.1080/14755610.2012.658426

Huang, C. J., E. Valussi and D. A. Palmer. 2011. 'Gender and Sexuality'. In *Chinese Religious Life*, edited by D. A. Palmer, G. Shive and P. L. Wickeri, 107–123. Oxford, UK: Oxford University Press. https://doi.org/10.1093/acprof:oso/9780199731398.003.0007

Huang, C. J. and R. P. Weller. 1998. 'Merit and Mothering: Women and Social Welfare in Taiwanese Buddhism'. *The Journal of Asian Studies* 57 (2): 379–396. https://doi.org/10.2307/2658829

Jansen, T. 2017a. 'Embodied Spirituality and Self-Divinization: A Re-reading of the *Legend of Princess Miaoshan*'. In *Exploring the Materiality of Food "Stuffs": Transformations, Symbolic Consumption and Embodiment(s)*, edited by L. Steel and K. Zinn, 103–117. London: Routledge.

Jansen, T. 2017b. 'Review of Barend Ter Haar, *Practicing Scripture: A Lay Buddhist Movement in Late Imperial China*'. *Journal of Chinese Religions* 45 (2): 222–224. https://doi.org/10.1080/0737769X.2017.1369708

Kieschnick, J. 2005. 'Buddhist Vegetarianism in China'. In *Of Tripod and Palate: Food, Politics, and Religion in Traditional China*, edited by R. Sterckx, 186–212. New York: Palgrave. https://doi.org/10.1057/9781403979278_10

King, U. 1997. *Christ in All Things: Exploring Spirituality with Teilhard de Chardin*. London: SCM.

Leonardi, J. 2010. 'What We Are Meant to Be: Evolution as the Transformation of Consciousness'. In *The Human Being Fully Alive: Writings in Celebration of Brian Thorne*, edited by J. Leonardi, 58–75. Ross-on-Wye, UK: PCCS Books.

Lin, W. 2014. *Building a Sacred Mountain: The Buddhist Architecture of China's Mount Wutai*. Seattle, WA: University of Washington Press.

Mather, R. B. 1981. 'The Bonze's Begging Bowl: Eating Practices in Buddhist Monasteries of Medieval India and China'. *Journal of the American Oriental Society* 101 (4): 417–424. https://doi.org/10.2307/601214

Pu, C. 2014. *Ethical Treatment of Animals in Early Chinese Buddhism: Beliefs and Practices*. Newcastle upon Tyne, UK: Cambridge Scholars Publ.

Qin, W. 2000. 'The Buddhist Revival in Post-Mao China: Women Reconstruct Buddhism on Mt. Emei'. PhD dissertation, Harvard University.

Rogers, C. R. 1961. *On Becoming a Person: A Therapist's View of Psychotherapy*. London: Robinson.

Rogers, C. R. 1980. *A Way of Being*. New York: Houghton Mifflin.

Ruegg, D. 1980. 'Ahimsa and Vegetarianism in the History of Buddhism'. In *Buddhist Studies in Honour of Walpola Rahula*, edited by S. Balasooriya, A. Bareau, R. Gombrich, S. Gunasingha, U. Mallawarachchi and E. Perry, 234–241. London: Gordon Fraser.

Sangren, P. S. 1983. 'Female Gender in Chinese Religious Symbols: Kuan Yin, Ma Tsu, and the "Eternal Mother"'. *Signs* 9 (1): 4–25. https://doi.org/10.1086/494021

Steel, l. and K. Zinn (eds.). 2017. *Exploring the Materiality of Food "Stuffs": Transformations, Symbolic Consumption and Embodiment(s)*. London: Routledge. https://doi.org/10.4324/9781315673851

Sterckx, R. 2011. *Food, Sacrifice, and Sagehood in Early China*. Cambridge, UK: Cambridge University Press.

Topley, M. 2011. *Cantonese Society in Hong Kong and Singapore: Gender, Religion, Medicine and Money*. Singapore: NUS Press. https://doi.org/10.5790/hongkong/9789888028146.001.0001

Wielander, G. and D. Hird (eds.). 2018. *Chinese Discourses on Happiness*. Hong Kong: Hong Kong University Press. https://doi.org/10.2307/j.ctvfxv929

Wing, S. 2011. 'Gendering Buddhism: The Miaoshan Legend Reconsidered'. *Journal of Feminist Studies in Religion* 27 (1): 5–31. https://doi.org/10.2979/jfemistudreli.27.1.5

Wu, H. 2013. *Leading the Good Life: Peng Shaosheng's Biographical Narratives and Instructions for Buddhist Laywomen in High Qing China (1683-1796)*. Unpublished PhD dissertation, University of Pittsburgh.

Xu, M. 2016. *Crossing the Gate: Everyday Lives of Women in Song Fujian (960-1279)*, Albany, NY: State University of New York Press.

Yang, L. and D. An. 2005. *Handbook of Chinese Mythology*. Santa Barbara, CA: ABC Clio.

Yü, C. 2001. *The Chinese Transformation of Avalokiteśvara*. New York: Columbia University Press.

Yu, J. 2012. *Sanctity and Self-Inflicted Violence in Chinese Religions, 1500-1700*. Oxford, UK: Oxford University Press. https://doi.org/10.1093/acprof:oso/9780199844906.001.0001

Yue, I. 2013. 'Tasting the Lotus: Food, Drink and the Objectification of the Female Body in Gold, Vase, and Plum Blossom'. In *Scribes of Gastronomy: Representations of Food and Drink in Imperial Chinese Literature*, edited by I. Yue and S. Tang, 97–112. Hong Kong: The Chinese University Press. https://doi.org/10.5790/hongkong/9789888139972.003.0009

Chapter 5

Spiritus contra spiritum: Spirituality, Belief and Discipline in Alcoholics Anonymous

Wendy Dossett

The fellowship and programme of Alcoholics Anonymous (AA)[1] occupy an ambiguous place within the range of available and validated approaches to addiction recovery. Objections are levelled at various of its features, in particular at the use of religious language and rituals. Terms such as 'God', 'a power greater than ourselves' and 'spiritual awakening' appear in the Twelve Steps. Moral (or even moralistic) language regarding 'character defects', 'moral inventory-taking' and 'amend-making' also appear. Personal prayer and meditation are recommended to practitioners, and communal prayer is practised in meetings.[2] AA's own assertion that it is a spiritual and not religious programme notwithstanding, this inevitably clashes with prevailing medical models of addiction and recovery. In a culture where clear lines are invoked between secular and religious spheres, little or no legitimacy is afforded to apparently religious language manifesting in what is patently a secular health care (if not a criminal justice) setting (Peele, Bufe and Brodsky 2000; Lewis 2015; Szalavitz 2017). This controversy has considerable implications for people suffering with addictions whom AA could potentially help. It is also of obvious interest within a discursive tradition of religious studies which considers categories of 'religion', 'spirituality' and 'the secular' to be mutually constituted and contingent, and deployed in ways that reflect social and political rather than substantive realities. This chapter interrogates those categories as they manifest explicitly and implicitly in the narratives of Twelve Step fellowship members, in order to expose the ways in which, individually, they fail to fix a position for AA within the contemporary religious/spiritual/secular landscape.

The claim made by AA and other Twelve Step Mutual Aid groups, that addiction is a 'spiritual malady' requiring a 'spiritual awakening', can be presented in (at least) two ways. Firstly, it can assume that the secular/religious binary is real and argue that religious language is indeed salient in this discourse, and even that secular health care discourse is less, or even not, salient. This assertion precisely mirrors the assertion outlined above made from a secular clinical perspective, which argues that AA language is substantively religious and therefore must be relegated to a private (irrational and dubious) realm. This kind of 'religion-positive' articulation is forwarded by some pro-AA writers, epitomized by the controversial figure Dick B[3]. It is also made by some members of AA, and in fact there are sub-movements within AA which seek to re-discover or re-emphasize what they claim to be its original Christian nature (Kurtz and White 2015, 61). However, the 'spiritual malady/awakening' claim can also be presented in a form that is suspicious of a strong secular/religious binary. In this more discursive account, religious language is not substantive or exclusive, it simply provides an alternative vocabulary for features of the addiction and recovery experience which could just as well be both mediated and described clinically. An account positioned in this way is open to the possibility that recovery in AA is influenced by sources drawn from culture outside of AA, as well as by those authoritative sources from within. It focuses more on the quotidian life-world of members and the ways they adopt, reproduce, interpret, mould, recast and discard elements of official 'doctrines'. It explores how their identities as AA members in recovery intersect (and sometimes conflict) with other identities that they possess or participate in. It examines the day to day practices which they incorporate into their lives to maintain their ongoing abstinence and deepen, as they see it, their recovery. In this construal, AA appears not as a homogenous, conservative and moralistic form of pseudo-Christianity, but much more multifaceted. Whilst it clearly includes Christian voices, these are one grouping in a whole range of expressions, many of which are more aligned with contemporary wellbeing spirituality; sometimes Deist, sometimes Perennialist, but often not particularly hospitable to labels at all. An ethnographic lens, which diminishes the focus on authoritative and historically fixed textual statements about AA 'beliefs' in favour of a focus on lived contemporary AA practices, generates this picture of spiritual diversity. At the same time, and paradoxically, a stronger focus on day-to-day lives uncovers the practice of, arguably austere, 'disciplines' of AA. This in turn generates stark contrasts with the more individualistic, self-affirming/soothing and 'subjective-life' (Heelas and Woodhead 2005, 3) elements of contemporary wellbeing spirituality.

Positioning AA as religious, spiritual or secular is inevitably far more complex than those who claim its religious features disqualify it from serious consideration as a recovery modality would wish it to be. Widen the lens further and it is clear that medical discourse itself is not simplistically secular. Health care is rooted in religious history, and churches are the largest non-governmental providers of health care globally (Cadge 2012). Under the equality and diversity agenda, public health care has become more open to notions of spirituality; at least instrumentally, insofar as it accepts that care is enhanced by considering and accommodating the self-identified spiritual/religious needs of patients. However, it may, at the same time, have a financial vested interest in casting AA as dubious and irrational. The arguably radical phenomenon of people getting well 'for free' (Humphreys and Moos 2001) through naturally occurring, community-based AA could theoretically undermine client supply.[4] In an area of health care which, even in the UK, has become progressively privatized, this is potentially problematic. Of course, clinicians want people to get well, but they may be unwilling to signpost AA because (amongst other reasons) 'keeping clients engaged with services' is the measure of success (Laudet 2003). Losing them to other freely available methods makes providers redundant. Thus, it may suit a certain clinical defensiveness to assert a secular/religious binary, and then to cast the clinical approach as secular and legitimate and AA's as religious and therefore dubious. A critical religious studies approach which considers the identification of phenomena as 'religious', 'spiritual' or 'secular', as strategic rather than substantive, provides some insight into the power dynamics at work here. Ethnography offers a useful corrective because it avoids (a) affirming the binary and (b) either critiquing or mounting an apologetic defence of a 'religious' style of addiction recovery. Rather, it offers an account of contemporary practice underpinned by a resistance to drawing those sorts of theoretical boundaries too easily.

This chapter first explores AA's rationale for its explicit claim that addiction is a 'spiritual malady' requiring a 'spiritual awakening'. Textual and historical material is supplemented with ethnographic data from the Higher Power Project[5], a qualitative project undertaken amongst contemporary (mostly UK based) members of AA and other Twelve Step Fellowships by the author and a team from the University of Chester. This data exemplifies some of the diverse ways that members interpret these key notions, and how they draw on some aspects of popular, self-help and mind–body–spirit culture to inform their interpretations. The chapter then shifts in focus from beliefs to practices and outlines some of the disciplines to which many AA members commit, in order to show how these set AA apart as a phenomenon from contemporary wellbeing spirituality.

Spiritual Malady and Spiritual Awakening

Problematic substance use is considered in Alcoholics Anonymous[6] to be merely a symptom of an underlying 'spiritual malady' (AAWS [1939] 2001,

64). This is controversial on two counts. First, 'spiritual' might be considered to have little conceptual traction or public currency. Secondly, 'malady' might suggest 'disease', a concept which has a long history of controversy within public discourse about alcohol problems. Much contemporary clinical discourse adheres to the so-called 'disease model' of addiction[7], with which, it is often wrongly assumed AA agrees. However, the founders of AA were not clinicians, and they made modest claims for the significance of their insights[8]. They did not speak in terms of a disease as defined in pathological or anatomical terms, nor of the now widely accepted genetic predisposition for the condition[9]. They did speak of an 'illness', which the sufferer was not responsible for contracting, but for which the sufferer must become accountable in order to recover. As AA historian, Ernest Kurtz put it:

> ... the use of that vocabulary [*disease*] no more implies deep commitment to the tenet that alcoholism is a disease in some technical medical sense than speaking of sunrise or sunset implies disbelief in a Copernican solar system. (Kurtz 2002, 6)

The use of 'disease' in the clinical model refers to alleged abnormalities[10] in the brain. When members of Alcoholics Anonymous use the word 'disease', the implication is that whatever it is, it is neither 'choice' nor 'weakness' nor 'moral failure'. It is 'like' any other disease, insofar as the sufferer cannot help having it. Thus, in calling it a disease, they do not make a clinical diagnosis, but throw a functional moral lifeline to people whose crippling sense of inadequacy and failure has so far contributed effectively to their ongoing harmful drinking. In one of the 'stories' (accounts of recovery written by early members of AA) in the main text *Alcoholics Anonymous* a physician in recovery explains:

> It helped me a great deal to become convinced that alcoholism was a disease, not a moral issue; that I had been drinking as a result of a compulsion, even though I had not been aware of the compulsion at the time; and that sobriety was not a matter of willpower. (AAWS [1939] 2001, 416)

Maria, one of the participants in the Higher Power Project, said:

> I thought I was stupid, weak and bad, and I had so much guilt. It took me a while to accept that I was not stupid or weak or bad, I was sick. I am less hard on myself these days.

Not only is the idea that addictive disorder is an illness or malady controversial, so is the idea that it is an illness with a 'spiritual' character. The claim for a spiritual dimension to addiction and recovery centres on the concept of powerlessness. Sufferers are understood within the twelve-step *épistème* to be powerless over the substance or behaviour which causes harm. Members speak of knowing, on the one hand, that their substance use results in significant adversity for themselves and others, yet, on the other, being utterly unable to desist. The momentary relief from emotional (or sometimes physical) pain offered by the substance is so overwhelmingly compelling that no amount of ordinary willpower is sufficient to battle the compulsion. Members often talk of being strong-willed in other areas of their life, but of needing to reach a point of 'despair' of their own willpower in relation to mind-altering substances. In fact, they describe the insistence on the positive use of willpower by caring professions and family members as profoundly damaging. It is only when the limits of their own power are finally acknowledged (members speak of 'surrendering') that effective power (in their words, 'higher power' or 'power greater than myself') can be accessed. In this presentation of the addiction problem, the idea that the will might be strengthened and the problem thereby overcome is mere hubris. Despair of personal willpower, followed by the complete reliance upon a higher power is essential.

AA was founded in 1935 in the United States. The co-founders, Bill Wilson and Dr Robert Smith (known devotionally in AA as 'Bill W' and 'Dr Bob') were both self-described 'alcoholics'[11], and both associated in different ways with the Oxford Group. Ernest Kurtz (1979) explains that they met in Akron in 1935, some months after Bill Wilson had experienced a dramatic epiphany in a New York drying-out hospital which had allegedly released him from the compulsion to drink. This experience is recounted in the 1957 volume *Alcoholics Anonymous Comes of Age*:

> Suddenly the room lit up with a great white light. I was caught up into an ecstasy there are no words to describe ... And then it burst upon me that I was a free man .... All about me and through me there was a wonderful feeling of Presence [capital letter in original], and I thought to myself, "So this is the God of the preachers!" (Alcoholics Anonymous World Services 1957: 63)

However, months later in Akron on a business trip, Wilson felt he was certain to relapse, until, through the offices of a mutual friend, he met with surgeon proctologist, member of the Oxford Group, and still drinking 'alcoholic' Dr Robert Smith. The communication which passed between them was the 'identification of one alcoholic with another', which members describe as so central to AA's efficacy. Wilson did not relapse and Smith stopped drinking soon after. They credited their own sobriety neither to Smith's piety nor to Wilson's experience, but to their support of each other and the practice of working with others still suffering. Together, and with the other early members, they developed the Twelve Steps; namely the "programme" of Alcoholics Anonymous, which was later adopted by Narcotics Anonymous and the dozens of other Twelve Step fellowships. Anne Taves offers a persuasive account of the balance between the significance of Wilson's personal religious experience, Oxford Group practices, and what she identifies as the 'mutuality' (Taves 2016, 117) of the fellowship, in the development of a movement that ultimately sought not to be defined theologically. The Oxford Group, a form of conservative protestant evangelism, later to become Moral Re-Armament, and known for its Four Absolutes of Honesty, Purity, Unselfishness and Love, undoubtedly provided the inspiration and model for the development of the Twelve Steps. Oxford Group ideas fed into early AA through a variety of routes, not only through Smith's own membership (see Dick B 1992). Distinctive Oxford Group practices which persist to the present day were adopted from the beginning; for example, the allegedly first-century Christian practices of morning reading and contemplation, and regular communal rehearsal of shortcomings. However, as Kurtz (1979) and Taves (2016) record, AA quickly severed formal connections with the Oxford Group and explicitly positioned themselves as independent of religion.

Some passages in AA's main text *Alcoholics Anonymous* (1939) (known by members as the 'Big Book') seem to engage the language of religious conversion (for example the 'three pertinent ideas'[12]); other passages in the Big Book talk of a 'psychic' or 'personality' change required for the development of sobriety. Even within the main text, there is an ambiguity regarding the precise nature of the change necessary for abstinence to be achieved. Emphasizing personality change (AAWS [1939] 2001, 567), the Jungian term 'psychic change' (ibid, xxix), and William James's 'educational variety' of spiritual awakening (ibid, 567) over the so called 'hot flash' dramatic type of experience had by Wilson, several early members (including agnostics and an atheist, as well as Wilson himself) sought to widen the appeal for potential sufferers uncomfortable with narrow religiosity.

They claimed that 'God' need not be the God of Christianity; only that there must be reliance on a power 'greater than the self'. Whilst the phrase 'God, as we understand Him' is retained, the term 'Higher Power' is also found frequently in much of the AA literature. The lack of relationship with any formal religious tradition is made explicit in the Preamble[13], read at every AA meeting, which announces independence from 'sect, denomination, politics, organization or institution'. In the UK, AA is legally unable to receive any donations or bequests from any organization, church or government body, or to receive donations of more than £10,000 pounds from individuals[14]. It is not funded by nor does it promote any denominational worldview. This commitment to independence and corporate poverty means it has nothing to sell and it does not need to 'recruit', thus ensuring that it is never in competition with any other method of describing the problem or solution.

In the late 1920s/early 1930s, long before the founding of AA, Dr Carl Jung had treated an American patient at his Swiss clinic, a Harvard educated Rhode Island textile magnate called Rowland Hazard III.[15] Jung had diagnosed Hazard as suffering with alcohol dependence so extreme that he was beyond the help of medicine. In a statement viewed by later members of AA as signifying the immense humility of this giant of medicine and psychology, Jung said that Hazard's only hope was what he described as a 'vital spiritual experience', but added that such things were 'comparatively rare' (AAWS 1984, 382). Nevertheless, Hazard sought out the Oxford Group and stopped drinking. Along with fellow religionists, Hazard then managed to bring Ebby Thatcher, a well-to-do New Yorker who was summering in New England, to the Oxford Group and to sobriety also, thus preventing, at the last minute, his admission into the Vermont Asylum for the Insane. Ebby had been a drinking partner of alcohol-dependent stock-broker Wilson, who was initially horrified to learn that his friend had stopped drinking. Wilson, who had by then acknowledged that drinking was a problem for him, was sure that he would never 'get religion', but Ebby's example was to be hugely influential in Bill's later sobriety following the experience in his hospital room.

In 1961, more than a quarter of a century after the founding of AA, and having already recorded the events of Hazard's release from alcoholism in the Big Book (AAWS [1939] 2001, 26–8), Wilson, now retired, wrote to Jung to thank him for his role in the course of events which had led to the development of AA. He received an immediate reply[16]. This letter is not surprisingly widely quoted, to indicate that the 'celebrated physician' (as Jung is described in the Big Book [ibid, 26]) supported the argument that a spiritual experience or awakening of some kind is the solution to alcoholism. Jung's phrase *spiritus contra spiritum* ('spirit', in the sense of the numinous or holy—against 'spirits'—alcohol) is an arresting epigram. However, a close reading of the letter indicates that Jung actually attributes Hazard's recovery from alcohol addiction to 'personal and honest contact with friends'. Jung states that the journey of what he calls this 'unrecognized spiritual need' into perdition can be arrested in two ways—by 'real religious insight', or by the 'protective wall of the human community'. Engagement with other human actors is as much a solution to alcoholism as is a vital spiritual experience.

The research amongst people in Twelve Step style recovery from addictions undertaken at the University of Chester under the banner of the Higher Power Project demonstrates that contemporary members use (in line with Jung's observation) a whole range of ways of understanding and articulating the profound affective change they have experienced, and the lifestyle which they maintain 'a day at a time'. A very small proportion of the 107 participants identify a dramatic religious experience with apparently supernatural features as part of their recovery. Joe[17] is one. He described an auditory experience, which he described as 'spiritual', coupled with a spectacular sense of release and relief:

> J: And I think what actually happened was, when I went through the programme of recovery and went through the erm, when I knelt down with my sponsor[18], and said the Step Three Prayer. It was that night, I went home, and I was living by myself, and I err, a voice said to me 'Joseph, we love you'. As clear as anything.
> I: Uh hu.
> J: And I thought I was, I was going back to the psychiatric department, so I asked it to go away and come back in the morning but when I, when I woke up that next morning, it was as though everything had changed for me, I got a massive sense of release. And relief. For nine months then as I, as I've said in the err, in me description [Joe refers here to his questionnaire in which he briefly mentions 'hearing voices' and then 'being on Cloud Nine for nine months'] I felt I was on cloud nine, I was just floating really.
> I: Yeah, could you describe that spiritual experience in a little more detail?
> J: Err, yeah, really it was just a sense of erm, lightness and errm, expansiveness I suppose [...] it was almost as if all sorts of erm, well, as if the shackles had been er released and I was, I was free. You know, there, there was no fear, there was no need for a, that that, was when the erm, the need to have a drink or even the thought to have a drink, it was completely taken away from me from that point.

A greater number talk about interpreting what might be considered coincidences as the working of a higher power in their life. Nick, for example, in a story that brings to mind Bill Wilson's own trip to Akron, when his sobriety was saved by his fortuitous meeting with Dr Bob, talks about his intense anxiety about going to the US on a business trip when only a couple of months sober, arriving at his hotel in the destination city, and seeing a sign 'Orange County's Alcoholics Anonymous Convention':

> N and the interviewer laugh.
> N: I'm not joking, there must've been two thousand alcoholics[19] in that hotel!

I: [laughing] yeah.
N: And I thought, if there isn't a God, I'll eat my bloody hat [...]. And it went on like that. I couldn't believe it, things happened to me, that just, either, I, I, they were so coincidental it was just a ... it ... they and all that lot did was to reinforce for me, that a) there was a God, something outside was looking after me. And, that I was doing the right thing.

Many of the accounts indicate an interpretation of spirituality rooted in human community and the power of friendship, reminiscent of Jung's reference to the same. Here, Carol explains her grappling with the notion of higher power. We enter this conversation as Carol is describing the meeting she attended in her early days:

C: What I really want to deal with now is to stop drinking and errm, talk to these sober women, there were a lot of sober women. Well, 4 or 5. In this meeting. Who were regulars.
I: Mmm.
C: So I, fell among them, and they looked after me. And after a few months I got a sponsor that was a lady who eventually took me through the steps and everything. So, she was my higher power and the meeting was my higher power.
I: And that, that group of friends?
C: Yes, I didn't know how this business of staying sober was going to work ...
I: Mmm
C: And I had to just, put a foot in and trust that if I did what they suggested it would work. I, was lucky in that it never occurred to me to question, to rebel, to argue, I did what was suggested. No-one suggested anything outlandish so I didn't have to think about it too much so it was just sensible stuff. Erm, a copy of Living Sober[20], a copy of the Big Book. Erm, my sponsor talking to me, now at that point I think, I don't know, *sighs* I took AA as my higher power. There was absolutely no doubt about it.
I: Mmmm.
C: And it had to be what I could see in the rooms.
I: Yeah.
C: Erm, I couldn't at that stage put my faith in something I didn't know anything about and hadn't, didn't, didn't know anything about really. And what I did know about was, the rooms and the sober women and the programme and my sponsor and I just kept ... They say keep it simple! So I kept it simple. [...] And it was the programme and it needed to be done and I needed a sponsor to take me through it and I needed to attend meetings and then eventually I needed to be doing something within the meeting and that was service. And

> frankly that was enough to be going on with. So I actually payed no attention to the word God.
> I: Great, great. The other thing is, when you came to work the steps with your sponsor erm, presumably the concept of higher power reared its head again?
> C: No, I, I, I kept it as AA.
> I: Yeah, you just kept it the same and erm, um, and that was perfectly acceptable and to your sponsor? I mean, it wasn't challenged in any way?
> C: She didn't. She was a very pragmatic woman. Very common sense. A very strong sponsor.

Carol's approach is typical of many we have interviewed. Their higher power is simply the community of other sober 'alcoholics' following the same path, and in Carol's case (as in the majority of cases amongst our participants) that was considered acceptable by her sponsor. Several said that for them God was the **G**roup **O**f **D**runks, or **G**ift **O**f **D**espair. Many participants speak of a 'composite' notion of higher power. Here, Ruby writes a questionnaire response to the question 'Please describe your concept of a Higher Power (if you have one) in one sentence':

> something greater, the group, the ground of all being, the universe, the 'unknown mystery of things', nature, not me—or at least, not my self-serving ego.

Spiritual beliefs and spiritual experiences or awakenings are of obvious interest for an analysis of the AA programme, but a fuller picture is seen when these are not the only foci. In this respect, the turn to everyday and vernacular religion, as seen in the work of Leonard Primiano (1995, 2012) and Marion Bowman and Ülo Valk (2012), is helpful, insofar as it prioritizes practices over beliefs, and people over concepts. In Primiano's words, 'It shifts the way one studies religion with the people becoming the focus of the study, not "religion" or "belief" as abstractions' (Primiano 2012, 384). Amongst the many ways in which everyday or vernacular religion can be explored is to investigate what people read. Dick B undertook significant research to establish what sources the early AA members read to inform their viewpoints (Dick B 1998). Dawn Llewellyn's 2015 volume *Reading, Feminism and Spirituality* establishes how various critical and selective ways in which people (in her case women) read canonical and non-canonical texts expose cultural commitments, cultivate shifts, nourish multiple identities and create new canons.

Inspired by Llewellyn's work and curious to explore how reading habits have changed since Dick B's study, we asked participants what sources they drew on to inspire their development of a concept of higher power.

Not all our participants were readers of course, and many referenced non-textual sources of inspiration. Readers amongst the participants make intensive use of what the fellowships call 'Approved Literature'. Those that find reading challenging are nevertheless participating in an oral community saturated by references to this literature. All of them say they have used fellowship literature or the ideas within it in some way in their development of their concept of higher power. These sources are strongly authoritative within this community. However, almost all *also* say they seek inspiration from elsewhere in addition, and some fascinating patterns emerge. Participants speak about a wide range of music, films and poetry, including classical, religious and popular culture sources. Space does not permit an analysis of all this material here, but I draw out some significant sources for situating the ideas of contemporary members within the religion–spirituality–secular matrix.

Just under a quarter of the 107 project participants identify themselves as belonging to a Christian denomination, but well over a third refer to Christian literature including scripture, as a source of inspiration. A number of biblical passages are specifically referred to, including the Sermon on the Mount, well-known passages about love from the Gospels and from 1 Corinthians 13, and the line from Isaiah 36 'A bruised reed He will not break'. This is an interesting, but not surprising finding, about the significance and reach of biblical literature outside of the directly affiliated context. A great deal of the most commonly used literature in the fellowships is Christian in origin. The so-called *Serenity Prayer*—'God Grant me the serenity to accept the things I cannot change, the courage to change the things I can and the wisdom to know the difference' is claimed by the fellowships not just as a kind of mascot or slogan, but as a spiritual practice with life-changing effects. The *Prayer of St Francis*, sometimes called the *Step Eleven Prayer*, which seeks the power to understand rather than to be understood, to love rather than to be loved, is cited as important to them by several participants, including by those who want to make it very clear that they are not Christians. The *Footprints* poem (for authorship see Stuever 2008) is popular. Max Ehrmann's 1927 prose poem *Desiderata*—not necessarily a Christian text but used by many Christians is also used by people in Twelve Step fellowships. The work of the Franciscan friar Richard Rohr is appreciated by both Christians and non-Christians in the fellowships. Related to this literature is an interest in the literature of New Thought Religion, the nineteenth century American phenomenon. There are historical and cultural reasons for this as Emmet Fox's book *The Sermon on the Mount* (1934) and William James's *Varieties of Religious Experience* (1902) was on the reading list of early members of AA, and as with other spiritual communities, there is a fascination around the alleged experiences and reading of founders and early members. Amongst our participants a few mention Mary Baker Eddy and Swedenborg as influential.

After Christian spirituality the next most popular traditional spiritual source is Buddhism. In fact, Buddhist sources are cited at nearly the same frequency as Christian sources. Some refer to canonical texts, but more popular are the works of Buddhist teachers writing for anglophone audiences—Thich Nhat Hanh, the Dalai Lama, Ajahn Sumedho, Pema Chödrön and Jack Kornfield—and references to particular meditation practices such as *mettā bhāvanā* (lovingkindness) meditation. Several explicitly mention the Buddhist notion of the interconnectedness of all things as an influence on their higher power notion, leading, they say, to greater awareness of the consequences of their behaviour.

The next category of literature referred to by participants is a very broad genre of contemporary Mind–Body–Spirit literature, that draws on practices, sometimes associated with mindfulness, which assign a high value to living 'in the present moment', and to building the foundations of action on love rather than fear. Many of these are written by contemporary guru figures with significant transnational followings. Central is Eckhart Tolle; his *The Power of Now* (1997) was referred to by more than a tenth of our participants. Marianne Williamson is also popular; a writer (and politician) who has made her career promoting the phenomenon known as *A Course in Miracles*, which is an allegedly divinely inspired text, the words of Jesus channelled by Helen Schucman (1975). Williamson is currently exploring the possibility of seeking the Democratic nomination in 2020, on a manifesto that America needs to reclaim its loving spiritual heritage (see https://marianne.com/), and she embodies a contemporary spirituality flavoured in part with the long tradition of American Transcendentalism, and with contemporary feminist self-care spirituality. A couple of participants indicated the importance to them of the fact that Williamson is in recovery herself. Jill, who had experienced what she described as 'a dry period' (meaning abstinent from alcohol) as a practising Christian and then relapsed before finding recovery again told us:

> [...] Marianne Williamson, particularly as she's in recovery y'know and it's her recovery journey and it it sort of makes more, umm, seems to make much more sense to me cos I had a period when I was very frightened in the relapse that that God had given me this sort of recovery, my first recovery, and that I'd thrown it away [...] and so I was sort of looking for something that sort of fitted y'know a God that was gonna be more forgiving and caring [...] and, and loving.

Also mentioned by participants is the Positive Thinking/Law of Attraction programme *The Secret* (Byrne 2006). Other writers in this mind–body–spirit category are Caroline Myss, another contemporary American spiritual teacher; P. D. Ouspensky, the Russian Esotericist, and Jalaluddin Rumi, the thirteenth century Persian sufi mystic poet. Amongst novels mentioned are Paul Coelho's *The Alchemist* (1993) and Richard Bach's *Jonathan Livingston Seagull* (1972).

There is a section of self-help literature typified by Melody Beattie, who writes for people with co-dependency issues, and Karen Casey and Stephanie Covington who write primarily for women with addictions. They are published by the enormous American-based multinational recovery organization the Hazelden Foundation. In a broadly similar vein is M. Scott Peck whose *The Road Less Travelled* (1978) was mentioned by more than a handful of our participants. Kurtz and Ketcham's the *Spirituality of Imperfection* (1992) is also popular, it being no coincidence that Ernest Kurtz is a well-known historian of AA.

Also frequently mentioned is Neale Donald Walshe and his series of books Conversations with God. God is depicted in these texts in pantheistic and panentheistic terms. These ideas are reflected in much of what participants tell us about their concept of higher power, and in the resources they select. The classic example is the reference to the Star Wars idea of 'the Force', that appears several times in our research participants' accounts.

Roger said:

> the Star Wars thing came in fairly early on[21], it, it, it made a lot of sense to me [...] Just the idea that there was something there that was, round through everything and everybody that made an awful lot of sense to me; a sort of synergy that was sort of there and all they had to do was tap into it.

A number of participants cite New Atheist literature as influential in their development of a concept of a higher power. Dawkins, Hitchens, Harris, all get mentions, as do Charles Darwin and Bertrand Russell. Most of these references come from self-identified agnostics or atheists who have found these sources reassuring in their development of non-spiritual concepts of higher power. Sophia's account here shows how the development of a concept of higher power is an autonomous negotiation, not simply an uncritical adoption and reproduction of theistic or deistic ideas:

> Ricky Gervais is a well-known Atheist and I've read what he has written on the subject. Also Stephen Fry, David Mitchell and Germaine Greer are

all people I'm interested in so I've listened to what they've said about Religion / God, as well as discussing it with friends. I've heard 'The Force' in Star Wars being compared to HP[22] and I quite like that, I guess it had some influence. The people in the fellowship have had a huge influence over my version of an HP, mainly by me not agreeing (for me) with a lot of HP versions I hear in AA. So by defining what my HP is NOT it has helped me define what it IS.

This short investigation into the ways contemporary AA members draw on a range of sources goes some way to demonstrating that any attempt to position AA in simple terms as either religious or secular, or even 'spiritual but not religious' is inevitably inadequate. All our participants (including atheists) said that a higher power was important or essential, but how that was described varied hugely. Inspiration was sought as much from popular mind–body–spirit culture as it was from explicitly Christian sources. Clinicians who dismiss AA because it is 'too Christian' may be surprised to learn how closely aligned it is to contemporary wellbeing spirituality, though that may be perceived as equally dubious. However, if an ethnographic approach illuminates the ways in which the beliefs of contemporary AA members are diverse, liberal, subject to change over the recovery life-course, and accommodating of the secular; this relativism is challenged and confounded when focus turns to the practice of the Steps themselves.

AA's Disciplines

Not all members of AA 'work' the Steps, though the folk wisdom of the fellowship holds that those who work the Steps get well. The putative need to undertake this work relates to the characterization of the underlying problem, or the malady of which the substance use is merely the symptom, as 'self-centered fear' (AAWS [1952] 1981, 77) and 'self-will run riot' (AAWS [1939] 2001, 62). Addressing this, according to members, requires the discipline, self-examination and self-giving which comprise AA's programme of recovery.

The Twelve Steps are:

1. We admitted we were powerless over alcohol[23]—that our lives had become unmanageable. 2. Came to believe that a power greater than ourselves could restore us to sanity. 3. Made a decision to turn our will and our lives over to the care of God as we understood Him. 4. Made a searching and fearless moral inventory of ourselves. 5. Admitted to God, to ourselves, and to another human being the exact nature of our wrongs. 6. Were entirely ready to have God remove all these defects of character. 7. Humbly asked Him to remove our shortcomings. 8. Made a

list of all persons we had harmed, and became willing to make amends to them all. 9. Made direct amends to such people wherever possible, except when to do so would injure them or others. 10. Continued to take personal inventory, and when we were wrong, promptly admitted it. 11. Sought through prayer and meditation to improve our conscious contact with God as we understood Him, praying only for knowledge of His will for us and the power to carry that out. 12. Having had a spiritual awakening as the result of these steps, we tried to carry this message to alcoholics, and to practice these principles in all our affairs.[24]

Practitioners typically work through the Steps, often over a period of months or even years, with the help of a sponsor. 'Working' the steps requires the practitioner to gain an understanding of each step, and apply it to their own life and circumstances. In Steps 1–3, the programme deals with the question of powerlessness and the need for higher power, namely the issues so far discussed in this chapter. Thus, a practitioner begins working on Step 1 by considering (and possibly listing) what evidence they have of powerlessness over alcohol (or other drugs) and that their lives have become unmanageable. They stay focused on each step until they are sure that they recognize its significance in their own life and they are ready to move to the next. In Step 2 they consider what for them might function as 'a power greater than myself' and in Step 3 what 'turning their will and their life over' might look like in their case. In Steps 4 and 5 the programme tackles the denial thought to be present in the sufferer. It is assumed that unconscious mental strategies are employed to justify their continued substance use; minimizing the damage to self and others, minimizing the extent of the problem or the severity of the compulsion, justifying the behaviour on the grounds of personal difficulties or suffering (perhaps involving the exaggeration of these). An inventory of resentments, fears and damage done[25] enables the sufferer to emerge from denial not only about the personality distorting effects of substance use but of the difficult underlying emotions and characteristics (or 'spiritual malady') thought to be driving the substance use. In other words, it facilitates a process of becoming honest, and owning the harm done. Undertaking a Step 4 usually requires of practitioners significant, emotionally challenging writing. Various styles of Step 4 have emerged, but in general terms practitioners survey their past, both in terms of negative experiences perpetrated upon them by others (individuals and institutions), their reactions to these, and the harms they have perpetrated themselves. This survey must be 'searching and fearless' and takes considerable courage, humility and honesty to undertake seriously. This 'moral inventory' is designed to uncover what the programme calls 'character defects' and the practitioner identifies were they have been self-centred, prideful, jealous, vindictive, lazy etc. In Steps 6 and 7 the spiritual malady is addressed through working on those defects or characteristics with a view to improvement. In Steps 8 and 9 the practitioner commits to doing what they can to mend damaged relationships, where this might be of benefit to others. Given the extent of damage done to close relationships in addiction, this too requires discipline, discernment and courage, and often goes far beyond apologies and asking forgiveness. Practitioners sometimes speak about undertaking amends for life. In Steps 10 to 12 they maintain a daily programme of self-examination, contemplation, selfless action (which includes assisting those still suffering), and, as they see it, ongoing growth. Practitioners of the Steps amongst our participants commonly referred to a personal 'daily programme' which included readings, prayers or contemplation time, calling or texting newcomers or struggling peers, writing gratitude lists, writing Step 10 inventories, planning events to ensure they are not at risk of drinking or of engaging in anti-recovery behaviours (e.g., getting 'hungry, angry, lonely or tired') and so on. Practitioners 'working' their Step 12 typically attend as many meetings as they can to 'carry the message', they do service (undertake responsibilities for running meetings and take on roles within the service structure of AA), and they sponsor newcomers, which can represent a significant emotional and time commitment. One participant, an academic, told us that working with a sponsee was like supervising a PhD student 'only with much more at stake'. The discipline and commitment involved in this programme is considerable, and most practitioners describe it as a lifetime journey which continues long after the substance has been eliminated from their lives.

Conclusion

Whilst the *beliefs* involved in AA are open to interpretation to such a degree that atheists, deists, Christians, Buddhists and practitioners of alternative spiritualities all feel at home in AA rooms[26], the *disciplines* and *practices* (if taken up), are by contrast challenging, demanding, and counter-cultural. Even highly-committed religious people may baulk at the rigour of the self-examination required of a Step-practising AA member; a rigour that is certainly out of step with the elements of the holistic milieu which seek release from stress and self-affirmation. Practising the Steps has more in common with Ignatian Spiritual Exercises than it does with the kind of individualistic, commodified wellbeing spirituality critiqued by Carrette and King in *Selling Spirituality* (2005), despite the fact that interest in those forms is evidenced in the eclectic reading practices of members. The answer to the question of whether AA is secular, spiritual or religious depends not only on the conceptual framework and political agenda of who is asking it, but also on which element of the AA lifeworld is under scrutiny.

That very question, whether AA is secular, religious or spiritual has recently been investigated by Harvard Medical School's John F. Kelly (Kelly 2017). It is significant that as an addiction scientist he identifies AA's spiritual components as being amongst its effective mechanisms. Kelly's work focuses largely on the role of positive spiritual beliefs resulting in positive feelings. These may indeed be a significant part of what makes spirituality 'work' in AA, but as noted elsewhere (Dossett 2017), attention must also be given to the challenging practices, daily activities, and disciplines of AA, and recovery life-course ethnography has much to offer in this regard. It may seem improbable that an apparently spiritual approach to what is thought to be a health or criminal justice issue should be effective. However, *clinical* research shows that participation in AA leads to increased levels of abstinence, improved wellbeing and increased self-efficacy (Donovan et al. 2013). Furthermore, 'full' engagement (doing service, engaging a sponsor, working the Steps; rather than mere attendance) has been shown to result in decreased likelihood of relapse (Humphreys et al. 2004). Clinical research speaks in the language of recovery capital deficits, adaptive social networks and self-efficacy. Fellowship members, on the other hand, speak of defects of character, fellowship and spirituality. Jung's *spiritus contra spiritum* sounds mystical and otherworldly, but the clinical language and the language of spirituality (whether that be Christian, Buddhist, alternative, or wellbeing spirituality) may simply be considered alternative lexica for the same phenomenon. AA offers religious studies a case study which exposes the provisionality and inadequacy of its central analytical categories, a finding with practical significance beyond the scope of religious studies itself.

Biographical Note

Wendy Dossett is Associate Professor of Religious Studies and Programme Director of the MA Religious Studies at the University of Chester, UK. She is a former Associate Director of the Alister Hardy Religious Experience Research Centre. She has published in the fields of Buddhist studies, religious education and recovery spirituality, and her research is centred on the intersecting nature of the categories 'religion', 'spirituality' and 'the secular'. She is Principal Investigator of The Higher Power Project; a large qualitative project exploring spirituality amongst people in twelve-step recovery from addictions. Her most recent publication in this field is 'Twelve Step Mutual Aid: Spirituality, Vulnerability and Recovery', in S. Harvey, S. Steidinger and J. Beckford (Eds.), *New Religious Movements and Counselling: Academic, Professional and Personal Perspectives* (2018).

Notes

1. Alcoholics Anonymous (AA) is described by its members not as an organization, but as a 'fellowship'. Membership is self-selecting (members are so because they say they are). Addiction Studies literature tends to refer to the fellowships as 'mutual aid', (in other words, self-help, but in groups). The programme of recovery in AA is comprised of 'the meetings' (there are more than 4000 weekly AA meetings in the UK) and the Twelve Steps (see pp. 126–127), which members may or may not (their choice) take up and apply to their lives. AA is free, (attenders may make a voluntary contribution to refreshments and room rent). It is not 'selling' a particular form of treatment, and is naturally occurring in communities.
2. In the UK meetings are commonly closed with a communal recitation of the Serenity Prayer (a prayer open to Deistic interpretation), often standing up and holding hands in a circle. People are free not to participate, but the norm is to do so. In the US and the Republic of Ireland, it is more common for the Serenity Prayer to be recited communally early in the meeting, and the more explicitly Christian 'Lord's Prayer' is used to close the meeting.
3. For a discussion see Beech 2018.
4. At the beginning of a half-day course for professionals introducing them to Twelve Step fellowships, we asked participants to list their concerns about them, and one said 'If we refer our clients to Mutual Aid, what will we do? We won't have jobs' (Wrexham, January 2015).
5. Dossett 2013, 2015, 2017, 2018. See also www.csarsg.org.uk. The Higher Power Project was generously funded by the Sir Halley Stewart Trust.
6. Alcoholics Anonymous was the first Twelve Step 'fellowship', founded in 1935. It was followed by Al-Anon, a Twelve Step fellowship for friends and family members, founded in 1951, and Narcotics Anonymous in 1953. There are now dozens of Twelve Step fellowships which use twelve steps very similar to those developed in Alcoholics Anonymous, but focused on different substances or behaviours. Examples include Cocaine Anonymous, Gamblers Anonymous, Sex Addicts Anonymous, Anorexics and Bulimics Anonymous and Overeaters Anonymous.
7. The American National Institute on Drug Abuse, NIDA, website www.drugabuse.gov describes addiction as follows: 'addiction is defined as a chronic, relapsing brain disease that is characterised by compulsive drug seeking and use, despite harmful consequences'.
8. The foreword to the second edition of the main text *Alcoholics Anonymous* (first published in 1939 and known by members as 'The Big Book') states, 'In all probability, we shall never be able to touch more than a fair fraction of the alcohol problem in all its ramifications. Upon therapy for the alcoholic himself [sic], we surely have no monopoly.' (AAWS [1939] 2001, xxi).
9. National Institute on Alcohol Abuse and Alcoholism's *Collaborative Studies on Genetics of Alcoholism (COGA) Study* provides a gateway to some of the research in this area: https://www.niaaa.nih.gov/research/major-initiatives/collaborative-studies-genetics-alcoholism-coga-study (retrieved December 30, 2018).

10. A claim which itself is controversial (Lewis 2015).
11. The terms 'alcoholic' and 'addict' are usually avoided in academic literature. Alcohol Use Disorder (AUD) is the preferred nomenclature, and 'alcoholism' is not a recognized academic term. When speaking of sufferers, person-first language is (rightly) preferred 'person suffering with/living with AUD (or SUD, Substance Use Disorder, for other drugs). However, the terms are sometimes used in this chapter to reflect emic usage. For members of Twelve Step fellowships, the claiming of the identity is considered as central in the recovery process: 'my name is ..., and I'm an alcoholic'. Furthermore, fellowship members usually think of these terms applying for life, and to be unrelated to abstinence. Thus, people who have not had an alcoholic drink for 30, 40, 50 years or more will still announce themselves in meetings as 'my name is ..., and I'm an alcoholic'.
12. Much of the 'Big Book' is written in the third person as it comprises a report of what the early members did (rather than a set of instructions about what members 'should' do). The 'three pertinent ideas' are 'a) That we were alcoholic and could not manage our own lives; b) That no human power could have relieved our alcoholism, and c) That God could and would if he were sought.' (AAWS [1939] 2001: 60).
13. The Preamble: 'Alcoholics Anonymous is a fellowship of men and women who share their experience, strength and hope with each other that they may solve their common problem and help other to recover from alcoholism. The only requirement for AA membership is a desire to stop drinking. There are no dues or fees for AA membership; we are self-supporting through our own contributions. AA is not allied with any sect, denomination or politics, organization or institution; does not wish to engage in any controversy, neither endorses nor opposes any causes. Our primary purpose is to stay sober and to help other alcoholics achieve sobriety'.
14. The Alcoholics Anonymous Dispositions Act of 1986 in the UK made AA immune from the legal compulsion to accept bequests. http://www.alcoholics-anonymous.org.uk/Members/Service/Disciplines/Finance
15. The most complete account of Jung's relationship with Hazard, and his indirect influence on AA is recorded in *Pass It On: The Story of Bill Wilson and How the AA Message Reached the World* (AAWS 1984: 381–386).
16. The text of Jung's letter may be read here: http://www.silkworth.net/aahistory/carljung_billw013061.html
17. Participants choose the name by which they wish to be referred to in the research. In many (but not all) cases it is their own first name.
18. A 'sponsor' is a person in the fellowship who is experienced in practising the Twelve Steps. Many members (but not all) ask a sponsor to help them through the steps. The role is not dissimilar to that of spiritual friend in some Buddhist and Christian traditions.
19. Members of AA refer to themselves as 'alcoholics' regardless of time elapsed since the last drink they took, since it is a condition they consider they have for life. Nick's use of the term here does not imply 'drinking alcoholics' but other members of AA. As a newly sober person, it would have been

profoundly reassuring to Nick to find himself in the company of people who understood the challenges he faced on that trip.
20. This volume (AAWS 1975) is practical advice for staying sober, which does not outline the Twelve Step programme, yet is 'AA-approved'.
21. By '[coming] in fairly early on', Roger means 'making sense to him fairly early in his recovery'.
22. HP is a commonly used acronym for Higher Power.
23. Other Twelve Step programmes replace this with the relevant substance or behaviour, e.g., drugs.
24. Reproduced with permission from the General Service Board UK of Alcoholics Anonymous.
25. These are sometimes separated into sexual harms and other harms.
26. This is true in the UK, but in the USA atheists report greater levels of alienation in some AA meetings (Roger C 2017).

Bibliography

Alcoholics Anonymous World Services (AAWS). [1939], 2001. *Alcoholics Anonymous. The Story of How Many Thousands of Men and Women Have Recovered From Alcoholism* (4th edn). New York: Alcoholics Anonymous World Services.

Alcoholics Anonymous World Services (AAWS). [1952] 1981. *Twelve Steps and Twelve Traditions*. New York: Alcoholics Anonymous World Services.

Alcoholics Anonymous World Services (AAWS). 1957. *Alcoholics Anonymous Comes of Age: A Brief History of A. A.* New York: Alcoholics Anonymous World Services.

Alcoholics Anonymous World Service (AAWS). 1975. *Living Sober.* New York: Alcoholics Anonymous World Services.

Alcoholics Anonymous World Services (AAWS). 1984. *Pass It On: The Story of Bill Wilson and How the A.A. Message Reached the World.* New York: Alcoholics Anonymous World Services.

Bach, R. 1972. *Jonathan Livingston Seagull.* London: Turnstone Press.

Beech, J. 2018. 'How Accurate Is the Dick B Narrative of Early Akron AA?'. *The Fix*, May 24, 2018. Retrieved January 1, 2019, from https://www.thefix.com/how-accurate-dick-b-narrative-early-akron-aa

Bowman, M. and U. Valk (eds.). 2012. *Vernacular Religion in Everyday Life: Expressions of Belief.* London: Routledge.

Byrne, R. 2006. *The Secret.* New York: Simon & Schuster.

Cadge, W. 2012. *Paging God: Religion in the Halls of Medicine.* Chicago, IL: University of Chicago Press. https://doi.org/10.7208/chicago/9780226922133.001.0001

Carrette, J. R. and R. King. 2005. *Selling Spirituality: The Silent Takeover of Religion.* London: Routledge. https://doi.org/10.4324/9780203494875

Coelho, P. 1993. *The Alchemist: A Fable About Following Your Dream.* London: HarperCollins.

Dick, B. 1992. *The Oxford Group & Alcoholics Anonymous.* Kihei, HI: Paradise Research Publications.

Dick, B. 1998. *The Books Early AAs Read for Spiritual Growth* (7th edn). Kihei, HI: Paradise Publications.

Donovan, D. M., M. H. Ingalsbe, J. Benbow and D. C. Daley. 2013. '12-Step Interventions and Mutual Support Programs for Substance Use Disorders: An Overview'. *Social Work in Public Health* 28 (3–4): 313–332. https://doi.org/10.1080/19371918.2013.774663

Dossett, W. 2013. 'Addiction, Spirituality and 12-step Programmes'. *International Social Work* 56 (3): 369–383. https://doi.org/10.1177/0020872813475689

Dossett, W. 2015. 'Reflections on the Language of Salvation in Twelve Step Recovery'. In *Alternative Salvations: Engaging the Sacred and the Secular*, edited by H. Bacon, W. Dossett and S. Knowles, 21–30. London: Bloomsbury Academic.

Dossett, W. 2017. 'A Daily Reprieve Contingent on the Maintenance of Our Spiritual Condition'. *Addiction* 112: 942–943. https://doi.org/10.1111/add.13731

Dossett, W. 2018. 'Twelve Step Mutual Aid: Spirituality, Vulnerability and Recovery'. In *New Religious Movements and Counselling: Academic, Professional and Personal Perspectives*, edited by S. Harvey, S. Steidinger and J. Beckford, 221–235. New York: Routledge. https://doi.org/10.4324/9781315598086-16

Fox, E. 1934. *The Sermon on the Mount: The Key to Success in Life*. San Francisco, CA: Harper & Row.

Heelas, P. and L. Woodhead. 2005. *The Spiritual Revolution: Why Religion is Giving Way to Spirituality*. Oxford, UK: Blackwell.

Humphreys, K. and R. Moos. 2001. 'Can Encouraging Substance Abuse Patients to Participate in Self-Help Groups Reduce Demand for Health Care? A Quasi-Experimental Study'. *Alcoholism: Clinical and Experimental Research* 25 (5), 711–716. https://doi.org/10.1097/00000374-200105000-00012

Humphreys, K, S. Wing, D. McCarty, J. Chappel, L. Gallant, B. Haberle, A. T. Horvath et al. 2004. 'Self-Help Organizations for Alcohol and Drug Problems: Toward Evidence-Based Practice and Policy'. *Journal of Substance Abuse Treatment* 26 (3): 151–158. https://doi.org/10.1016/S0740-5472(03)00212-5

James, W. 1902. *The Varieties of Religious Experience*. London: Longmans, Green and Co. https://doi.org/10.1037/10004-000

Kelly, J. F. 2017. 'Is Alcoholics Anonymous Religious, Spiritual, Neither? Findings from 25 Years of Mechanisms of Behavior Change Research'. *Addiction* 112 (6): 929–936. https://doi.org/10.1111/add.13590

Kurtz, E. 1979. *Not-God: A History of Alcoholics Anonymous*. Center City, MN: Hazelden Educational Services.

Kurtz, E. 2002. 'Alcoholics Anonymous and the Disease Concept of Alcoholism'. *Alcoholism Treatment Quarterly* 20 (3–4): 5–39. https://doi.org/10.1300/J020v20n03_02

Kurtz, E. and K. Ketcham. 2014. *Experiencing Spirituality: Finding Meaning Through Storytelling*. New York: Tarcher, Penguin.

Kurtz, E. and W. White. 2015. 'Recovery Spirituality'. *Religions* 6 (1): 58–81. https://doi.org/10.3390/rel6010058

Laudet, A. B. 2003. 'Attitudes and Beliefs About 12-Step Groups Among Addiction Treatment Clients and Clinicians: Toward Identifying Obstacles to Participation'. *Substance Use & Misuse* 38 (14): 2017–2047. https://doi.org/10.1081/JA-120025124

Lewis, M. 2015. *Biology of Desire: Why Addiction is Not a Disease*. New York: PublicAffairs.

Llewellyn, D. 2015. *Reading, Feminism, and Spirituality: Troubling the Waves*. New York: Palgrave Macmillan. https://doi.org/10.1057/9781137522870

Peck, M. S. 1978. *The Road Less Travelled: A New Psychology of Love, Traditional Values and Spiritual Growth*. London: Arrow.

Peele, S., C. Bufe and A. Brodsky. 2000. *Resisting 12-Step Coercion: How to Fight Forced Participation in AA, NA or 12-Step Treatment*. Tucson, AZ: See Sharp Press.

Primiano, L. 1995. 'Vernacular Religion and the Search for Method in Religious Folklife'. *Western Folklore* 54 (1): 37–56. https://doi.org/10.2307/1499910

Primiano, L. N. 2012. 'Manifestations of the Religious Vernacular: Ambiguity, Power, and Creativity'. In *Vernacular Religion in Everyday Life: Expressions of Belief*, edited by M. Bowman and U. Valk, 382–94. London: Routledge.

Roger C. 2017. *A History of Agnostics in AA*. Toronto: AA Agnostica.

Schucman, H. 1975. *A Course in Miracles*. Mill Valley, CA: Foundation for Inner Peace.

Stuever, H. 2008. 'Search to Divine Authorship Leads "Footprints" to Court'. *The Washington Post*, June 1, 2008. Retrieved Jan 1, 2019 from http://www.washingtonpost.com/wp-dyn/content/article/2008/05/31/AR2008053101998.html

Szalavitz, M. 2017. *Unbroken Brain: A Revolutionary New Way of Understanding Addiction*. New York: Picador.

Taves, A. 2016. *Revelatory Events. Three Case Studies of the Emergence of New Spiritual Paths*. Princeton, NJ: Princeton University Press. https://doi.org/10.23943/princeton/9780691131016.001.0001

Tolle, E. [1997] 2001. *The Power of Now: A Guide to Spiritual Enlightenment*. London: Hodder and Stoughton.

Section Three:
The Diversity of Perspectives

Chapter 6

Narratives of Spirituality and Wellbeing: Cultural Differences and Similarities between Brazil and the UK

Bettina E. Schmidt

Introduction

Wellbeing and its siblings, happiness and life satisfaction, are perceived depending on a range of factors, including income, social position, gender, age and cultural context. In Latin America, the term widely used for wellbeing in Spanish speaking countries is *buen vivir*, which is roughly translated as 'living well' (see e.g., Fatheuer 2011), while in Brazil (Portuguese speaking) the most common term is *bem estar* which can be translated literally as 'being well'. Rodríguez explains that 'Living well is a holistic concept rooted on principles and values such as harmony, equilibrium and complementarity, which from an indigenous perspective must guide the relationship of human beings with each other and with nature (or Mother Earth) and the cosmos' (Rodríguez 2016, 279, endnote 1).

Inspired by this understanding of wellbeing as 'living well', Sarah C. White proposes 'relational wellbeing' as a more appropriate term and argues that a relational view of wellbeing challenges the dominant conceptions of wellbeing by underlying the positioning of wellbeing (2016b, 29). Referring to Atkinson et al. (2012) she writes that 'the starting point of relational wellbeing is that notions of wellbeing are seen as socially and culturally constructed, rooted in a particular time and place' (White 2016b, 29). Instead of approaching wellbeing in universal terms, it is important to investigate how wellbeing is understood by the people who are subjects of the research. Hence, wellbeing belongs to and emerges through relationships with others (White 2016b, 29, referring to Christopher 1999).

While relational and connectivity models of wellbeing find increasing attention in psychological studies about wellbeing (Delle Fave et al. 2016, 19, referring to Wissing 2014), one needs to be aware of the danger of a nostalgic projection of 'the good life' in traditional societies and avoid the Orientalist trap of a West–East (i.e., West–South) opposition which influences some studies. The paradox of happy but poor peasants in South America and miserable millionaires in the Northern hemisphere, which is based on a comparison of their subjective perception of a satisfied and happy life (e.g., Graham 2009), is misleading as anthropological studies have shown. The study by Maria Susana Cipolletti and Hanna Heinrich (2015) shows that the traditional feeling of contentment among the eighteenth century indigenous people has been replaced by a feeling of dissatisfaction with their place in the contemporary globalized economic system. They argue that the traditional concept of a good life in South America which has showed similarities with central teachings of the Ancient Greek philosopher Epicurus who put the values of self-sufficiency, ascesis, refusal of the longing for material possession and a secluded life into the centre of his philosophy, has been replaced by a more materialistic perception. Despite attempts to return to the ancient perception of 'living well' and to reunite happiness with self-sufficiency, the perception of 'being poor' outshines the traditional understanding of 'living well'.

Nonetheless, the indigenous perception of living well together has achieved some political impact in South America, in particular in 'rights-based struggles against the dominance of the political elites, the United States and neo-liberal capitalism' (White 2016b, 15). In some countries (e.g., Ecuador and Bolivia) the indigenous concept of living well is now officially recognized and even incorporated in the national constitution (Rodríguez 2016, 260). The implementation of this political aim is however still far away as the translation of it into practice is very complex, partly due to the uncertainty of what wellbeing, or living well together, actually means. Following White, who argues in favour of a reflective approach that acknowledges the diversity of social and cultural constructions of wellbeing (White 2016b, 1–2), this chapter looks at narratives of wellbeing that derived from a study of the place of spirituality in therapy in Brazil and the UK. Brazil is usually portrayed with the greater acceptance of alternative spirituality and healing that should support a more holistic understanding of wellbeing. However, the study has shown little evidence for the acceptance of spirituality within the medical context in Brazil. Comparing subjective definitions of wellbeing from Brazilian and British spiritualists and other people involved in mediumistic religions, this chapter highlights the cultural framework of these narratives and discusses similarities and differences, following White's call for 'greater intercultural dialogue about what matters for people to live well together' (White 2016a, xi). In addition, it reflects why the apparently unbreachable wall between the medical sector and faith, whether it is spirituality or religion, makes it so difficult to challenge the dominance of the Western understanding of wellbeing.

Wellbeing, Religion and Medicine

Recent studies of wellbeing challenge the common approach to the study of wellbeing which seems to assume that we in the West are the measure of all things. Referring to the Dalai Lama, Michael H. Cohen gives a good example that demonstrates the ethnocentricity of the Western approach to science. In his keynote lecture at the opening of the First International Congress of Tibetan Medicine held in the US the Dalai Lama challenged the designation 'First' as it ignored the various international congresses of Tibetan Medicine held in Asia. Cohen states that ethnocentrism is embodied in modern scientific efforts within the Western hemisphere to understand indigenous and other medical traditions (Cohen 2007, 1). Researchers adhere too rigidly to the Western scientific model and tend to imagine that the medical system 'authoritatively can filter, understand, and synthesise other medical traditions' (Cohen 2007, 2). Cohen highlights that the Dalai Lama was not criticizing the power of medicine and science 'but rather the exclusive claim these disciplines hold on our epistemological framework - on what we hold to be true, real and valid' (Cohen 2007, 2). In the Western way of thinking, everything that does not fit into the Western scientific framework is excluded. In the tradition of William James who challenged 'medical materialism' in his renowned *Varieties of Religious Experience* (1902), Cohen argues in favour of a bridge between seemingly opposite parts of the world of healing, some to be objective and others subjective. However, as this chapter shows, there is still a long journey ahead of us. Studies about wellbeing rarely mention religion or spirituality. The common understanding is that healing is achieved by a scientific medical practice.

Among the few studies about the relationship between health (or healing) and spirituality (e.g., Suave 1997) studies of specific spiritual practices such as meditation, praying and yoga (e.g., Carneiro et al. 2017) dominate. Vernacular practices are usually overlooked. Another problem is, as Eyber writes, that the spiritual dimension of illness is usually tucked under the umbrella of cultural and traditional practices that neglects the importance of religion as a resource of wellbeing (Eyber 2016, 199). Hence, while scholars mention in studies of wellbeing its multifaceted features and acknowledge that concepts of wellbeing vary according to the cultural and social setting, religion and spirituality do not feature in a prominent place. There are exceptions, of course. Eyber points, for instance, at the work of Wessells and Monteiro (2000) and Honwana (1997) that include the spiritual dimension in relation to war. But even in these studies religion is just seen as a sub-category of other cultural practices. While this approach reflects the common anthropological definition of religion as a cultural system (Geertz 1966), 'ignoring religion and spirituality undermines', as Eyber argues, 'the commitment to take local understanding of wellbeing as an essential starting point for understanding the suffering of displaced populations' (Eyber 2016, 199).

The problem is the underlying secular framework of the wider medical sector[1] which features two assumptions: that religion is backward and should be (or will be) replaced by more reasonable worldviews and that religion is a private matter. Researchers as well as practitioners are consequently reluctant to even mention religion or spirituality. Eyber states that 'the medical and clinical training that many practitioners undergo assumes a rationalistic, evidence-based approach to mental health and psychosocial wellbeing which excludes perspectives on spirituality and religion' (Eyber 2016, 201). Many practitioners not only see it as inappropriate even to mention religion, it is even regarded as unethical as it may be seen as a way to promote one's own interest (Dein at al. 2010, 63). However, as Eyber (2016), Woods (2008) and others have demonstrated, ignoring religion and spirituality excludes 'a significant element in how people construct their own wellbeing'. And Eyber continues her profound challenge of a systematic form of bias in the discussion of wellbeing by stating that 'Religion and Spirituality is evident in every aspect of daily life in many countries and constitutes as much part of everyday discussions as does talk about poverty, conflict, family problems, health and illness and other daily topics of conversation. If we are to take an emic perspective on how people conceptualise wellbeing we cannot afford to "pick and choose" aspects of local understandings that we approve of, feel confident to handle, or can understand' (Eyber 2016, 202). At the same time it is also important to avoid a purely functionalist or instrumentalist approach to religion. Religion cannot be studied only as a possible resource for healing or life satisfaction. To just study 'what can religion do for people's wellbeing' limits the understanding of both religion and wellbeing as it would judge, as Eyber highlights, religious participation 'purely on what it contributes on material and social levels (Ager and Ager 2011). As an alternative worldview it is relegated to a marginalised position in relation to the dominant secular one' (Eyber 2016, 212). Eyber is pessimistic in her prognosis and sees the marginalization as ongoing despite an increasing recognition of the role of religion. While it is probably the case in her field, development studies, there are some new researches ongoing that will hopefully have a long-term impact on the conceptualization of wellbeing that derives from local multiple understandings of wellbeing instead of a Western-dominated universalist view.

Research Setting

At this point I move to my research about spirituality and wellbeing in Brazil and the UK. I conducted two online surveys in order to find out how people speak about these issues. Despite the use of an online survey the data is not by any means quantitative. The technology was only used to help with the data collection across the Atlantic. The survey was originally based on a questionnaire Jeff Leonardi used for his in-depth interviews of Person-centred counsellors and trainees in the UK. In collaboration with Leonardi I converted his questionnaire into an online survey that was no longer aimed only at Person-centred counsellors but targeted a wider group of medical professionals. After I sent it to a few individuals to test the method, I translated the survey into Portuguese and after discussing the translation with colleagues it was then circulated to various mailing lists of professional practitioners in Brazil with the help of Everton Maraldi, psychologist at the University of São Paulo.

Most of the questions allowed for long answers that led some respondents to add informative narratives about their understanding of wellbeing and the place of religion in medical or therapeutic workplaces. The high response rate for the Brazilian survey and the interesting replies inspired me to develop a second survey that was aimed at religious and spiritual practitioners. Once again, I developed it first in English and, after a test run in the UK, translated it and circulated it via social media and other personal networks to people in Brazil. Similar to the first survey it gave space for longer replies and focused on their understanding of wellbeing and their experience when discussing their faith in a medical or therapeutic context.

Despite the encouraging number of replies (over 100 people responded to the second survey in each country, the UK and Brazil) the collected data is not quantitative nor includes any measurable data on wellbeing and spirituality (Likert-type scales were only used to collect general background data). Instead they enabled me to gain a better insight into the local understandings of wellbeing and of the relevance attributed to religion and spirituality within a specific cultural context. For the purpose of this chapter I selected replies specifically to illustrate the complexity of the discourse on wellbeing and its link to spirituality and religion. Though my research focus is on Brazil I include in this chapter data from the British replies in order to illustrate similarities and differences between the two groups in order to highlight the locality of the conceptualization of wellbeing.

Previous research experiences in Brazil (e.g., Schmidt 2016) influenced my assumption that there would be a difference between the discourse about the significance of religion and spirituality for the conceptualization of wellbeing in Brazil and the UK due to the cultural differences between the two countries. Brazil is usually portrayed as having greater acceptance of alternative spirituality and healing than the UK which should support (theoretically) a more holistic understanding of wellbeing. While the 'religious marketplace' in relation to healing is widespread and has been described also for the UK (e.g., Bowman 1999), Brazil has some of the best studied examples, from 'Spiritist surgeries' (e.g., Greenfield 2008) and 'Spiritist hospitals' (e.g., Araújo Aureliano 2011) to 'faith healing' (e.g., King 2014) and 'Orixás hospitals' where healing is linked to African deities (e.g., Gomberg 2011). I assumed therefore that the local perceptions would be affected by the relative openness towards spiritual healing in Brazil and the huge popularity of spiritual healers. However, the replies painted a different picture.

In particular the replies to questions about whether they had any experience (positive or negative) of discussing spiritual experiences and religious practices with medical practitioners were similar in the UK and Brazil. While I assumed a difference due to the cultural context, I had overlooked that the medical sector in Brazil is based on the same bio-medical understanding of health as in the UK. Every medical practitioner is trained as a student in the same bio-medical and secular framework for the treatment of patients, whether in the UK or Brazil. The result is that even in Brazil religious devotees shy away discussing their experiences with medical practitioners and that medical practitioners who declare themselves to be religious or spiritual distinguish sharply between their faith and their medical work. This bio-medical approach to treatment was even visible when I discussed my research with a group of students in psychology at the Catholic University of Brasilia in 2016. They openly challenged a lack of training about spirituality during their degree and how it might impact on their future therapeutic practice. Despite the fact that Brazil is home to a range of spiritual traditions with specific offers of healing (Rabelo 1993), these forms of spiritual healing are linked to subjective notions of healing that as already discussed are usually ignored within a bio-medical context as they cannot be measured in a conventional manner (see O'Connell and Skevington 2007). It should have not surprised me therefore that the overall approach to wellbeing and spirituality showed many similarities despite some local-culture-specific features such as the reference to specific religious traditions and spiritual entities.

An interesting difference in the replies was a higher number of references to God in the Brazilian replies than in the British replies. Once again my expectations were different. I had assumed that a survey about spirituality and wellbeing would attract more interest in the UK among people who are highly involved in a religious community, so-called 'church goers'. And I also expected that in Brazil where spiritual healing is a vast sector among vernacular religious traditions more people at the fringe of mainstream religions would be interested in my survey. However, the replies I got were much more diverse and to a certain degree unexpected. A result was a greater openness to speak about the impact of the divine on wellbeing in Brazil than in the UK.

Another difference was a more frequent mentioning of the importance of community and relationship among the Brazilian replies though relationship was also mentioned in some British replies. This outcome is to a certain degree corroborated by Antonella Delle Fave's study about the lay definitions of happiness across nations (Della Fave et al. 2016). While the UK was not included in this project, interpersonal relation scored relatively high in Brazil. However, the answers to my survey show that in addition to interpersonal relation the relation to the spiritual entities was also seen as important, something that the study by Della Fave et al. did not capture despite also listing spirituality and religion as a factor for the definition of happiness. While several British respondents mentioned that they dropped out of Church and became more spiritual than religious, the commitment to a community seems very important for Brazilian respondents, whether it is a church, a Spiritist group or a *terreiro*[2] of an Afro-Brazilian religion. This difference supports the information from the literature (see above) that highlights the importance of relations as expressed in the phrase 'living well together' as a definition of wellbeing.

The replies are, of course, not representative for Brazilian or British society. I did not take the social or ethnic stratification of the societies into consideration when setting up the surveys, and the survey specifically targeted people who identified themselves as religious or spiritual, hence the growing number of 'nones' were not included in the second survey but were to a certain degree in the first one. Among the respondents in Brazil were a high number of people categorizing themselves as spiritualist, Spiritist or member of one of the many Afro-Brazilian religious traditions, though some also described themselves as Christian. While in the national census only three per cent of Brazilians identified themselves as belonging to Spiritism, Umbanda or one of the other Afro-Brazilian traditions, they were overwhelmingly represented in the survey: only 12 identified themselves as Catholic (Catholicism is still the predominant religion in Brazil), 10 as Evangelical or Pentecostal (the second largest religion in Brazil), and 53 as belonging to a Afro-Brazilian tradition and 16 as Kardecists or Spiritists. One also needs to consider that many Kardecists do not perceive Kardecism as a religion or belief but as a science or communication technique which is not based on belief (Schmidt [forthcoming 2019]). Hence, while the majority would tick the box 'spiritual' when describing themselves, they would link their form of spirituality not (only) to Kardec's teachings but to their wider interest in alternative spiritualities. Among the 39 respondents who ticked the box for 'other' were several people who identified themselves with Harekrisha or even Umbanda, one of the many Afro-Brazilian traditions, indicating therefore that they did not agree with the general label Afro-Brazil.

Among the British replies the vast majority identified themselves as spiritual instead of religious (249 out of 297). Only a few replied that they belong to a specific Christian denomination in the UK while several mentioned instead 'lapsed CoE'. When asked for specific identification, 72 of the British respondents wrote Spiritualist and 24 Pagan, Druids or Wicca. Several indicated a syncretic belief and did not want to be identified with just one, while others indicated a former Christian background. Only 55 mentioned one of the many Christian denominations though often with an explanation that they no longer practise it. Among the rest were a few Jewish respondents, some Buddhists, Hindus and Quakers.

Overall, in both surveys, the mix of traditions does not correspond to the figures about religious belonging from the national census data; quite the opposite is the case. In particular the British survey where the majority (157 out of 297) stated that they practise their religion or spiritual practice daily, does not correspond to the decline of religion in the UK that is documented not only in the census figures but also by several sociological studies (e.g., Bruce 2002, Day 2011). And even in Brazil researchers have noticed an increase in secularization, while the survey data indicates that the vast majority of respondents (112) practise their faith daily (69) or weekly (33). While national census figures have to be taken with caution when it comes to religious commitment and belonging (see Schmidt 2014), this discrepancy highlights that the survey data is not representative for the societies but gives insight into the understanding of the relationship between wellbeing and spirituality on an individual level.

What Matters to People

Moving on to the narratives, I begin with replies to the question 'How would you describe wellbeing?'. A common aspect of these replies was that wellbeing was perceived as multifaceted. Physical health was not sufficient to describe wellbeing. In addition, people referred to balance, mental features, the divine, living in harmony, peace and more. A common feature in the British as well as Brazilian replies was the mention of harmony and peace when defining wellbeing. Once again, this outcome reflects Della Fave's study as the group also expressed their surprise at how frequently harmony was mentioned in definitions of happiness and suggests a broadening of wellbeing studies 'by including the still overlooked psychological construct of inner harmony' (Della Fave et al. 2016, 20). However, as already indicated, more often than in the UK, Brazilian respondents referred to the presence of the divine (or God) as an important element of wellbeing. One defined wellbeing for instance as 'Communion with God, with others and with oneself' which points towards a relational perception of wellbeing that includes the divine. Overall the replies ranged from 'Feeling satisfied with your life and content' to 'being happy' and 'good health' and 'Balance in body, mind and spirit'. A female respondent highlighted for instance that 'Wellbeing is something that gets us in peace with ourselves ... with nature ... with others and with God, at last is happiness and joy different from the one we usually feel because it lasts' (#7, Brazil, 50 years old, female).

Apart from the link to physical health and the divine, several people referred to happiness and to the importance of being a member of a community and to being part of something greater than oneself. One male respondent, for instance, wrote that 'Wellbeing is the feeling of belonging to the whole and that everything is connected. When we understand and practice it, we feel that we are part of something bigger. By knowing this, daily problems become small' (#75, Brazil, 54 years old, male). This relational aspect that links wellbeing with being part of something greater was mentioned by others too. A woman wrote that 'Wellbeing is to feel well with oneself and at the same time to know that one is not alone. It is to feel supported although we don't see those who take care of us' (# 31, Brazil, 45 years old, female). And a male respondent wrote that wellbeing 'is to feel happy and satisfied with what one has. The harmony with people and the peace should walk hand in hand' (# 29, Brazil, 20 years old, male). Comparing these answers with White's definition of wellbeing as 'living well together' presented above, it is evident that for many respondents 'living well together' is not restricted to interpersonal relations, hence human beings, but includes spiritual entities.

Among the British respondents were several that highlighted balance. For instance, wellbeing was defined as 'A state of general balance and harmony in body, mind, and spirit—where one maintains the best level of health that they can given any limitation of their physical bodies. An approach to life and living that takes the Whole into consideration, and seeks to cure from the root, rather than simply identify and treat symptoms of imbalance' (#53, UK). Another respondent made an interesting comment about wellbeing of a dying person and wrote that wellbeing is 'more about state of mind than physiology. A mortally or terminally ill person can achieve wellbeing. Acceptance of the things you can't change. Love of self. Respect for ones surroundings. These are telltale signs of wellbeing. Being happy with where you are in life while not stagnating'. Wellbeing is therefore more than physical health—even when physically ill one can experience a sense of wellbeing.

A follow-up question asked about the importance of spirituality or religion for the wellbeing of a person. Once again, I noticed similar features in the replies that gave insights into the way spirituality can help to improve wellbeing. The responses often began by yes, followed by a short explanation. For instance, 'yes, spirituality helps create a focus beyond oneself, provides mental and emotional wellbeing and stability'. The replies highlighted a sense of purpose, knowing that one is not alone, that life is eternal. Some also mentioned impact on the physical body and some mentioned some practices, hence highlighting that coming together as a group has an impact on wellbeing. One of the British replies stated that 'Spirituality is essential for the wellbeing of a person, as it reinforces the recognition that love, the most powerful force there is, keeps us alive, heals us, and enables us to complete our life-plans here whilst we are in our physical bodies' (#16, UK survey). In Brazil people responded similarly though once again a higher number of people in Brazil referred to aspects of the divine (or God). One woman, for instance, wrote: 'Yes. Because through the connection with the divinity and with the other side of life it is possible to better understand the natural difficulties of human life and to search a wider sense for existence' (#55, Brazil survey, 41 years old, female).

Another interesting outcome is that the respondents often explained the importance of spirituality for wellbeing with reference to other people, the community or society, while some also referred to the importance of one's own development. For instance, one man wrote 'Yes, spirituality is the connection with oneself, fundamental to self-knowledge and consequently to achieve happiness and wellbeing' (#3, Brazil, 49 years old, male). And one woman stated that 'Yes, living spiritually invites us to better our relationship with the world and people. Always considering that we have a reason to be encarnated. The reason is to improve ourselves and others, which is the main one' (#4, Brazil, 51 years old, female). This aspect of self-improvement is interesting as it is a strong feature within Spiritist teachings. However, it was not only Spiritists that mentioned it, but also people describing themselves more broadly as spiritualist.

Bearing in mind the importance spirituality has for the wellbeing of the respondents, the replies to the question about whether they would speak about their faith to their doctor reflect the strong separation of the medical sector and the private life. In Brazil only 11 out of 96 said yes, while in the UK only 27 out of 294 replied affirmatively. Hence, the vast majority of the respondents would not discuss their faith with anyone working in the medical sector (the question did not distinguish between nurses, medical doctors or other therapists). One reason is the perception that religion is private. Indeed, several explained that they would not discuss their faith with doctors as religion (or spirituality) is private. However, some also mentioned negative responses or that the doctor would not be interested. Once again I noticed strong similarities between the UK and Brazil. Hence, although many Brazilian medical doctors and nurses are involved in Kardecism, are even members of the Association of Medical-Spiritism and volunteer in one of the many Spiritist hospitals around the country (see Hess 1991), there is widespread reluctance to discuss religion with a doctor or nurse.

In a follow-up question I asked whether they had mentioned their religious or spiritual practices to a nurse or a doctor in the past. The majority wrote no and explained it with the general perception of their faith. For instance, one wrote 'No. I would be too embarrassed, that they would think I'm a nutter' (#43, UK). Another wrote 'No, I feel they would discriminate against me' (#50, UK), and someone else wrote 'No. Afraid he could think I am little crazy' (#12, UK). When they had spoken about it the majority had had a negative experience. For instance, #37 (UK) wrote 'My husband did and was treated as though he was having hallucinations or having a mental breakdown!' and #94 (UK) wrote 'Yes. I got rather harsh and sceptical comments thrown at me, so have learnt to be careful as to what I say to anyone else about my experiences'. However, a few also mentioned a positive experience, in particular in relation to death and dying (e.g., in a hospice). I got similar responses in Brazil where also the majority would not discuss faith within the medical sector. Only 20 out of 111 wrote that they had mentioned their belief to their doctors. When asked for past experiences some mentioned that they discussed their belief with a psychologist during a phase of depression, or with a neurologist or a doctor open to alternative therapies. In these cases the experience was usually perceived positively. In a very few cases the respondents even commented that the doctor was also a Spiritist like they were which would not happen in the UK. Nonetheless, the vast majority of Brazilian respondents did not mention any experience as they would not discuss it with any medical practitioner, despite the importance of it for their perception of wellbeing.

The Medical Sector

In order to understand the reluctance to discuss religious beliefs within the medical sector I will look at the replies from the other survey that was sent to medical practitioners. Initially the target group was therapists, psychologists and counsellors[3] though the Brazilian survey went to a wider group of medical practitioners. Their replies reflected on one side the separation between spiritual or religious belonging and the medical treatment which the religious practitioners described. But it also indicated that medical practitioners are often more open towards different religious beliefs than their patients might expect.

After some basic background questions, one of the first questions was whether religion or spirituality plays a part in their work. The majority of replies denied it, even when initially the respondent had identified themselves as being religious or spiritual. One respondent, a psychologist with 20 years of work experience, wrote categorically that spirituality (and religion) does not have a place in the workplace. Another one gave a longer explanation:

> In my personal upbringing, yes and in professional practice, no. Spirituality is in me, integrated in everything. When I listen to a person with focus, attention, care, trained, thoughtful, with ethical values, without judgments and criticism, accepting the reality of the other in their context, in a way, this is also spirituality in practice. However, I do not express the spiritual discourse and practice to the outside because my professional academic training and practice require other demands, knowledge, explanations, ethics and code of professional conduct etc., although they are integrated in me, in my spirituality. I never speak to a patient or client about spirituality ... about God ..., or rather, I do not approach spiritual matters because this is spiritual rather than therapeutic care. Each practice has space, time and place, and should not to be confused. Both knowledge is fused and not confused. It is also necessary to know and to respect the different. Here in Brazil we are more eclectic, ecumenical. (#52, Brazil)

Another respondent who just began working in the medical sector a year ago and was much younger than the earlier respondent also dismissed the presence of spirituality in the workplace and stated quite technically, 'The analyst's spirituality should not interfere with the session. The significance of what the analyzing process exposes has to be worked out' (#56, Brazil). In a follow-up question one clarified that one has to separate anything religious from the therapeutic context: 'No, not in the area of health. Many behaviours, in any area, may have a spiritual origin and commitment, but it is not possible for a psychologist to address this or treat [a patient] with a focus on spirituality, otherwise one risks losing

6 Narratives of Spirituality and Wellbeing

being a psychologist and become a spiritual advisor or counsellor. Each one needs to work in their area and not intertwine' (#52, Brazil). Hence, the overall understanding is that faith is something private and does not belong in the medical sector, which is seen as secular.

Nevertheless, some respondents mention that some of their patients spoke about their religious or spiritual experience. One therapist, for instance, wrote:

> There was a patient who saw smoke, figures and heard voices, and mentioned them from the start, already in the first sessions. However, during the psychotherapy, the patient spoke about the maternal grandmother and that she was a Gypsy, and a member of an Afro-Brazilian religion. But the patient denied these roots and did not admit having the gift [of mediumship]. It made me reflect on my own resistance to such religions that enchant me, but also frighten me. (#20, Brazil)

Hence, while treating a patient the therapist realized their own feelings towards religion, in particular vernacular religious traditions which are still perceived as peripheral.

The attitude towards the faith of their patients became even more open in the replies to a follow-up question about whether a patient has mentioned religion or spirituality and how they reacted. Here the overwhelming response was—even among respondents who deny the importance of discussing religion within a medical setting—that they would react with respect or neutrality for the belief of their patients. Several respondents reflected on the importance of knowing more about their patients as their religious behaviour would have implications for the treatment. For instance, one wrote when asked about experiences with patients speaking about their faith (question 10), 'yes, I try to understand the role of religious practices and beliefs and what this has to do with their process of self-awareness' (#84, Brazil). Another respondent explained it in more detail:

> Yes, very often. I allow the patient to tell me details of their [religious] practice, since it often helps me to understand how the psyche of the individual works. Many seek religion as a way of transferring responsibility for treatment to others, while others seek it to cope with (or, being more technical, sublimation) the disease. At the beginning, it is generally necessary to reduce the power of religious thought for the individual appropriate the treatment, whereas later religion must be reinforced as a form of therapeutic assistance. In this way, I believe it is possible to improve the outcome of the treatment. (#92, Brazil)

Hence, while their own belief is kept outside the treatment, the beliefs of their patients are valuable elements for their treatment. Sometimes the respondents refer to specific religions, saying that among their patients are Christians, Adventists, Buddhists, Spiritists and so on. Several insist that they would approach the patients' disclosure with respect and would not let their own belief interfere, for instance:

> Yes, it does not surprise me. I seek meaning for it and do not interpret it [=what my patients tell me] from my beliefs and attitudes. Meanings are always rich either through dreams, choices and actions. Religion strengthens me and gives me the foundation [explanation] of some misfortunes in life but at work ... the needs of the patient comes first. (#66, Brazil)

Some others are perhaps less understanding. One respondent wrote that 'Yes, many declare themselves Christians and tell me of the promises made to them in their churches. Promises, according to them, that God would heal them. I try to react naturally, legitimizing the patient's hope, but transferring their thoughts to treatments that we can make on this earth' (#16, Brazil).

Another question asked whether any patient has mentioned religious or spiritual experiences. While only a few mentioned specific experiences of their patients, several mentioned experiences often related to near-death experience. For instance, one listed 'out of body experiences, near-death experiences, premonitions and premonitory dreams, telepathy, meditations, etc.', and then the respondent added a comment that 'I understand that these reports can be relatively common when clients realize that the therapeutic setting is welcoming rather than judgmental' (#40, Brazil). Some replied with a more generic 'Yes, several' but without any details while others referred to general mediumistic experiences or experiences with the Madonna. Someone replied 'Yes. Some [mention] situations like the sensation of floating during sleep, or they even reported what doctors or nurses said while they were in coma or sedated during surgical procedures. But they were always afraid of criticism' (#34, Brazil). One respondent mentioned in more detail a difficult experience with a patient in the emergency room that could be resolved with a jointly spoken prayer:

> [...] a patient in the ICU had extreme difficulty in relating to the team [of doctors and nurses], complaining about everything and not allowing procedures. I went to try out physiotherapy, and when I put my hands under her chest, the patient asked to remove the hands, claiming extreme pain. I argued that I had not started the exercises just by touching it. She said she could not stand the pain because when I touched her, my pain had mingled with hers and she could not bear it. The family was standing on the other side of the bed and I asked if she was Catholic.

6 Narratives of Spirituality and Wellbeing

They said yes and then I suggested that she says 'Our father' to dissolve this pain she mentioned and that I would accompany her in prayer. She agreed. (#14, Brazil)

Some were more critical about the long-term impact of these experiences. One respondent for instance writes:

> Yes. In the clinic of alcohol and other drug abuse these experiences are frequent. There was one patient who considered himself a *pai de santo*[4] and for the first time he felt comfortable reporting his mediumship without being labelled schizophrenic. This patient recovered satisfactorily from a severe depression when rediscovering what he believed to be his spiritual mission. Another patient, on the other hand, described spiritual attacks that seemed to be closely related to his symptoms of schizophrenia. This patient did not achieve significant improvement during the treatment. Often chemically dependent patients embraced the gospel due to family pressure or by desperation, without further questioning, which in the medium term resulted in many relapses. (#61, Brazil)

After these questions about experiences with religion and spirituality within the medical workplace the questions moved on to wellbeing. One question asked whether spirituality or religion is seen to be of importance to wellbeing. While several respondents replied in the negative (e.g., 'Not necessarily. This is a particular point of view. It depends on how one views the role of spirituality in one's life' (#59, Brazil)), the majority confirmed that spirituality is important. One respondent, for instance, replied:

> I consider it important, because, like what I have said before, they are human experiences and as such they must be integrated, welcomed, understood (in any way). Of course, if a person is atheist and has no religion or spiritual experiences, somehow this person will still have significant symbolic experiences and that is what will be worked out in the session, but I realize that they are not spiritual or mystical experiences. What I mean is that the experience of mystical union with nature that a meditator feels will never be felt by an atheist simply because the paradigmatic system that the latter uses to signify reality does not allow this kind of experience. (#40, Brazil)

Another respondent declared even more openly that 'of course, it is part of health. There is no separation. We divided [the experience from ordinary experiences] didactically, creating an illusion of separation, but in fact we need to learn that [the experiences] cannot be separated' (#73, Brazil). Interestingly some also described a kind of relational wellbeing, for instance, 'Yes, I do [consider it significant]. Spirituality is fundamental because it deals with issues of acceptance and confrontation. It improves the inter- and intra-individual relationship' (#34, Brazil). Another one wrote that:

> Yes, I think that spirituality is very much related to the sense that the person has for him/herself (meaning of life). Contemporary society is wrong (deluded) into believing that reason would reveal the key to the secrets of life, and consequently we fell into a void of meaning, which was left by religions, the lack of meaning or plan for the future cause serious illnesses, such as depression. (#72, Brazil)

Comparison Between British and Brazilian Replies
Due to the small number of British replies to this survey it is impossible to draw informative comparison to the Brazilian replies. While the separation between faith and medicine seems more rigidly applied in the UK, it seems to be quite porous in near death situations, when a patient is dying. In particular, in hospice and palliative care facilities or when looking after bereaved patients, medical practitioners in the UK seem to be more open to speaking about faith than in other contexts. Nevertheless, despite the limited number of replies, I will suggest some similarities and differences between the Brazilian and the British situations by putting the replies from medical professionals in context with the replies of religious practitioners from the UK.

The few British replies indicate an awareness of the impact of spirituality on the wellbeing of patients which does not correspond with the awareness of religious practitioners about the attitude of their doctors and therapists. In Brazil the attitude of the medical practitioners was influenced to a certain degree by their own faith which was also hinted at by some religious practitioners who felt more enabled to mention spiritual experiences when they knew that the doctor or therapist shared the same faith such as spiritism. Nevertheless, the vast majority of Brazilian medical practitioners strongly separated between their personal faith and the medical practice, an attitude one would also expect to see in the UK. Despite cultural differences the surveys therefore confirmed a similar secular attitude towards the place of spirituality in the medical context.

On the other hand, however, the surveys also showed cultural differences when discussing the impact of spirituality on wellbeing in the UK and Brazil. Not only was the frequent references to the divine—or God in particular—an interesting feature among the Brazilian replies but also the higher number of medical practitioners acknowledging personal faith. It shows openness towards spirituality even in such a secular sector of society as the medical one despite an ongoing separation between faith that is perceived as private and medicine that is perceived as public and secular. There was also a strong awareness of a relational understanding of wellbeing, whether it was linked to the religious community or the divine. Hence, wellbeing was perceived not in isolation but in relation to either other human or spiritual beings. Interestingly, a feature which was common among British and Brazilian respondents was a reference to harmony, peace or balance when describing wellbeing.

Conclusion

The discussion of cultural differences and similarities in a study of spirituality and wellbeing furthers our understanding of the importance of the local context. However, the comparison of data from Brazil and the UK also showed how widespread secular understanding of the medical sector is. Outsiders often have the impression of Brazil as a society open for alternative healing. However, as Rocha criticizes in her study of a spiritual healer known as John of God (Rocha 2017), this reflects an ethnocentric or even orientalist portrayal of Brazil and its healing scene. Brazil is a secular and highly diverse society, quite like other countries with a range of secular bio-medical therapies on offer as well as various so-called alternative healing practices such as reiki, channelling and more (see Toniol 2018). Hence, the offers of alternative or complementary therapies (CAM) are quite similar in the UK and Brazil, despite the intriguingly wide range of offers of spiritual healing in Brazil. Even Spiritist Hospitals which are widespread in Brazil look from the outside like 'normal' (secular/bio-medical) hospitals but offer treatments by embodied spirits (mediums) as well as other alternative therapies (e.g., meditation). Nevertheless, Brazilians perceive their society as secular, in particular the medical sector, and when visiting a 'normal' bio-medical centre they, like their British counterparts, shy away from speaking about their faith.

This reluctance was also a common feature in the interviews I began to conduct in the summer of 2018 in São Paulo. I asked, for instance, someone who had practised Candomblé for decades what he would do in the case of an illness, and he replied that he would seek the advice of his *pai de santo* first. But when speaking to his doctor he would not mention his faith. When I asked him whether he would ask his *pai de santo* to come to the hospital if he had to have surgery, he replied yes but he would introduce him as a friend and not as his priest. While some hospitals that are linked to the Roman Catholic Church appear more open towards religion, the openness is usually restricted to Christianity and Judaism and does not include the Brazilian religions such as Candomblé and would happen only in some hospitals with a religious foundation (interview July 2018).

And another person who described himself as Kardecist and spiritual, explained how before heart surgery he not only searched for a surgeon who was also a Spiritist (he found one in the list provided by his health insurance) but he also asked the spirits for approval of his surgery before going to the hospital (interview August 2018).

Looking back at my former study on spirit possession and trance the outcome of this survey surprised me to a certain degree. While I struggled in earlier studies (e.g., Schmidt 1995, 2008) to find someone to speak openly about their religious practices involving mediumship (e.g., Spiritists in Puerto Rico and *Vodouissants*[5] in New York City), I had fewer problems in Brazil. Why are Brazilians therefore not more open to speaking about faith when speaking to a medical doctor while they perceive spirituality as an important part of wellbeing? Why do they insist that religion has nothing to do with medicine, despite the engagement of numerous therapists, nurses and medical doctors in Spiritism or other beliefs? Anthropologists always highlight the importance of studying the cultural framework for our understanding of Other cultures. To a certain degree the surveys seem to indicate that we have more in common than we assume, which might be the result of the globalization of higher education and in particular medical science which has led to the spread of the Western ideas of secularization. However, the narratives tell another story. While a common thread was reference to 'religion has no place in therapy' it became evident that spirituality places high significance on the understanding of personal wellbeing. Hence, when we look at the narratives—from each sector—it is possible to extrapolate what matters to people—and their faith, as well as a wider understanding of relationship, are core concepts that pop up again and again.

The particular understanding of spirituality depends on the cultural framework. Brazilians refer more often to the divine, whether it is God or *axé*, the spiritual force that is at the heart of Afro-Brazilian religions, and also put more emphasis on community, hence relationships whether to human beings or spiritual entities are perceived as crucial for wellbeing. British respondents refer more often to a general understanding of spirituality against religion and do not put so much emphasis on community and relations which is in line with the wider picture about the place of religions in the UK. But even they acknowledge in their narratives the importance of spirituality for wellbeing. Hence, while the exact understanding of spirituality and wellbeing depends on the cultural setting, the narratives indicate an overarching agreement in the significance of a wider—and culturally subjective—understanding of wellbeing which is perceived as interconnected with other human beings (such as family or communities) and spiritual entities.

Biographical Note

Bettina E. Schmidt is professor of study of religions at the University of Wales Trinity Saint David and Director of the Alister Hardy Religious Experience Research Centre in Lampeter, UK. Her research area is anthropology of religion with special focus on Latin American, the Caribbean and its diaspora. Among her more recent publications is *Spirits and Trance in Brazil: An Anthropology of Religious Experience*.

Notes

1. The term 'wider medical sector' includes medical practitioners in a wider sense, hence including therapists and psychologists, but also humanitarian aid and development agencies.
2. *Terreiro* is the commonly used term for the ceremonial place of an Afro-Brazilian religious community.
3. As outlined, the survey was developed based on the questionnaire used by Jeff Leonardi for his research on Person-centred counselling.
4. A commonly used term for a priest in an Afro-Brazilian religion such as Umbanda and Candomblé.
5. The term for practitioners of the Haitian religion Vodou.

Bibliography

Araújo Aureliano, Waleska de. 2011. *Espiritualidade,Saúde e as Artes de Cura no Contemporâneo: Indefinição de margens e busca de fronteiras em um centro terapêutico espírita no sul do Brasil*. PhD thesis in anthropology, Federal University of Santa Catarina, Brazil.

Bowman, Marion. 1999. 'Healing in the Spiritual Marketplace: Consumers, Courses and Credentialism'. *Social Compass* 46 (2): 181-189. https://doi.org/10.1177/003776899046002007

Bruce, Steve. 2002. *God is Dead: Secularisation in the West*. Oxford, UK: Blackwell.

Carneiro, Élida Mar, Luana Pereira Barbosa, Jorge Marcelo Marson, Júverson Alves Terra, Claudio Jacinto Pereira Martins, Danielle Modesto, L. Rodrigues De Resende and Maria de Fátima Borges. 2017. 'Effectiveness of Spiritist "passe" (Spiritual Healing) for Anxiety Levels, Depression, Pain, Muscle Tension, Well-Being, and Physiological Parameters in Cardiovascular Inpatients: A Randomized Controlled Trial'. *Complementary Therapies in Medicine* 30: 73-78. https://doi.org/10.1016/j.ctim.2016.11.008

Christopher, J. 1999. 'Situation Psychological Well-Being: Exploring the Cultural Roots of Its Theory and Research'. *Journal of Counselling and Development* 77: 141-154. https://doi.org/10.1002/j.1556-6676.1999.tb02434.x

Cipolletti, María Susana and Hanna Heinrich. 2015. 'El "buen vivir": Una perspectiva diacronica de la nocion de bienestar de los Tucano occidentales del noroeste amazonico a la luz de la doctrina de Epicuro'. *Anthropos* 110 (1): 1-11.

Cohen, M. H. 2007. *Healing of the Borderland of Medicine and Religion*. Chapel Hill: The University of North Carolina Press.

Day, Abby. 2011. *Believing in Belonging: Belief and Social Identity in the Modern World*. Oxford, UK: Oxford University Press. https://doi.org/10.1093/acprof:oso/9780199577873.001.0001

Dein, S., C. C. H. Cook, A. Powell and S. Eagger. 2010. 'Religion, Spirituality and Mental Health'. *The Psychiatrist* 34 (2): 63–64. https://doi.org/10.1192/pb.bp.109.025924

Della Fave, Antonella, Ingrid Brdar, Marié P. Wissing, Ulisses Araujo, Alejandro Castro Solano, Teresa Freire, María Del Rocío. 2016. Lay Definitions of Happiness Across Nations: The Primacy of Inner Harmony and Relational Connectedness. *Frontiers in Psychology* 7 (30): 1–23. https://doi.org/10.3389/fpsyg.2016.00030

Eyber, C. 2016. 'Tensions in Conceptualising Psychosocial Wellbeing in Angola: The Marginalisation of Religion and Spirituality'. In: *Cultures of Wellbeing: Method, Place, Policy*, edited by S. C. White with C. Blackmore, 111–121. Basingstoke, UK: Palgrave Macmillan. https://doi.org/10.1057/9781137536457_8

Fatheuer, Thomas. 2011. *Buen Vivir. Eine kurze Einführung in Lateinamerikas neue Konzepte zum guten Leben und zu den Rechten der Natur*, Schriften zur Ökologie 17. Berlin, Germany: Heinrich-Böll-Stiftung.

Geertz, C. 1966. ,'Religion as a Cultural System'. In: *Anthropological Approaches to the Study of Religions*, edited by M. Banton, 1–46. Edinburgh, UK: Tavistock Publications.

Gomberg, Estélio. 2011. *Hospital de Orixás: Encontros terapêuticos em um terreiro de Candomblé*. Salvador, Brazil: Edufba.

Graham, Carol. 2009. *Happiness Around the World. The Paradox of Happy Peasants and Miserable Millionaires*. Oxford, UK: Oxford University Press. https://doi.org/10.1093/acprof:osobl/9780199549054.001.0001

Greenfield, S. M. 2008. *Spirits with Scalpels: The Culturalbiology of Religious Healing in Brazil*. Walnut Creek, CA: Left Coast Press.

Hess, David J. 1991. *Spirits and Scientists: Ideology, Spiritism, and Brazilian Culture*. University Park: Pennsylvania State University Press.

Honwana, A. 1997. 'Healing for Peace: Traditional Healers and Post-War Reconstruction on Southern Mozambique'. *Peace and Conflict: Journal of Peace Psychology* 3 (3): 293–305. https://doi.org/10.1207/s15327949pac0303_6

James, William. [1902] 2008. The Varieties of Religious Experience: A Study in Human Nature. Rockville, MD: Arc Manor. https://doi.org/10.1017/CBO9781139149822

King, Lindsey. 2014. *Spiritual Currency in Northeast Brazil*. Albuquerque: University of New Mexico Press.

O'Connell, Kathryn A. and Suzanne M. Skevington. 2007. 'To Measure or Not to Measure? Reviewing the Assessment of Spirituality and Religion in Health Related Quality of Life'. *Chronic Illness* 3: 77–87. https://doi.org/10.1177/1742395307079195

Rabelo, M. C. 1993. 'Religião e Cura: Algumas Reflexões Sobre a Experiência Religiosa das Classes Populares Urbanas'. *Cad. Saúde Públ.* 9 (3): 316–325. https://doi.org/10.1590/S0102-311X1993000300019

Rocha, Cristina. 2017. *John of God: The Globalization of Brazilian Faith Healing.* Oxford, UK: Oxford University Press. https://doi.org/10.1093/acprof:oso/9780190466701.001.0001

Rodríguez, I. 2016. 'Historical Reconstruction and Cultural Identity Building as a Local Pathway to "Living Well" Among the Pemon of Venezuela'. In *Cultures of Wellbeing: Method, Place, Policy*, edited by S. C. White with C. Blackmore, 260–280. Basingstoke, UK: Palgrave Macmillan. https://doi.org/10.1057/9781137536457_11

Schmidt, Bettina E. 1995. *Von Geistern, Orichas und den Puertoricanern: zur Verbindung von Religion und Ethnizität.* Marburg, Germany: Curupira.

Schmidt, Bettina E. 2008 *Caribbean Diaspora in the USA: Diversity of Caribbean Religions in New York City.* Aldershot, UK: Ashgate.

Schmidt, Bettina E. 2014. 'The Problem with Numbers in Study of Religions: Introduction'. *DISKUS, The Journal of the British Association for the Study of Religions* 16 (2): 1–4. http://www.religiousstudiesproject.com/DISKUS/index.php/DISKUS/article/view/36/34 https://doi.org/10.18792/diskus.v16i2.36

Schmidt, Bettina E. 2016. *Spirits and Trance in Brazil: Anthropology of Religious Experience.* London: Bloomsbury.

Schmidt, Bettina E. [forthcoming 2019]. '"Incorporation Does Not Exist": The Brazilian Rejection of the Term "Possession" and Why it Exists Nonetheless'. In *Spirit Possession: European Contributions to Comparative Studies*, edited by Éva Pócs and András Zempléni. New York: Central European University Press.

Suave, Juanita. 1997. 'Healing the Spirit from the Effects of Abuse. Spirituality and Feminist Practice with Women Who Have Been Abused'. MA thesis in Social Work. Carleton University, Ottawa, Canada.

Toniel, Rodrigo. 2018. *Do Espírito na Saúde: Oferta e uso de terapias alternativas/complementares nos serviços de saúde pública no Brasil.* São Paulo, Brazil: Editora LiberArs.

Wessells, M. and C. Monteiro. 2000. 'Healing Wounds of War in Angola: A Community-Based Approach'. In: *Addressing Childhood Adversity*, edited by D. Donald, A. Dawes and J. Louw. Cape Town, South Africa: David Philipps.

White, S. C. 2016a. 'Preface'. In *Cultures of Wellbeing: Method, Place, Policy*, edited by S. C. White with C. Blackmore, xi–xiv. Basingstoke, UK: Palgrave Macmillan.

White, S. C. 2016b. 'Introduction: The Many Faces of Wellbeing'. In *Cultures of Wellbeing: Method, Place, Policy*, edited by S. C. White with C. Blackmore, 1–44. Basingstoke, UK: Palgrave Macmillan. https://doi.org/10.1057/9781137536457_1

Wissing, Marie P. 2014. 'Editorial: Meaning and Relational Well-Being in Cross-Cultural Perspective'. *Journal of Psychology in Africa* 24 (III–VI). https://doi.org/10.1080/14330237.2014.904092

Woods, Richard. 2008. *Wellness: Life, Health and Spirituality.* Dublin: Veritas Publications.

Chapter 7

Using Autoethnography to Explore the Experience of Spirituality in Epilepsy

Louise N. Spiers

Autoethnography as a Research Method

Autoethnography has arisen from the so-called 'narrative turn' in the social sciences which involved a shift in the way that human society and experience is considered (Polkinghorne 1988). The narrative turn challenges a view where the researcher stands outside the social reality being examined and looks instead toward socially contextualized narratives of individuals and groups (Goodson and Gill 2011). Autoethnography embodies this relationship between the self and other, emphasizing its socially-conscious status (Adams and Holman Jones 2008) and some see it as a return of the social sciences to their promise to help solve individual and societal problems (Polkinghorne 1988). This qualitative methodology honours the perception and the meaning of experience (Smith, Harré and Van Langenhove 1995) and in doing so, offers insight into a rich and detailed account of phenomenology (lived experience) from an insider perspective (Hayano 1979). Giving voice to under-represented groups (particularly, feminist researchers who have used it as a methodology to explore their experiences, e.g., Ettorre 2005), autoethnography wants readers to care and respond (Campbell 2017).

As both methodology and the resulting product of research, autoethnography avoids 'categorisation or simplification of experience' (Ellis and Bochner 2000, 739) and has been found valuable when considering anomalous experiences (Raab 2013). It is useful in researching non-linear states such as those found in mystical and spiritual experiences (Chapman-Clarke 2016). Previously, autoethnography has been used to explore how it is to have epilepsy (Scarfe and Marlow 2015) and its hidden nature (Marcalo 2012). The result is both personal and intellectual (Brooks 2011) with a fuller empathic understanding of the subject matter (Behar 1996). Autoethnography is particularly well-suited to challenging the traditional healthcare perspectives of stigmatized medical conditions that include controversial and disputed content. Often, such conditions lack a personal voice in the literature, and autoethnography offers this voice (Frank 1995). This can also be the case with spiritual and mystical experiences, making autoethnography a highly appropriate method to use in researching and exploring the relationship between spirituality and health.

Health research into epilepsy, even of a qualitative nature, is often concerned with third-person perspectives of conformity to medication regimes (e.g., Honnekeri et al. 2018) and social aspects of the condition (e.g., Jacoby, Snape and Baker 2005). In the rest of this chapter, I will write from a first person, autoethnographic, perspective. I will illustrate the application of autoethnography to spiritual experiences in epilepsy by sharing material from my own PhD research, demonstrating how autoethnographic narrative can embody experiences of EFEs in a unique manner.

Here, I use spirituality as a broad term that covers both spiritual and religious experiences. Spirituality in epilepsy is often attributed to delusions or hallucinations symptomatic of the condition, often seen as a form of psychosis. The narrative presented here suggests that spirituality in epilepsy may contribute in a fundamental way to understanding the human condition and, specifically, the process by which we derive meaning and purpose from our experience of life. Autoethnography enables the researcher to question and challenge a materialist understanding of these spiritual experiences. Its varied range of data enables it to be highly relevant to those researching the connections between spirituality and health, because it can use personal data that cannot be encompassed by other data collection and analysis methods. Autoethnography enables the researcher to consider spiritual experiences from the perspective of those who have them and enables us to understand the role of wellbeing arising from what may be otherwise considered an illness.

In producing an autoethnographic account I used Chang's (2016) criteria for ensuring effective autoethnography in healthcare, which centre around data trustworthiness, the process, ethics and the integration of cultural commentary. Below, I have demonstrated how they can be met.

I began by identifying suitable autobiographical material providing authentic and trustworthy data. Once collated, a time period was agreed that would be sufficient to provide a 'thick' description of the nature of my experience. A chronological sequence was devised to create an engagingly evocative narrative for the reader (Ellis 2004). The data were analysed using a process of refinement and collaborative discussion between myself and my PhD supervisors, who contributed to the composition, impact and socio-cultural aspects of the narrative, and the resulting discussion.

For the artist David Hockney (cited in Stephens and Wilson 2017), paintings are not concerned with a literal, photographic view but, rather, a composite from memory and emotion. Similarly, in autoethnography the truthfulness and evocation of essence is vital in a narrative (Medford 2006). I have approached the presentation of my data by drawing memories from real events, with trustworthy accounts, even if the retelling may not be literal (Short 2013). As a reflexive account, the exposure of my emotional responses and personal meaning is embodied, but this also makes me personally vulnerable (Behar 1996).

Ethical approval was granted for this study by my university and sensitivity maintained for everyone implicated in the research, following best practice (Tolich 2010). As it is, by its very nature, an act of self-disclosure, the autoethnographic material presented has been carefully evaluated with regards to risk to the researcher, whilst simultaneously acknowledging that sharing reflexive writing is an uncomfortable but necessary feature of the approach (Tenni, Smyth and Boucher 2003). As a psychotherapist, I have used reflexive writing as a feature of my professional work for many years. It enables me to work honestly and openly—to both understand and effect change in my responses to feelings and events. I draw on reflexive writing here to embody my experience and connect the deep, and not necessarily comfortable relationship between my personal experience and culture (Reed-Danahay 1997). Where appropriate, pseudonyms are used, although I have chosen not to use one. Photographs have been cropped to remove the faces of individuals I am no longer in contact with and all identifying features of consultants and hospital appointments have been erased.

Just as I and my experience comprise my data (Davies 2007), so the society I am situated within and reflect is an inextricable element of the research—implicitly and explicitly. By aiming to understand spiritual experiences in epilepsy within the socio-cultural context they are lived through, my autoethnography emphasizes the use of personal experience to not only examine the self (Frank 1995), but also wider socio-cultural responses (Sparkes 1996). The intention is for the reader to consider their own response to the material and how this reflects socio-cultural aspects of the narrative, perhaps offering a new lens for engagement, even if this is a subject matter that was previously known (Ellis 2000).

In this autoethnography, I employ an approach that subverts the usual manner in which neurological cases are presented in epilepsy patient reviews (e.g., Stefan et al. 2012). Such reviews collect history, comment on investigations and end with an assessment and diagnosis. Here, pictures, emotion and narrative are used in the case study sections as a deliberate contrast to the medical terminology and diagnostic criteria that usually populate these reports. References are made to relevant neurological, psychiatric and transpersonal literature alongside this narrative. In this manner, I tie my experiences to the relevant literature and its cultural attitudes, and I problematize the ways in which spiritual experiences in epilepsy are usually understood.

Campbell (2017) identifies one criticism of autoethnography: that the autoethnographer's personal involvement is a contaminant of research; a narcissism. However, Dwyer and Buckle (2009) state that researchers always have *some* form of connection with their subject matter and often feel personally involved. Lived experience, conveyed empathically, may even be best enabled by an 'insider' (Gair 2011). Perhaps, there is a form of critical awareness which is impossible without having lived through that experience oneself (Kelly, Burton and Regan 1994). An individual's experience is not necessarily representative; as an 'insider' I may hold different views or understanding of similar experiences (Letherby and Zdrodowski 1995). However, what my insider status can do is provide a deeper understanding, based on my heartfelt, embodied personal experience (Grant, Short and Turner 2013). Merriweather (2015) emphasizes how the subsequent knowledge emerges through a different type of engagement; one with the non-verbal, reflexive self, critically reviewing and demanding transformation.

Epilepsy

Epilepsy is one of the oldest and most common neurological conditions, affecting fifty million individuals globally (Reynolds 2002). As such, it is an important area of interest for those interested in health and wellbeing. Epilepsy is identified as a spectrum disorder (Fisher et al. 2014), where an individual will have an enduring tendency for recurrent seizures. With at least 40 variations of different symptoms and causes (Fisher et al. 2005), individuals can experience multiple types of seizure, ranging in severity from infrequent momentary absences to, at the most extreme, sudden seizure-related death (Joint Epilepsy Council 2011).

The Babylonians regarded epilepsy as a supernatural affliction (Wilson and Reynolds 1990) and the Greek notion of a 'sacred disease' persisted through the Middle Ages (Temkin 1994). Symptoms were understood as possession, lunacy and mental illness, and treatment involved a combination of cauterization, trepanning, magical cures and herbal remedies until the development of asylums, when epileptics were removed from society (Devinsky and Lai 2008). Despite the emergence of a physiological understanding of the condition, the religious connection continued well into the nineteenth century (Temkin 1994). The history of epilepsy has been seen as '4000 years of ignorance, superstition and stigma followed by 100 years of knowledge, superstition, and stigma' (Kale 1997, 12). Consequently, it is obvious that the diagnosis of epilepsy is an important life-event (Schneider and Conrad 1983), often involving a sense of personal meaning (Schachter2008) and central to the wellbeing of those with the condition.

Temporal Lobe Epilepsy (TLE) is the most common form of epilepsy, characterized by seizures that originate in the temporal lobe area of the brain, accompanied by a short period of impaired consciousness (Fenwick and Fenwick 1996). Some individuals with TLE have feelings and sensations associated with a state that is qualitatively different from anything that they have in normal waking consciousness (Åsheim Hansen and Brodtkorb 2003). These experiences are described as mystical (Ramachandran and Blaksee 1999), cosmic (Dolgoff-Kaspar et al. 2011), and ecstatic (Åsheim Hansen and Brodtkorb 2003). Individuals sometimes struggle to portray the experience because of its ineffable and numinous quality, sitting outside a shared reality (Dolgoff-Kaspar et al. 2011). Descriptions include déjà-vu (Picard and Craig 2009), jamais-vu (Sacks 2012), out-of-body experiences and altered states of consciousness (e.g., Neppe 2011; Palmer and Neppe 2003). Such experiences are understood by experients to have spiritual connotations that can involve a felt presence (Persinger 2001), talking with, or feeling God's reality (Dewhurst and Beard 2003). Experients regard them as a spiritual experience that contributes towards their overall wellbeing, including no longer fearing death, seeing the world in a different way, and feeling a deep sense of harmony with the universe (Picard and Craig 2009). In this chapter, I refer to all such experiences as Epileptiform Events (EFEs)—a more neutral description than the medically oriented terms 'seizure' or 'aura', the colloquial term 'fit' and the somewhat pejorative term 'outburst' (Admi and Shaham 2007).

It has been suggested (Ananthaswarmy 2014) that those with epilepsy go to great lengths not to experience another seizure. However, some individuals greatly value the non-shared reality EFEs proffer. Dewhurst and Beard (2003) reported six cases of individuals with epilepsy with what they termed a 'sudden religious conversion', which included: a feeling of bliss, feeling God's reality, a land of peace, talking to and hearing God's voice. Dostoyevsky saw his EFEs as a gift (Alaljouanine 1963), claiming 'this feeling is so strong and so sweet that for a few seconds of this enjoyment one would readily exchange ten years of one's life—perhaps even one's whole life' (p. 212).

The prudence of stigmatizing any experiences that sit outside a shared experience of reality has been questioned (Kaminker and Lukoff

2013). EFEs are regarded, in common with other spiritual experiences, as 'anomalous' in the sense that they are individually and culturally unlike usual, 'ordinary' or expected experiences (Braud 2012; Palmer and Marcusson-Clavertz 2015). They are classified by neurologists and psychiatrists as an unwanted symptom of epilepsy-related psychosis (Trimble, Kanner and Schmidt 2010). The experience of these so-called hallucinations, delusions or illusions has been regarded as being neurologically based, because those who experience them have epilepsy, and only the experient can perceive them (Kasper et al. 2010).

William James (1902) noted that all thoughts and feelings originate from the physical brain; he rejected biological materialism as wholly explanatory. Fenwick (1996) concurs, remarking that such reductionism demands neurocognitive accounts of all experience, when no such thing is yet possible. This is particularly pertinent when cross-cultural attitudes are considered; for example, in anthropological examples of shamans with epilepsy (Temkin 1994).

Ignoring or pathologizing spiritual experiences is not new to the medical establishment (Lukoff, Lu and Turner 1992). As such, EFEs are deemed to be neither genuine nor appropriate, and the typical reaction of the medical profession to an individual with epilepsy reporting an EFE is to regard it as, at best, delusional (e.g., Kasper et al. 2010) or hallucinatory (Penfield and Jasper 1954). At worst, it is seen to be symptomatic of Temporal Lobe Personality Disorder (Waxman and Geschwind 1975), otherwise known as Geschwind syndrome (this behavioural diagnosis is now controversial but is still used by some clinicians, e.g., Veronelli et al. 2017). It is identified by the diagnostician's perception of the patient as having hyper-religiosity (intense religious beliefs or experiences that are deemed to interfere with normal functioning), irritability, hypergraphia (an intense desire to write or draw), hyposexuality (inhibited sexual excitement) and an intense mental life (Trimble and Freeman 2006).

It has been noted that those in the helping professions are often ill-equipped to provide support for the emotional reactions that individuals have to spiritual experiences (Braud 2012) and I would add EFEs to this. There is therefore value for those concerned with researching the relationship between spiritual experiences and health in exploring the tension between their causation and the manner in which they are experienced and understood by experients.

The purpose of this chapter is to provide a first-hand autoethnographic account of the lived experience of epilepsy and EFEs, in order to demonstrate how autoethnography can be a valuable methodology for researching these spiritual experiences. The use of personal data that allows the experient to explore and explain the nature of their spiritual experience and the role that it has in their life means that it is applicable to many forms of spirituality and a broader understanding of health and wellbeing than those defined by narrow medical terms. By showing how autoethnography works with one very specific example of spirituality, I demonstrate how other forms of spiritual experience that have a relationship with health and wellbeing can also be considered using this research method.

Autoethnographic Narrative

Clinical History

Figures 1 and 2 are photographs of me just before and after my diagnosis of epilepsy. I include them here, at the start of my narrative, as I have chosen them as artefacts that take me back to the start of my journey with epilepsy, evoking my emotional response at that time.

Figure 1. 'Normal' me—Blenheim Palace, Oxford, UK, 1988.

Figure 2. 'Abnormal' me—Louvre, Paris, France, 1989.

I was diagnosed with epilepsy at the age of 18, in the middle of my 'gap' year between school and university. Living abroad, I had been found on more than one occasion unconscious in the front gardens of the people I lived with. They thought that I had fallen, drunk; that I was irresponsible and selfish. The first time it happened, I slept for four days straight. I had a relentless headache that was so painful it hurt to move my head, and my limbs ached as if I had been in a fight. After the third or fourth occasion, I was hurting myself badly; there were bumps, cuts and a bloody face.

No-one wanted to talk about it and they certainly didn't want me living with them. I felt as if I was sent away; I returned home for investigations. I felt rejected and punished and this transformed into anger. Scans and tests followed, culminating in a diagnosis of epilepsy and medication. I felt bemused.

Around this time, a private member's bill – the so-called Alton Bill as it was raised by a member of Parliament called Alton - was debated in Parliament, aiming to reduce abortions to 18 weeks (HC Deb 24 April 1990), potentially leaving women without the choice of whether to abort children with birth defects. No-one seemed to care about anything but my compliance to medication. I noted from the side effects accompanying my tablets that women who take medication for epilepsy have a higher risk of foetal abnormalities that include cleft lips and palates, congenital heart defects, malformations of the face and slow development (Fenwick and Fenwick 1996); I became a protester.

General History

In the autumn of 2012, the breakdown of my marriage forced me into extreme levels of stress and emotional vulnerability. I began to question my sense of self-identity and, unravelling emotionally and psychologically, the condition that I had always rejected became a serious concern. I experienced uncontrolled and damaging seizures, something that I had not suffered from in over two decades. I never embraced my condition, but I took the tablets. I didn't tell people about it, it was a secret I chose mostly not to disclose. People didn't know unless something went wrong. In an attempt to stabilize my condition, I requested an appointment with a neurologist.

Examination

Diary entry July 2014

'The consultant is very late, I am so sorry', says the secretary. 'He is flying in, you see'. I look up from my hands. I realise that I have not been listening, that I have been wandering for an hour, lost in the dreamy world of what-ifs and how-cans. 'Would you mind if his registrar saw you instead?' I take no time to consider and chirp out 'Oh no, that's fine' brightly, not knowing whether or not this will be of any use. I haven't been here for many years and the return is not a welcome one. I start the conversation; I know what I want—I need an MRI scan. So, I tell the young (very young, it seems) woman. We talk about our research. It is too scary to talk about my own experiences. 'So, why are you here?' says the perky young doctor. It takes my breath away. You have to do this, I remember, trying to be calm, not to lose composure. 'I have had seizures, out of the blue'. I know the next question so add on quickly 'I am fully compliant with my medication'. Big, fat, soft tears begin to drop from my eyes, the room is swimming, I can't talk. Slowly and gently, I talk about my situation, about the seizures, my fear, the need to explore what is happening. And then, surprising myself, I admit the experience I have been having for years, the details that I haven't told anyone, because I feared they would say this was something very, very, bad. 'I leave my body, I go into the cosmos, I can see the earth from the stars' I blurt out. The neurologist looks lost, she wants to do something but feels embarrassed, out of her depth. She can't engage with my fear; the cheeriness has gone. She says, 'I think you need a scan'.

Although EFEs vary, accounts often include a sense of accessing a joyful and harmonious state. Dostoyevsky (cited in Alaljouanine 1963) recounted feeling 'such a happiness that it is impossible to realize at other times, and other people cannot imagine it. I feel a complete harmony within myself and in the world' (p. 212). It can be experienced as a non-shared reality (Schachter 2008). One woman said: 'it is such a different place it is beyond reality' (p. 77.) unlike anything else experienced (Åsheim Hansen and Brodtkorb 2003), which medical professionals find difficult to engage with. One person explained their transformative nature as seeing the world differently and meaning one no longer fears death (Picard and Craig 2009).

Descriptions and experiences of EFEs share a phenomenological similarity with other mystical and spiritual experiences (Neppe 1983; Persinger and Makarec 1993). Anomalous experiences in non-epileptic populations are also seen as irrational or pathological (Walsh and Vaughan 1993) and can be seen as dangerous, or 'an abomination' (Michael 1999, 53). Roxburgh and Evenden (2016) observe that individuals fear mentioning anomalous experiences as they expect to be labelled as mentally ill. It is hardly surprising, therefore, that individuals with EFEs are reticent to discuss them, or keep them secret for fear of judgement (Åsheim Hansen and Brodtkorb 2003).

Special Studies

Diary entry Sept 2013

I am sitting in a business meeting with my manager. I am telling her about the work I am doing currently. It is a normal day, we are discussing nothing special. In the space of a moment, my heart sinks and I feel woozy. I feel my mind move. It is as if it tips to the back of my head. I try to grab onto it, to keep hold of it. But I have slipped away. I have to sit back. I need to take a deep breath, to ground myself. My mouth produces saliva, I have the need to swallow, but no ability. A fear ominously rises from the pit of my stomach. 'I know you, old friend' I think. I look around me—the colours are brighter, sounds are louder, there is a quality of the unreality about the everyday. It feels too much. I feel sad, very sad. Everything is carrying on as normal, but I am not. I feel my body transported a long, long way away. I am in the outer cosmic regions of space, looking down on the earth. It is blue and covered with clouds that swirl and move over its surface. The tiny ants of humanity move over its surface, moving fast, going nowhere. I sit amongst the planets. Darkness abounds. No sounds, no smells. But I know how it is connected. I know how the universe works. And I feel calm, at peace.

EFEs are largely dismissed as merely symptomatic of the condition (Jackson and Coleman 1898) and professionals dismiss patient worries and concerns as exaggerated (Goldstein, Seidenberg and Peterson 1990). This is identified by the psychiatric profession as epilepsy-related (ictal) psychosis (Gaber 2017). In the *Diagnostic and Statistical Manual of Mental Disorders* (American Psychiatric Association 2013) used by psychiatrists worldwide, specific codes are given for this form of psychosis (codes 293.81 and 293.82: Psychotic Disorder Due to Another Medical Condition). Wooffitt (1992) highlights how individuals who have anomalous experiences create an identity to support or validate the reliability of their experience. Even the most understanding members of the medical establishment comment on how these experiences manifest as psychotic symptoms (e.g., Brett et al. 2014).

Neuropsychological assessment
Witnessing a seizure can be disturbing for onlookers. My epilepsy is unpredictable, generally completely absent. Whilst some individuals have a warning, or aura, the seemingly erratic nature of seizures, even with mostly effective medication, can be a distressing feature of the condition (Jacoby, Snape and Baker 2005). This poem reflects my feelings about a haphazard seizure before a new lover; it encapsulates many of my emotions concerning my body's ability to suddenly fall into seizure activity with no prior warning—and other people's responses.

Show and tell

When I told you
That I am sometimes not here
That I travel to another place
You thought I meant a daydream
When I told you
That you will feel helpless
That you will realise this is real
You didn't know what I meant

When I told you
That this is not straightforward
That it is deep
You thought I was being poetic
When I asked you
If you want to go now
You showed me love
And held your nerve
When I showed you
You could not travel with me
And were left to watch
You were scared

Image Findings

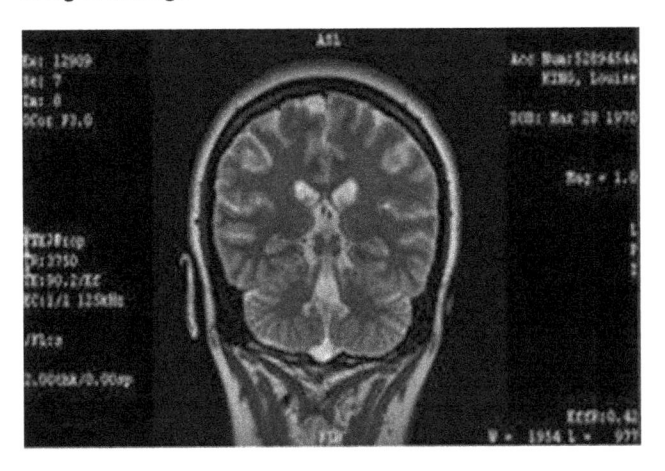

Figure 3. MRI scan, 30 June 2014.

Diary entry 25 Sept 2014

I am late for the appointment. The NHS, it seems, cannot accommodate delay from its patients. They make me wait 2 hours until the end of the clinic. Ushered in, the consultant's face makes it clear he is not in the mood to engage. Fixing my gaze, dreading his response, I tentatively ask 'what did the MRI scan show?' I am expecting some collaborative examination of impenetrable imagery. This neurologist is well respected. I want him to bring me into the world of my illness.

'The scan shows nothing', he replies. 'But you have had auras. Auras are seizures, so you will need to take double the prescribed dose'. I look down at my shoes, and cry. I feel I am infantilised; he has the authority, I am being told how it is. My responsibility is to comply without commotion. 'What about the effects, how about my mental confusion and tiredness?' I ask. He looks up from his sheet, his brow is dark, eyebrows knotted together; he resents my intrusion into his consultation. 'If you are feeling anxious, I prescribe benzodiazepine, don't take them more than 3 days in a row'. He writes a prescription, there is an arrogant flourish in his off-handedness. I feel an uncontrollable adolescent anger rising in my throat, I become indignant, feeling incensed. 'What's their current black-market value?' I joke, tauntingly. The consultant responds without humour: 'You cannot sell these, they are not for those who have not had them prescribed', pompously rising in his seat to claim the authority of his position. I feel belittled and look at my shoes. I immediately drop my handbag and scrabble on the floor to collect loose items of make-up, pens, keys, bits of fluff, old train tickets. The consultant turns away and starts to speak into his Dictaphone, repeating the medical details of the conversation.

So that's it. The consultation is over. I leave the room. I am stunned. Following the signs blindly, I remember the prescription. I turn around, retrace my steps to the pharmacy and stand waiting patiently. The pharmacist chats to a colleague about a film they have seen, handing me the tablets. I examine the sticker on the box, remember what they are and put them straight in the bin. London roars outside, offering anonymity. Limply, I join the slipstream.

There is a power dynamic in medical encounters (Charon 2008) that can act as a catalyst for isolation and a 'privatizing' experience (Schneider and Conrad 1980). Patients can feel shame, humiliation, bewilderment and insignificance, such that arriving late can seem as important as the illness itself (Lazare 1987).

Diagnosis

I receive a copy of the letter to my GP, the result of that conversation with the consultant. I have no difference in size between my hippocampi and have been prescribed an increased dosage of medication. This is not what I took away from our meeting.

Follow Up

Diary entry 25 Sept 2014

When I visit the neurologist for my follow-up six months later, I tell him I am visiting the Tablet Room at the British Museum and show him a picture of The Sakikkū, explaining what it is. In the Sakikkū, a symptom of epilepsy is that 'a man evolves his own religion' [Reynolds and Kinnier Wilson 2008, 1489]. He says he has only ever heard about it, never seen it. Suddenly we have a shared passion, a delight. We start to talk, as equals. He is excited, wants to know about it. Emboldened by this disclosure, I guardedly mention my research into spiritual experiences in epilepsy. And then something changes; he shifts in his chair

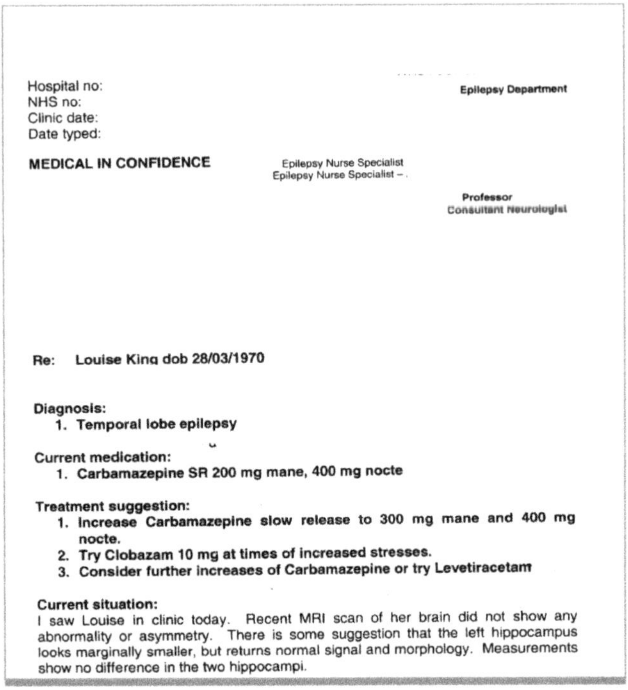

> Hospital no:
> NHS no:
> Clinic date:
> Date typed:
>
> **MEDICAL IN CONFIDENCE**   Epilepsy Nurse Specialist
>   Epilepsy Nurse Specialist – .
>
>   Epilepsy Department
>
>   Professor
>   Consultant Neurologist
>
> Re: Louise King dob 28/03/1970
>
> **Diagnosis:**
>   1. Temporal lobe epilepsy
>
> **Current medication:**
>   1. Carbamazepine SR 200 mg mane, 400 mg nocte
>
> **Treatment suggestion:**
>   1. Increase Carbamazepine slow release to 300 mg mane and 400 mg nocte.
>   2. Try Clobazam 10 mg at times of increased stresses.
>   3. Consider further increases of Carbamazepine or try Levetiracetam
>
> **Current situation:**
> I saw Louise in clinic today. Recent MRI scan of her brain did not show any abnormality or asymmetry. There is some suggestion that the left hippocampus looks marginally smaller, but returns normal signal and morphology. Measurements show no difference in the two hippocampi.

Figure 4. Consultant letter, 25 September 2014.

and is reminding me about people who have temporal lobe epilepsy and commit violent acts—his professional persona is back and the connection we had, momentarily, is lost. I leave the follow-up feeling just as frustrated as ever. But this time it is for a different reason, because this time I did see a flash of the healer, the human, the father, the husband; I saw that he was more complex than just a pantomime baddie. And then he deliberately put his mask back on and pushed me away, so I was no more complex than the submissive patient.

The Tablet Room

The appointment clerk looks up, momentarily
I wait for you again
In the bustling antechamber of the brain
The room where heads are categorized
Experience is stigmatized
A stratigraphy of shame
The sands of time have shifted
My distress wasn't buried in your memory
You may think you heal
Measuring with tests and scans

But what your excavation reveals
Is that I am gifted
Dusty Nineveh, just a breath away
In hushed, hallowed halls
They knew it all before, this malaise
Their tablets wiser than yours
You can't see what's inscribed in my mind
Cuneiform reveals meaning today

Discussion

The narrative that I have presented demonstrates that autoethnography is a highly suitable method for exploring spiritual experiences, as it allows the researcher to subtly interweave the phenomenology of their experience and its meaning. Autoethnography allows us to consider the cultural significance of such an experience. For individuals with EFEs, there is the potential for a damaging mismatch in encounters with healthcare professionals, as expectations differ. From the perspective of the patient, there is a desire to have their experience met and validated, but a fear of judgement. Patients see the encounter as highlighting defects, making them physically and psychologically vulnerable (Lazare 1987). For the healthcare professional, the focus is to control seizures through a medical regimen, seeking answers from pre-determined diagnostic criteria (Devinsky 2008). Metaphysical worldviews can collide when the causes of illness are understood very differently (Charon 2008). So Western American doctors may diagnose abnormal neural activity, and the Hmong, a shamanic culture, would instead understand perturbed ancestral spirits (Fadiman 2012).

Autoethnography enables the researcher to engage with less seen or understood experiences. With epilepsy, this includes its ambiguous and complex status as an 'invisible' disability (Rhodes et al. 2008). Individuals ignore their condition or hope it will subside in order to be 'normal' (Admi and Shaham 2007). Frequently, they choose to conceal; some people are told, others not (Schneider and Conrad 1980). Often, not even friends and family are told (Hayden, Penna and Buchanan 1992), with secrecy creating feelings of isolation and separation (Schachter 2008). It is likened to the disclosure of 'coming out of the closet' (Schachter, Krishnamurthy and Cantrell 2008, 3). I have always hidden my epilepsy. Autoethnography provides a research method where I can valuably disclose the invisible, and I accept my vulnerability in doing so.

Autoethnography allows the researcher to honour experience whilst also considering the societal status of lesser understood experiences. For example, working with a chasm of misunderstanding, those with epilepsy manage their symptoms as well as their stigma and shame (Scambler and Hopkins 1986). Public perception and treatment of those with epilepsy continues to be poor and it remains 'a stigmatizing condition par excellence' (Baker et al. 1997, 353). Society has built a body of memory that depicts those with epilepsy as dangerous, unreliable, frightening and unable to function as adults (Schneider and Conrad 1980), pervasive across educational level, class, culture and geography (e.g., Aragon, Hess and Burneo 2009; Chung et al. 1995). It is hardly surprising that this creates a strong feeling of vulnerability and inadequacy (Schachter, Krishnamurthy and Cantrell 2008), where individuals often avoid engaging with the treatment for their symptoms, because they find the prejudice more difficult to engage with than their seizures (WHO 2017). This amplifies feelings of unworthiness and a self-identity (Schachter 2008) heavily influenced by societal barriers, erected to limit the possibility of a conventional life (Schneider and Conrad 1980).One woman said of her condition, 'I felt less than a person' (Schneider and Conrad 1980, 2).The consequence is a loss of social value (Jacoby, Snape and Baker 2005) and a feeling of spoiled social identity (Goffman 1963). No surprise, then, that those with EFEs fear judgement and keep their experiences secret.

Conclusion

In this chapter, I have shown how autoethnography can be used to explore spiritual experiences that are usually kept silent, for fear of judgement. Autoethnography is a flexible methodology that can encompass a range of data that would be inaccessible from other approaches, and this makes it an ideal candidate for research into spirituality. Oliver Sacks (2012) highlighted that a strictly biomedical perspective of EFEs offers no insight into the significance and the meaning that they have in people's lives. He also noted that spiritual experience may form an essential part of what it means to be human. Rabbi Mordechai Zeller, Jewish Chaplain at Cambridge University, challenges the received view that transcendental experiences, coming from outside the self, are regarded as God, and inner experiences are not (Carr 2018). He draws a parallel between the intensely emotional experiences of mystics, looking inward in a search for God, the Biblical prophets and individuals with EFEs. Here I have used autoethnography to explore EFEs, but if Rabbi Zeller is right, then autoethnography, offering as it does primacy to inner experience, is a very fitting approach for research into spiritual experiences of all types.

I have demonstrated how autoethnography uniquely captures what it feels like to have this type of spiritual experience and the meaning for experients. EFEs are like other spiritual experiences insofar as some involve a non-shared reality, where there exists a mismatch between how it is experienced, and how healthcare professionals view it. Ettore (2010) notes that autoethnography is particularly useful in considerations of health where there is a power dynamic between the patient and the professional. A similar thing could be said for experiences of spiritual awakening and spiritual crisis, where healthcare professionals hold the power to diagnose an individual as psychotic, with all of the consequences that this will have for their life (e.g., Clarke 2010; Razzaque 2014). Autoethnography has been shown to be an evocative approach that respects lived experience that may be judged in such instances as not 'normal'. I recommend that as well as health, autoethnography is a suitable method for the consideration of any ineffable or disputed experiences that are common in spirituality, because it rejects the simplification of experience and requires consideration from an embodied perspective.

In using autoethnography, I have challenged medical responses to EFEs and shown how seeing them as symptomatic of psychosis both reinforces antiquated stereotypes of individuals with epilepsy as mad and ignores how they can contribute to the experients' sense of wellbeing. Autoethnography has been adopted enthusiastically as a research method by a number of health-related disciplines including occupational therapy, clinical psychology and sport. In nursing, autoethnography has rapidly become a popular qualitative research method and this speaks to how it connects to an understanding of wellbeing. Its value lies in its ability to hold up a critical mirror to both self and culture (Merriweather 2015), and in doing so holds the voices of many—not just the researcher (Frank 2010). Autoethnography's reflexivity of narrative holds the seeds of change for the wellbeing of self, other, and community. It offers the researcher a method and subsequent analysis that is flexible enough to encompass a wide range of data types that explore the relationship between spirituality and health as it is lived and understood.

Biographical Note

Louise Spiers is a Senior Lecturer in Psychology and Counselling at the University of Northampton, UK, where she is a Doctoral candidate researching transpersonal understandings of spiritual experiences in epilepsy. She is interested in exceptional human experiences and their phenomenology and research methodologies that enable this. She is passionate about the use of autoethnography as a qualitative methodology for researching experiences that are otherwise pathologized or silenced. An Integrative Psychotherapist and Counsellor (UKCP, MBACP), Louise works as a transpersonal psychotherapist in private practice in London, where she uses therapeutic methods which include the use of creative expression, dreams and archetypal symbolism.

Acknowledgements

I am extremely grateful to my PhD supervisors Chris Roe, Elizabeth Roxburgh and Nigel Hamilton for their encouragement, critical commentary and guidance, Phil Clarke for his generous heart, and my parents and for their loving support in my journey with epilepsy.

Bibliography

Adams, T. E. and S. Holman Jones. 2008. 'Autoethnography is Queer'. In *Handbook of Critical and Indigenous Methodologies*, edited by Norman K. Denzin, Yvonna S. Lincoln and Linda T. Smith, 373–390. Thousand Oaks, CA: Sage.

Admi, H., and B. Shaham. 2007. 'Living with Epilepsy: Ordinary People Coping with Extraordinary Situations'. *Qualitative Health Research* 17 (9): 1178–1187. https://doi.org/10.1177/1049732307307548

Alajouanine, T. 1963. 'Dostoiewski's Epilepsy'. *Brain* 86 (2): 209–218. https://doi.org/10.1093/brain/86.2.209

American Psychiatric Association. 2013. *Diagnostic and Statistical Manual of Mental Disorders (DSM-5®)*. Washington, DC: American Psychiatric Publications. https://doi.org/10.1176/appi.books.9780890425596

Ananthaswamy, A. 2014. 'Diagnosing Dostoevsky: Understanding Ecstatic Seizures'. *New Scientist* 221 (2953): 44–47. https://doi.org/10.1016/S0262-4079(14)60189-5

Aragon, C. E., T. Hess and J. G. Burneo. 2009. 'Knowledge and Attitudes about Epilepsy: A Survey of Dentists in London, Ontario'. *Journal of the Canadian Dental Association* 75 (6): 450–450g. https://doi.org/10.1037/t21946-000

Åsheim Hansen, B. and E. Brodtkorb. 2003. 'Partial Epilepsy with "Ecstatic" Seizures'. *Epilepsy & Behavior* 4 (6): 667–673. https://doi.org/10.1016/j.yebeh.2003.09.009

Baker, G. A., A. Jacoby, D. Buck, C. Stalgis and D. Monnet. 1997. 'Quality of Life of People with Epilepsy: A European Study'. *Epilepsia* 38 (3): 353–362. https://doi.org/10.1111/j.1528-1157.1997.tb01128.x

Behar, R. 1996. *The Vulnerable Observer: Anthropology That Breaks your Heart*. Boston, MA: Beacon Press.

Braud, W. 2012. 'Health and Well-Being Benefits of Exceptional Human Experience'. In *Mental Health and Anomalous Experience*, edited by C. Murray, 107–124. New York: Nova Science Publishers.

Brett, C., C. Heriot-Maitland, P. McGuire and E. Peters. 2014. 'Predictors of Distress Associated with Psychotic-like Anomalous Experiences in Clinical and Non-Clinical Populations'. *British Journal of Clinical Psychology* 53 (2): 213–227. https://doi.org/10.1111/bjc.12036

Brooks, C. F. 2011. 'Social Performance and Secret Ritual: Battling Against Obsessive-Compulsive Disorder'. *Qualitative Health Research* 21 (2): 249–261. https://doi.org/10.1177/1049732310381387

Campbell, E. 2017. '"Apparently Being a Self-Obsessed C** t Is Now Academically Lauded": Experiencing Twitter Trolling of Autoethnographers'. *Forum: Qualitative Social Research* 18 (3): Art. 16.

Carr, C. 2018. Sunday. BBC Radio 4, 28 October. Available at: https://www.bbc.co.uk/sounds/play/m0000xml (accessed November 2018).

Chang, H. 2016. 'Autoethnography in Health Research: Growing Pains?'. *Qualitative Health Research* 26 (4): 443–451. https://doi.org/10.1177/1049732315627432

Chapman-Clarke, M. 2016. '"Discovering" Autoethnography as a Research Genre, Methodology and Method: "The Yin and Yang of Life"'. *Transpersonal Psychology Review* 18 (2): 10–18. Available from https://shop.bps.org.uk/publications/transpersonal-psychology-review-vol-18-no-2-autumn-2016.html (accessed August 2018).

Charon, R. 2008. *Narrative Medicine: Honoring the Stories of Illness*. Oxford, UK: Oxford University Press.

Chung, M. Y., Y. C. Chang, Y. H. C. Lai and C. W. Lai. 1995. 'Survey of Public Awareness, Understanding, and Attitudes Toward Epilepsy in Taiwan'. *Epilepsia* 36 (5): 488–493. https://doi.org/10.1111/j.1528-1157.1995.tb00491.x

Clarke, I. (Ed.) 2010. *Psychosis and Spirituality: Consolidating the New Paradigm*. Hoboken, NJ: John Wiley. https://doi.org/10.1002/9780470970300

Davies, C. A. 2007. *Reflexive Ethnography: A Guide to Researching Selves and Others*. New York: Routledge. https://doi.org/10.4324/9780203822272

Devinsky, O. 2008. 'Foreword'. In *Brainstorms—Epilepsy in our Words: Personal Accounts of Living with Seizures (Vol. 1)*, S. C. Schachter, xi–xiii. New York: Oxford University Press.

Devinsky, O. and G. Lai. 2008. 'Spirituality and Religion in Epilepsy'. *Epilepsy & Behavior* 12 (4): 636–643. https://doi.org/10.1016/j.yebeh.2007.11.011

Dewhurst, K., and A. W. Beard. 2003. 'Sudden Religious Conversions in Temporal Lobe Epilepsy'. *Epilepsy & Behavior* 4 (1): 78–87. https://doi.org/10.1016/S1525-5050(02)00688-1

Dolgoff-Kaspar, R., A. B. Ettinger, S. A. Golub, K. Perrine, C. Harden and S. D. Croll. 2011. 'Numinous-Like Auras and Spirituality in Persons with Partial Seizures'. *Epilepsia* 52 (3): 640–644. https://doi.org/10.1111/j.1528-1167.2010.02957.x

Dwyer, S. C. and J. L Buckle. 2009. 'The Space Between: On Being an Insider-Outsider in Qualitative Research'. *International Journal of Qualitative Methods* 8 (1): 54–63. https://doi.org/10.1177/160940690900800105

Ellis, C. 2000. 'Creating Criteria: An Ethnographic Short Story'. *Qualitative Inquiry* 6 (2): 273–277. https://doi.org/10.1177/107780040000600210

Ellis, C. 2004. *The Ethnographic I: A Methodological Novel About Autoethnography*. New York: Rowman Altamira.

Ellis, C. S., and Bochner, A. 2000. 'Autoethnography, Personal Narrative, Reflexivity: Researcher as Subject'. In *The Sage Handbook of Qualitative Research* (2nd edition), edited by N. K. Denzin and Y. S. Lincoln, 733–768. London: Sage.

Ettorre, E. 2005. 'Gender, Older Female Bodies and Autoethnography: Finding my Feminist Voice by Telling my Illness Story'. *Women's Studies International Forum* 28 (6): 535–546. https://doi.org/10.1016/j.wsif.2005.09.009

Ettorre, E. 2010, 'Autoethnography: Making Sense of Personal Illness Journeys'. In *The Sage Handbook of Qualitative Methods in Health Research*, edited by I. Bourgeault, R. Dingwall and R. De Vries, 478–496. London: Sage. https://doi.org/10.4135/9781446268247

Fadiman, A. 2012. *The Spirit Catches You and You Fall Down: A Hmong Child, her American Doctors, and the Collision of Two Cultures*. New York: Farrar Straus & Giroux.

Fenwick, P. 1996. 'The Neurophysiology of Religious Experiences'. In *Psychiatry and Religion: Context, Consensus and Controversies*, edited by D. Bhugra, 167–177. London: Routledge. https://doi.org/10.4324/9780429490576-12

Fenwick, P. and E. Fenwick. 1996. *Living with Epilepsy. A Guide to Taking Control*. London: Bloomsbury.

Fisher, R. S., W. V. E. Boas, W. Blume, C. Elger, P. Genton, P. Lee and J. Engel. 2005. 'Epileptic Seizures and Epilepsy: Definitions Proposed by the International League Against Epilepsy (ILAE) and the International Bureau for Epilepsy (IBE). *Epilepsia* 46 (4): 470–472. https://doi.org/10.1111/j.0013-9580.2005.66104.x

Fisher, R. S., C. Acevedo, A. Arzimanoglou, A. Bogacz, J. H. Cross, C. E. Elger, J. Engel et al. 2014. 'ILAE Official Report: A Practical Clinical Definition of Epilepsy'. *Epilepsia* 55 (4): 475–482. https://doi.org/10.1111/epi.12550

Frank, A. W. 1995. *The Wounded Storyteller: Body, Illness, and Ethics*. Chicago, IL: University of Chicago Press. https://doi.org/10.7208/chicago/9780226260037.001.0001

Frank, A. W. 2010. *Letting Stories Breathe*. Chicago, IL: The University of Chicago Press. https://doi.org/10.7208/chicago/9780226260143.001.0001

Gaber, A. 2017. 'Semiological Bridge between Psychiatry and Epilepsy'. *Journal of Psychology and Clinical Psychiatry* 8 (1): 1–7. https://doi.org/10.15406/jpcpy.2017.08.00467

Gair, S. 2011. 'Feeling Their Stories: Contemplating Empathy, Insider/Outsider Positionings, and Enriching Qualitative Research'. *Qualitative Heath Research* 22 (1): 134–143. https://doi.org/10.1177/1049732311420580

Goffman, E. 1963. *Stigma: Notes on the Management of Spoiled Identity*. Englewood Cliffs, NJ: Prentice-Hall.

Goldstein, J., M. Seidenberg and R. Peterson. 1990. 'Fear of Seizures and Behavioral Functioning in Adults with Epilepsy'. *Journal of Epilepsy* 3 (2): 101–106. https://doi.org/10.1016/0896-6974(90)90158-U

Goodson, I. and S. Gill. 2011. *Narrative Pedagogy: Life History and Learning* (Vol. 386). Oxford, UK: Peter Lang.

Grant, A., N. P. Short and L. Turner. 2013. 'Introduction: Storying Life and Lives'. In *Contemporary British Autoethnography*, edited by N. P. Short, L. Turner and A. Grant, 1–16. Rotterdam, The Netherlands: Sense Publishers. https://doi.org/10.1007/978-94-6209-410-9_1

HC Deb (24 April 1990) vol. 171, cols 1–267. Available at: https://hansard.parliament.uk/Commons/1990-04-24/debates/5ea9dbab-9fa0-4037-8ec4-0cbc21731ab3/AmendmentOfLawRelatingToTerminationOfPregnancy?highlight=abortion%201988#contribution-e547d123-7b5a-4574-bd97-6f3308c92511 (accessed 22nd June 2019).

Hayano, D. M. 1979. 'Autoethnography: Paradigms, Problems, and Prospects'. *Human Organization* 38(1): 99–104. https://doi.org/10.17730/humo.38.1.u761n5601t4g318v

Hayden, M., C. Penna and N. Buchanan. 1992. 'Epilepsy: Patient Perceptions of their Condition'. *Seizure* 1 (3): 191–197. https://doi.org/10.1016/1059-1311(92)90025-V

Honnekeri, B., S. Rane, R. Vast and S. V. Khadilkar. 2018. 'Between the Person and the Pill: Factors Affecting Medication Adherence in Epilepsy Patients'. *Journal of The Association of Physicians of India* 66: 24.

Jacoby, A., D. Snape and G. A. Baker. 2005. 'Epilepsy and Social Identity: The Stigma of a Chronic Neurological Disorder'. *The Lancet Neurology* 4 (3): 171–178. https://doi.org/10.1016/S1474-4422(05)01014-8

Jackson, J. H. and W. S. Colman. 1898. 'Case of Epilepsy with Tasting Movements and "Dreamy State"—Very Small patch of Softening in the Left Uncinate Gyrus'. *Brain* 21 (4): 580–590. https://doi.org/10.1093/brain/21.4.580

James, W. 1902. *The Varieties of Religious Experience. A Study in Human Nature.* New York: Longmans, Green & Co. https://doi.org/10.1037/10004-000

Joint Epilepsy Council. 2011. *Epilepsy Prevalence, Incidence and Other Statistics.* Retrieved from http://www.jointepilepsycouncil.org.uk

Kale, R. 1997. 'Bringing Epilepsy Out of the Shadows'. *BMJ (British Medical Journal)* 315: 2. https://doi.org/10.1136/bmj.315.7099.2

Kaminker, J. and D. Lukoff. 2013. 'Transpersonal Perspectives on Mental Health and Mental Illness'. In *The Wiley-Blackwell Handbook of Transpersonal Psychology*, edited by H. L. Friedman and G. Hartelius, 419–432. Chichester, UK: Wiley-Blackwell. https://doi.org/10.1002/9781118591277.ch23

Kasper, B. S., E. M. Kasper, E. Pauli and H. Stefan. 2010. 'Phenomenology of Hallucinations, Illusions, and Delusions as Part of Seizure Semiology'. *Epilepsy & Behavior* 18 (1): 13–23. https://doi.org/10.1016/j.yebeh.2010.03.006

Kelly, L., S. Burton and L. Regan. 1994. 'Researching Women's Lives or Studying Women's Oppression? Reflections on What Constitutes Feminist Research'. In *Researching Women's Lives from a Feminist Perspective*, edited by M. Maynard and J. Purvis, 22–48, London:Taylor & Francis.

Lazare, A. 1987. 'Shame and Humiliation in the Medical Encounter'. *Archives of Internal Medicine* 147 (9), 1653–1658. https://doi.org/10.1001/archinte.147.9.1653

Letherby, G. and D. Zdrodowski. 1995. '"Dear Researcher": The Use of Correspondence as a Method within Feminist Qualitative Research'. *Gender & Society* 9 (5): 576–593. https://doi.org/10.1177/089124395009005005

Lukoff, D., F. Lu, and R. Turner. 1992. 'Toward a More Culturally Sensitive DSM-IV: Psychoreligious and Psychospiritual Problems'. *The Journal of Nervous and Mental Disease* 180 (11): 673–682. https://doi.org/10.1097/00005053-199211000-00001

Marcalo, D. R. (2012). 'Involuntary Dances'. *Research Ethics* 8 (1): 57–59. https://doi.org/10.1177/1747016112437686

Medford, K. 2006. 'Caught with a Fake ID: Ethical Questions About Slippage in Autoethnography'. *Qualitative Inquiry* 12 (5): 853–864. https://doi.org/10.1177/1077800406288618

Merriweather, L. R. 2015. 'Autoethnography as Counternarrative'. In *Autoethnography as a Lighthouse: Illuminating Race, Research, and the Politics of Schooling*, edited by S. Hancock, A. Allen and C. W. Lewis, 47. Charlotte, NC: IAP.

Michael, M. 1999. 'A Paradigm Shift? Connections with Other Critiques of Social Constructionism'. In *Social Constructionist Psychology: A Critical Analysis of Theory and Practice*, edited by D. Nightingale and J. Cromby, 52–64. Milton Keynes, UK: Open University Press.

Neppe, V. M. 1983. 'Temporal Lobe Symptomatology in Subjective Paranormal Experiments'. *Journal of the American Society for Psychical Research* 77 (1): 1–29.

Neppe, V. M. 2011. 'Models of the Out-of-Body Experience: A New Multi-Etiological Phenomenological Approach'. *NeuroQuantology* 9 (1): 72–83. https://doi.org/10.14704/nq.2011.9.1.391

Palmer, J. and D. Marcusson-Clavertz (Eds.). 2015. Parapsychology: A Handbook for the 21st Century. Jefferson, NC: McFarland & Company.

Palmer, J. and V. M. Neppe. 2003. 'A Controlled Analysis of Subjective Paranormal Experiences in Temporal Lobe Dysfunction in a Neuropsychiatric Population'. The Journal of Parapsychology 67 (1): 75–97.

Penfield, W. and H. Jasper. 1954. Epilepsy and the Functional Anatomy of the Human Brain. London: Churchill. https://doi.org/10.1097/00007611-195407000-00024

Persinger, M. A. 2001. 'The Neuropsychiatry of Paranormal Experiences'. The Journal of Neuropsychiatry and Clinical Neurosciences 13 (4): 515–24. https://doi.org/10.1176/appi.neuropsych.13.4.515

Persinger, M. A., and K. Makarec. 1993. 'Complex Partial Epileptic Signs as a Continuum from Normals to Epileptics: Normative Data and Clinical Populations'. Journal of Clinical Psychology 49 (1): 33–45. https://doi.org/10.1002/1097-4679(199301)49:1<33::AID-JCLP2270490106>3.0.CO;2-H

Picard, F. and A. D. Craig. 2009. 'Ecstatic Epileptic Seizures: A Potential Window on the Neural Basis for Human Self-Awareness'. Epilepsy & Behavior 16 (3): 539–546. https://doi.org/10.1016/j.yebeh.2009.09.013

Polkinghorne, D. 1988. *Narrative Knowing and the Human Sciences*. New York: State University of New York Press.

Raab, D. 2013. 'Transpersonal Approaches to Autoethnographic Research and Writing'. The Qualitative Report 18 (21): 1–18. Available from https://nsuworks.nova.edu/tqr/vol18/iss21/2/?/ (Accessed June 2019).

Ramachandran, V. S. and S. Blakslee. 1999. God and the Limbic System. Phantoms in the Brain: Probing the Mysteries of the Human Mind. New York: William Morrow.

Razzaque, R. 2014. *Breaking Down is Waking up: The Connection Between Psychological Distress and Spiritual Awakening*. London: Watkins Media Limited.

Reed-Danahay, D. 1997. Auto/ethnography. Rewriting the Self and the Social. New York: Berg.

Reynolds, E. H. 2002. 'The ILAE/IBE/WHO Epilepsy Global Campaign History'. Epilepsia 43 (6): 9–11. https://doi.org/10.1046/j.1528-1157.43.s.6.5.x

Reynolds, E. H. and J. V. Kinnier Wilson. 2008. 'Psychoses of Epilepsy in Babylon: The Oldest Account of the Disorder'. Epilepsia 49 (9): 1488–1490. https://doi.org/10.1111/j.1528-1167.2008.01614.x

Rhodes, P., A. Nocon, N. Small and J. Wright. 2008. 'Disability and Identity: The Challenge of Epilepsy'. Disability & Society 23 (4): 385–395. Available

from http://hdl.handle.net/10454/7051 (accessed May 2019). https://doi.org/10.1080/09687590802038910
Roxburgh, E.C. and R. E. Evenden. 2016. '"Most People Think You're a Fruit Loop": Clients' Experiences of Seeking Support for Anomalous Experiences'. *Counselling and Psychotherapy Research* 16 (3): 211–221.
Sacks, O. W. 2012. Hallucinations. London: Picador.
Scambler, G. and A. Hopkins. 1986. 'Being Epileptic: Coming to Terms with Stigma'. Sociology of Health & Illness 8: 26–43. https://doi.org/10.1111/1467-9566.ep11346455
Scarfe, S. V., and C. Marlow. 2015. 'Overcoming the Fear: An Autoethnographic Narrative of Running with Epilepsy'. Qualitative Research in Sport, Exercise and Health 7 (5): 688–697. https://doi.org/10.1080/2159676X.2015.1035741
Schachter, S. C. 2008. Brainstorms—Epilepsy in Our Words: Personal Accounts of Living with Seizures (Vol. 1). New York: Oxford University Press.
Schachter, S. C., K. B. Krishnamurthy and D. T. C. Cantrell. 2008. Epilepsy in Our Lives: Women Living with Epilepsy (Vol. 5). New York: Oxford University Press.
Schneider, J. W. and P. Conrad. 1980. 'In the Closet with Illness: Epilepsy, Stigma Potential and Information Control'. Social Problems 28 (1): 32–44. https://doi.org/10.2307/800379
Schneider, J. W. and P. Conrad. 1983. Having Epilepsy: The Experience and Control of Illness. Philadelphia, PA: Temple University Press.
Short, N. P. (2013. 'An Englishman Abroad'. In Studies in Professional and Work Volume 9: Contemporary British Autoethnography, edited by N. P. Short, L. Turner and A. Grant, 97–126. Rotterdam, The Netherlands: Sense Publications. https://doi.org/10.1007/978-94-6209-410-9_7
Short, N. P., L. Turner and A. Grant (Eds.). 2013. Studies in Professional Life and Work Volume 9: Contemporary British Autoethnography. Rotterdam, The Netherlands: Sense Publications. https://doi.org/10.1007/978-94-6209-410-9
Smith, J. A., R. Harré and L. Van Langenhove (Eds.). 1995. Rethinking Methods in Psychology. London: Sage. https://doi.org/10.4135/9781446221792
Sparkes, A. C. (1996). 'The Fatal Flaw: A Narrative of the Fragile Body-Self'. *Qualitative Inquiry* 2 (4): 463–494. https://doi.org/10.1177/107780049600200405
Stefan, H., E. Ben-Menachem, P. Chauvel and R. Guerrini (Eds.). 2012. Case Studies in Epilepsy: Common and Uncommon Presentations. Cambridge, UK: Cambridge University Press. https://doi.org/10.1017/CBO9780511706103
Stephens, C. and A. Wilson. 2017. David Hockney. London: Tate Publishing.
Temkin, O. 1994. The Falling Sickness: A History of Epilepsy from the Greeks to the Beginnings of Modern Neurology. (2nd edn). London: The John Hopkins University Press.
Tenni, C., A. Smyth and C. Boucher. 2003. 'The Researcher as Autobiographer: Analysing Data Written About Oneself'. The Qualitative Report 8 (1): 1–12. Available from http://nsuworks.nova.edu/tqr/vol8/iss1/1 (accessed May 2019).
Tolich, M. 2010. 'A Critique of Current Practice: Ten Foundational Guidelines for Autoethnographers'. Qualitative Health Research 20 (12): 1599–1610. https://doi.org/10.1177/1049732310376076

Trimble, M. and A. Freeman. 2006. 'An Investigation of Religiosity and the Gastaut-Geschwind Syndrome in Patients with Temporal Lobe Epilepsy'. Epilepsy & Behavior 9 (3): 407–414. https://doi.org/10.1016/j.yebeh.2006.05.006

Trimble, M., A. Kanner and B. Schmitz. 2010. 'Postictal Psychosis'. Epilepsy and Behavior 19 (2): 159–161. https://doi.org/10.1016/j.yebeh.2010.06.027

Veronelli, L., S. J. Makaretz, M. Quimby, B. C. Dickerson and J. A. Collins. 2017. 'Geschwind Syndrome in Frontotemporal Lobar Degeneration: Neuroanatomical and Neuropsychological Features over 9 Years'. Cortex 94: 27–38. https://doi.org/10.1016/j.cortex.2017.06.003

Walsh, R. E. and F. E. Vaughan (Eds.). 1993. *Paths Beyond Ego: The Transpersonal Vision*. New York: Perigee Books.

Waxman, S. G., and N. Geschwind. 1975. 'The Interictal Behavior Syndrome of Temporal Lobe Epilepsy'. Archives of General Psychiatry 32 (12): 1580–1586. https://doi.org/10.1001/archpsyc.1975.01760300118011

Wilson, J. V. and E. H. Reynolds. 1990. 'Texts and Documents. Translation and Analysis of a Cuneiform Text Forming Part of a Babylonian Treatise on Epilepsy'. Medical History 34 (2): 185. https://doi.org/10.1017/S0025727300050651

Wooffitt, R. 1992. Telling Tales of the Unexpected: The Organization of Factual Discourse. Lanham, MD: Rowman & Littlefield.

World Health Organisation (WHO). 2017. Epilepsy Factsheet (updated February 2017). Available from: http://www.who.int/mediacentre/factsheets/fs999/en/ (accessed August 2018).

Chapter 8

To Thine Own Self Be True: Alcoholics Anonymous, Recovery and Care of the Self

Lymarie Rodríguez-Morales

> I used to go out Friday nights and think, I'm the only one, I'm the only young person that can't drink or do drugs, look, look at them, they're all going out and having a good time, but slowly I found people like myself and you know that's the power of the meetings, relating to people. (Robert, an AA participant, 28 years old)

Over the past two decades there has been a growing examination of the role of spirituality in mental health, addiction recovery, and wellbeing. Research has linked spirituality to positive outcomes in psychological functioning, such as a greater sense of social support and belonging, recovery from mental distress, healthier lifestyles, and a more meaningful life (Diener and Biswas-Diener 2008; Koenig 2015; Moreira-Almeida et al. 2016). Spirituality generally refers to the meanings, values and practices which enable a greater appreciation of ourselves, our world, and our relationships with both, encompassing our philosophy of life or worldview. For instance, Robert Solomon (2002) suggests that spirituality, secular or religious, concerns the great many ways of experiencing life as *human beings*, and therefore, it is involved in all aspects of psychological transformation and healing. For most of the twentieth century, spirituality received little attention in psychological literature, with the exception of the humanistic and existential perspectives (for example, Viktor Frankl, Abraham Maslow, Carl Rogers among others), which predominantly considered spirituality as ways towards living a more meaningful life. Carl Jung (1876–1961) believed that spiritual experiences were important for developing our potential and fulfilling our innate longing for wholeness; similarly, Abraham Maslow (1908–1970) stated the importance of peak experiences (moments of ecstasy, harmony and fulfilment) and self-transcendence[1] (going *beyond* one's self) in order for people to develop and maximize their abilities and resources in service of humanity, nature and the cosmos. More recently, positive psychology, which studies what people do to live a more fulfilling and a happier life, has advocated a greater focus on spirituality as a key element of enhancing our wellbeing (Ahluwalia and Shaka 2018; Culpepper 2016; Peterson and Seligman 2004). Another prominent aspect of spirituality is its meaning-making function, and how this provides one's life with a sense of coherence (Antonovsky 1987). Ultimately, spirituality concerns our personal journey contemplating the ultimate questions about life (death, illness, suffering), about our search for meaning and about our place in the world, including our relationships with the sacred or transcendent.

Spirituality is central to the addiction recovery programme of Alcoholics Anonymous (AA) and Twelve Step fellowships (e.g., Narcotics Anonymous, Cocaine Anonymous). Originating in the United States, Twelve Step fellowships define addiction as a spiritual illness which only a spiritual experience can heal. These fellowships are now an important part of recovery policy and clinical guidelines for addiction treatment in the United Kingdom (Gossop, Stewart, and Mardsen 2008; NICE 2013). AA group meetings have been taking place in the UK since 1947. More recently, group meetings have been developed solely for young adults (18–30 years old), with a growing number of young people attending and seeking help for problematic substance use. This has prompted AA to appoint a Young Person's Liaison Officer and to provide more online services for young people (Alcoholics Anonymous, accessed May 5, 2017). Whilst participation is encouraged, little investigation or documentation has been carried out regarding young adults' experience of Twelve Step spiritual recovery in the UK. What is it that young adults find in these spiritual fellowships? What impact does this experience of spiritual recovery have upon their developing adult selfhood? Studies have reported high rates of recovery for young people participating in the fellowships but have so far appeared to overlook the actual practices which enabled young adults to recover successfully. This chapter presents some key findings from a study[2] with young adult men (22 to 35 years old) who were recovering from problematic substance use in the UK, illustrating how AA's spiritual recovery unfolded in the participants' lives. The aim of the study was to examine participants' identity and psychological transformation whilst transitioning to a life-world without substance use. One-to-one interviews and autobiographical stories of their recovery were collected and analyzed from a qualitative-experiential approach (Smith, Flowers, and Larkin 2009). Two research questions guided the inquiry:

- How do young adults experience and make sense of their recovery?
- What are the processes of change embedded in their recovery?

Alcoholics Anonymous and Recovery Spirituality

> If when you honestly want to, you find you cannot quit entirely, or if when drinking, you have little control over the amount you take, you are probably alcoholic. If that be the case, you may be suffering from an illness which only a spiritual experience will conquer. (Alcoholics Anonymous 1986, 44)

The concept of recovery from alcoholism was for some time almost exclusively promoted by AA and the Twelve Step fellowships, after Bill Wilson and Dr. Bob Smith, both recovering from alcoholism themselves, formed the program in the 1930s. The rest of the fellowships were inaugurated in the 1950s, 1960s and 1970s. It has been established that William James's *Varieties of Religious Experience* ([1902] 1982) was a major influence on the formation of the steps, especially when concerning the concepts of 'Higher Power'[3] and self-surrender experiences (Finlay 2000). Carl Jung[4] has been recognised as another significant contributor to the formation of AA, with his views on religious experience as an important source of healing and transformation influencing AA since its inception. The organization of AA meetings was in many ways inspired by the Oxford Group[5], which advocated self-examination, acknowledgement of one's character defects, restitution for harm done, and sharing with others (Alcoholics Anonymous 1986). The Oxford Group also stressed the importance of moral standards, guidance with a mentor, and surrender; as well as the idea that God had a plan for each person's life (Kurtz 1991). These fellowships have influenced the idea that recovery requires total abstinence from all mood-altering substances, generally excluding nicotine and caffeine. AA has been described as a scheme of beliefs and an interactional system where members use the term recovery to imply a holistic turnaround of lifestyle (Mäkelä 1991). Its main recovery processes are: admitting that one alone cannot control one's addiction; developing an understanding of a 'Higher Power' that can give strength; examining past errors with the help of a sponsor (an experienced Twelve Step member); making amends for these errors; learning to live a new life with a new code of behaviour; and helping others who suffer from the same addictions or compulsions. AA defines itself as:

> ... a fellowship of men and women who share their experience, strength and hope with each other that they may solve their common problem and help others to recover from alcoholism. The only requirement for membership is a desire to stop drinking. (Alcoholics Anonymous 1986: 1)

There are no fees for membership and all fellowships are supported through their members' contributions. AA views alcoholism as a 'four-fold' disease, composed of physical, emotional, spiritual and psychological features (Kassel and Wagner 1993). Its fundamental organizing principles are the group meetings, the Twelve Steps (see Figure 1) and the Twelve Traditions (see Figure 2). Whilst the Twelve Steps are the actual practice for each participant, The Twelve Traditions provide guidance for group governance. A sponsor is someone with experience in the fellowship to whom members can turn for guidance; members' relationships with him or her are an important element of the programme as the sponsor will support them in their engagement with the fellowship's recovery programme and help to facilitate socialization with the others in the group (Kassel and Wagner 1993). Meetings take place in both urban and rural areas and are thus to a great extent dependent on resource and member availability. Meetings may also vary in accessibility, as some are open to family members and those interested in supporting recovery (health professionals), whereas other meetings are 'members only'; and in content, between discussions of the steps, general topic discussions, or recent personal experiences.

1. We admitted we were powerless over alcohol—that our lives had become unmanageable.
2. Came to believe that a Power greater than ourselves could restore us to sanity.
3. Made a decision to turn our will and our lives over to the care of God as we understood him.
4. Made a searching and fearless moral inventory of ourselves.
5. Admitted to God, to ourselves, and to another human being the exact nature of our wrongs.
6. Were entirely ready to have God remove all these defects of character.
7. Humbly asked Him to remove our shortcomings.
8. Made a list of all persons we had harmed and became willing to make amends to them all.
9. Made direct amends to such people wherever possible, except when to do so would injure them or others.
10. Continued to take personal inventory and when we were wrong promptly admitted it.
11. Sought through prayer and meditation to improve our conscious contact with God, as we understood Him, praying only for knowledge of His will for us and the power to carry that out.
12. Having had a spiritual awakening as the result of these steps, we tried to carry this message to alcoholics, and to practice these principles in all our affairs.

Figure 1. The Twelve Steps of Alcoholics Anonymous.

> 1. Our common welfare should come first; personal recovery depends upon AA unity.
> 2. For our group purpose there is but one ultimate authority—a loving God as He may express Himself in our group conscience. Our leaders are but trusted servants; they do not govern.
> 3. The only requirement for AA membership is a desire to stop drinking.
> 4. Each group should be autonomous except in matters affecting other groups or AA as a whole.
> 5. Each group has but one primary purpose—to carry its message to the alcoholic who still suffers.
> 6. An AA group ought never endorse, finance, or lend the AA name to any related facility or outside enterprise, lest problems of money, property, and prestige divert us from our primary purpose.
> 7. Every AA group ought to be fully self-supporting, declining outside contributions.
> 8. Alcoholics Anonymous should remain forever non-professional, but our service centres may employ special workers.
> 9. AA, as such, ought never be organized; but we may create service boards or committees directly responsible to those they serve.
> 10. Alcoholics Anonymous has no opinion on outside issues; hence the AA name ought never be drawn into public controversy.
> 11. Our public relations policy is based on attraction rather than promotion; we need always maintain personal anonymity at the level of press, radio, and films.
> 12. Anonymity is the spiritual foundation of all our traditions, ever reminding us to place principles before personalities.

Figure 2. Twelve AA traditions.

Leighton (2008) addresses a well permeated academic perception of the philosophy and dynamics of Twelve Step programmes, stating that their reference to both the 'disease concept' and to 'spirituality' forges beliefs in the participants of an external locus of control. Some studies have found, however, that this is not the case. Christo and Franey (1995) found in their study of English participants of Narcotics Anonymous that their spiritual beliefs were not related to an external locus of control over their drug use; indeed, participants presented various interpretations of the disease concept and of 'God'. Spiritual beliefs and understanding of addiction as a disease were not prerequisites for attendance, thus their study signalled the multi-layered and complex nature of Twelve Step philosophy and practice, and demonstrated that attendees make sense of such 'higher' concepts in their own infinitely personal way. In the UK, the *Higher Power Project* has explored a variety of definitions and understandings of 'a Power greater than ourselves', illustrating a wide range of non-religious and non-theistic definitions of such from those who have participated in Twelve Step recovery programmes in the UK (Dossett 2013). More recently, Dossett (2017) has pointed out that the troubled interface between professional addiction treatments and Twelve Step fellowships lies partly in the failure of professional treatment bodies to work with the 'spiritual' language of AA. Such terminology, however, is found to be more 'experience-near' (Geertz 1974) to people's day-to-day involvement in recovery than the language of academic and professionalized recovery programmes (e.g., self-efficacy, recovery capital, relapse).

Young adults have the highest rates of substance use disorder in the general population and represent a significant proportion of treatment admissions (Kelly et al. 2014; Knight et al. 2016). Aftercare support is deemed critical to the enhancement of positive outcomes for young people with severe alcohol and other drug problems. A number of studies have reported positive outcomes for young adults participating in the Twelve Step fellowships (Kelly et al. 2014; Kingston et al. 2015; Labbe, Slaymaker and Kelly 2014). Similarly, findings from research in the UK suggest that young adult men derive benefits from engaging with the Twelve Step recovery philosophy, with the installation of hope and development of social networks supportive of their recovery being key features of their successful rehabilitation (Rodriguez-Morales 2017; Rodriguez and Smith 2014). More so, the spiritual aspects of recovery provided participants with a life-structure (or in AA's terms, 'a design for living') that facilitated an existential reorientation of their worldview and of their self-understanding. Through engagement with AA's spirituality and relationships with fellow recovering members, as well as Twelve Step's recovery practices such as journalling, meditation and prayer, participants were introduced to a healthier life-structure[6], free from their addictive substance use behaviour.

Young Men's Recovery in Twelve Step Fellowships

Successful recovery, as observed in this study, encompassed the transformation of a life-world centred on drinking or drug using (or usually, both); this intoxicating world had become so fundamental to participants' selfhoods as young men, that its transition involved paradigmatic shifts in their experience of life. Their experience of daily activities and social relations had to be actively employed and managed by each individual. All participants in this study needed to distance themselves from their former life-structure of a drink and drugs infused self and socialization and begin new daily relationships and activities (e.g., leisure time, getting work qualifications, life skills and newfound spiritual practices) to both replace their previous life-world and reinforce and sustain their new recovery identities. All of these activities imparted a sense of normality and progress in the young men and helped to reinforce their faith in both the desirability and the probability of their successful recovery.

A key conceptual issue that emerged regarding AA's spiritual worldview is *recovery as care of the self*. Participants presented their drug and alcohol abuse as by-products of or indeed as secondary to their problems in self-regulation: capacities for managing feelings, self-esteem, relationships and self-care were in perilous dearth. Drugs and alcohol were used to compensate for deficits in regulating their affective life, enabling the achievement and maintenance of states of feeling, such as soothing and calming themselves, that they could not access on their own; this naturally developed into an unhealthy dependence on such substances. Successful recovery arises as the result of a functioning care of the self, as a worldview. The participants' accounts regularly detailed how their self-care was the salient aspect of their recovery:

> I take better care of myself, I care about my surroundings, simple things like I have a shower every day, I brush my teeth twice a day, I make sure that I eat three meals a day, I pay my bills, yeah I'm paying my bills, I'm not just letting all the letters pile up. I actually open them now and read them ... I feel a lot more alive and healthy and I listen to my body more as well, when I'm tired I think right okay I'm going to sleep before I fight it. (James)

Care of the self here included being concerned with their health, becoming aware of their relational patterns and emotional expressions, and becoming more concerned with revisiting their expectations. Care of the self, as a worldview and life-structure, developed further into participants' recovery, where a focus on maintaining abstinence became less necessary and concern towards their relationships with others came to the fore, as illustrated in the following quotes:

> I want to keep knowing myself and have good relationships. I now really value my relationships. They are the most important thing in my life. (Sean)

> I started to re-evaluate my relationships with people in a lot of ways and look at the reasons, not necessarily with family but the reasons why I might be friends with such person. (James)

> [Recovery] makes me think about people. (Eric)

Participants experienced their new selfhood as being caring and compassionate towards others, and by expressing a healthy relatedness. They have taken on board commitment and responsibility in their relational roles, evidencing a growing psychological maturation. This also illustrates that having achieved a successful recovery and built a secure and satisfying life structure, participants were ready to assume a mentoring role for others, to share their skills and life experiences, for the greater good:

> Being around recovery and combining this with therapy has given me a deep faith in the power of being positive, loving and useful to other people. (Mark)

> I would like to see myself as useful to others. (Danny)

As participants engaged with the Twelve Steps and their recovery activities, such as keeping a journal and praying, they were introduced to practices of self-care. Dan and Tom used writing to gain insight into their drug use:

> Being able to talk about powerlessness and the manageability was very helpful at the start ... I sat with my sponsor, I've read it out and it's like God that's not make believe, this is real. (Dan)

> To write questions like, in what ways have you tried to control your addiction ... what you understand about manageable, how do you know your life is manageable. Like even in step two like it's just not nice to admit those sort of things, it's helpful in terms of working the program but it's not, it's not very pleasant to have to write it down ... But in saying that you know I'd not be feeling free if I hadn't have done it. (Tom)

Keeping a journal and writing facilitates an appraisal of AA's concepts, such as a powerlessness in light of their life story, and works towards the participants' assimilation of the discourse on addiction as a spiritual illness. Writing also facilitates insight into the consequences of their drug use, and the sense of acknowledgement that may be necessary to self-disclose their personal stories. Writing facilitates self-examination (Pennebaker 1990), ameliorating negative feelings of shame and guilt. The importance of gaining self-knowledge and the true worth of disclosing their drug use and drinking stories are both reinforced. The participants recognized the value of going through this challenging but beneficial experience as part of their healing process. Similarly, participants' accounts illustrated how praying has become part of their daily routine:

> The prayer really helps me because it sets me up for the day ... I remember you know [that] I'd taken step three, I made that decision to turn my life over before I've even come in contact with anyone else you know ... it gets me in contact with God. (Mike)

> It depends on specific prayers that you use, that you could use in your fellowship, it depends on what the day's been like ... I went to a cathedral, in fact I got on my knees and I just said a prayer of gratitude and a prayer of thanks and I just said please protect the ones I love from harm and pain ... it's a weird thing I don't know I used to shudder when I heard other people use a prayer, it's the experience of that, it's a beautiful thing really. It's just getting in touch with a higher conscience ... It's trying to sort of hear the words, speaking out loud the words that are personal and getting them out there, I can't put it into words really, it's, it carries a power. (Dan)

Praying enabled the participants to develop a positive mindset towards the world based on AA's recovery values. It gave them a sense of wellbeing and a feeling of gratitude, whilst at the same time relaxing feelings of anxiety through articulation and expression of their suffering. Through prayer, participants also *transact a relationship* with their 'Higher Power'[7]. That is, they enact a dialogue with what they themselves recognized or conceived of as their 'Higher Power' and the principles that come with it.

Some participants defined recovery in terms of an evolving sense of spirituality, often including reference to a 'Higher Power'; participants described developing a more genuine and meaningful spirituality. For instance, in the next quote from Danny, he asserts that the recovery journey has gifted him the opportunity to recover his spirituality and the possibility of revisiting his own preconceptions of religious notions:

> Recovery is the means by which I have re-gained spirituality when I had firmly closed any doors to any possible religiosity. (Danny)

Similarly, participants' accounts illustrate how spirituality is clearly embedded in an ethical stance of care and authenticity, as shown in the following quotes:

> I think spirituality for me is more about sitting down and relaxing you know, and taking that time and thinking about my day and what I could have done better the way I treated people, could I have treated people differently, would I have liked to be treated the way I treat other people and I think that's for me you know a big part of, a big part of the way I want to live my life. (James)

> Sometimes I just need to give myself some time and just hold on. Sometimes I can go deeper and sometimes I back off for a bit. I pray to a God of my own understanding, which I sometimes don't understand. I just feel it and it's alright and it works. (Sean)

As spirituality is a key concept in AA's recovery process, it seems that participants are gradually developing an understanding of recovery as an ethical project; the development of their spirituality is becoming guided and measured by their care towards others, and their concern for a higher ethical conduct. This is sustained by an evolving self-understanding of what it is to be spiritual, which was needed to overcome previous negative experiences around religion.

Participants in this study gave up on their life-world of addiction whilst internalizing new ways of living in recovery which became foundational to their transition into the adult world. Such new ways of being included knowing how to be intimate with others, developing healthy emotional expressions, and authenticity - all demanding fundamental changes in their sense of self and the development of new coping skills. Participants illustrated that greater feelings of authenticity were at the core of their recovery with expressions such as 'recovery above all else it just means being true to yourself', 'my experience now is being me', and 'recovery is like finding your own place in the world'. AA's recovery encourages authentic self-disclosure in the Twelve Step meetings through the sharing of members' stories of recovery. This is also exemplified in AA's one-year anniversary coin, 'To thine own self be true'. Likewise, developing an AA alcoholic identity allowed them entry into a social space that facilitated a new life without substance use. Once they had established a more-or-less stable early recovery, being supported by recovering fellows and community, they were able to address or at least ponder questions concerning their personal development and growth as young adult men; for some, love and intimacy became spoken matters of concern as their recovery progressed.

AA's alcoholic identity continues to be used, however, even when sober or abstinent for years, as it facilitates membership to the group and puts forth the addict identity as a way to frame and explain their addictive behaviours. Most participants referred to an initial conflict around the acceptance of the alcoholic or addict identity; such an acceptance, however, is a foundational element of acknowledging that their addictive behaviour and their selfhood makes up the root of their problem (as opposed to the substance). Some upheld a critical stance about its acceptance, indicating that this identity need only be used when asked about their recovery or when they are attending meetings, but that it need not be their principal identity. Participants more established in long-term recovery (eight years or more) showed that the AA recovery identity does not remain indefinitely meaningful to each individual, who may decide to employ it to a greater or lesser extent. That is, the AA and Twelve Step 'recovery identity' also works through transformations according to participants' normative biographical development (Rodriguez-Morales forthcoming).

The spiritual recovery of AA and Twelve Step fellowships seems to provide a tangible experience of connection that counteracts the existential isolation of the participants, particularly during their early days in recovery. AA's spirituality gives prominence to the development of recovery practices that effectively educate participants in their capacities of self-evaluation and self-regulation (i.e., writing, meditation, prayer). Spiritual practices are ways in which to facilitate a self-transformation - an exercise of self upon the self by which one attempts to develop and transform, in order to attain a certain mode of being and living. AA's recovery programme introduces participants into a new field of meanings and practices that are supportive of the participants' process of *transcending*[8] negative and unhealthy behaviours related to their substance use dependence. The participants' recovery journeys were deeply relational and social in nature, and facilitated by gaining a sense of belongingness, community and identity. Likewise, participants' engagement with AA's recovery facilitated care as a general orientation, and for some this enabled a greater a sense of coherence and wellbeing in their lives. Care had become, as Antonovsky wrote, 'a generalized way of seeing the world and one's life in it' (1987, 22). Similarly, the pragmatic foundation and strong focus on care and the development of healthy habits stand out as perhaps AA's most valuable features. The focus on spiritual practices is consonant with both John Dewey's and William James's psychological conception of habit as the basis of health and wellbeing. The pragmatic conclusion, that we must change our habits if we seek to work on the self, responds to the very practical knowledge that the Twelve Step fellowships promote.

Conclusion

I have explored young adult men's experience of AA and the Twelve Step spiritual recovery in the UK; the study's findings illustrate how this recovery programme introduced the participants to practices of self-care that supported their recovering journey, and facilitated self-transcendence, which was contingent upon developing a new worldview based on values of authenticity, social belonging, and *care*, both of the self and of others. Participants' accounts were examined from a hermeneutical-phenomenological approach in order to understand the spirituality of AA in the context of participants' day-to-day, lived, meaning-making experiences.

Biographical Note

Lymarie Rodriguez-Morales is a mental health practitioner and Lecturer in Psychology based at University of Wales Trinity Saint David. Her research addresses the emotional experiences that underpin recovery and wellbeing, the role of spirituality in mental health, and nature-based health interventions.

Notes

1. A rectified version of Maslow's hierarchy of needs has been proposed by Koltko-Rivera (2006) following a revision of the author's work, in which self-transcendence constitutes the next motivational level after self-actualization. In self-transcendence, a person 'seeks to further a cause beyond the self and to experience a communion beyond the boundaries of the self through peak experience' (303–304).
2. Some excerpts from participants' stories and analyses presented in the chapter first appeared in Rodriguez-Morales (2017), Rodriguez and Smith (2014) and Rodriguez-Morales (forthcoming).
3. Alcoholics Anonymous (1986) states that 'Most of us think this awareness of a Power greater than ourselves is the essence of spiritual experience. Our more religious members call it 'God-consciousness' (568). Although the words 'God' and 'Him' appear frequently in the text of AA, members are invited to substitute the concepts of 'Higher Power', 'Power greater than themselves', 'God of their understanding' and to develop their own meaning of this power.
4. Jung (1961) wrote the following in a letter to Bill Wilson: 'I am strongly convinced that the evil principle prevailing in this world leads the unrecognized spiritual need into perdition, if it is not counteracted either by a real religious insight or by the protective wall of human community'.
5. Wilson (Alcoholics Anonymous 1976, 39) acknowledged that 'The early AA got its ideas of self-examination, acknowledgement of character defects, restitution for harm done, and working with others straight from the Oxford Group and directly from Sam Shoemaker, their former leader in America, and from nowhere else'.
6. Life-structure is defined by Levinson (1978, 41) as 'the underlying pattern or design of a person's life at a given time'.
7. William James (1982 [1902], 464) stated that prayer is the 'very movement of the soul, putting itself in a personal relation of contact with the mysterious power of which it feels the presence – it may be even before it has a name by which to call it'.
8. I am using the word 'transcending' as defined by Ruschmann (2011, 430): '... one could use *transcending* for the process of "stepping beyond the ego boundaries," in all of its aspects, horizontally and vertically, and "transcendence" simply as a term for a "higher reality," of different ontological forms and relationships to the immanent'. Ruschmann also suggests that an alternative world could be 'self-transcendence'.

Bibliography

Alcoholics Anonymous. 1976. *Alcoholics Anonymous Comes of Age: A Brief History of AA*. New York: Alcoholics Anonymous World Services.

Alcoholics Anonymous. 1986. *Alcoholics Anonymous: The Story of How Many Thousands of Men and Women Have Recovered from Alcoholism*. New York: Alcoholics Anonymous World Services.

Alcoholics Anonymous Great Britain. 'First Meeting'. https://www.alcoholics-anonymous.org.uk/members/projects/young-people's-project/first-meeting (accessed May 5, 2017).

Ahluwalia, Gurvinder and Nimona Shaka. 2018. 'Spiritual Wellness and Holistic Personal Growth'. *International Journal of Current Research in Life Sciences* 7 (8): 2531–2535.

Antonovsky, Aaron. 1987. *Unraveling the Mystery of Health: How People Manage Stress and Stay Well*. San Francisco, CA: Jossey-Bass.

Christo, George and Christine Franey. 1995. 'Drug Users' Spiritual Beliefs, Locus of Control and the Disease Concept in Relation to Narcotics Anonymous Attendance and Six-Month Outcomes'. *Drug & Alcohol Dependence* 38 (1): 51–56. https://doi.org/10.1016/0376-8716(95)01103-6

Culpepper, Leslie Dawn. 2016. 'Positive Psychology and Spirituality'. *Journal of Psychology and Clinical Psychiatry* 6 (7): 00407. https://doi.org/10.15406/jpcpy.2016.06.00407

Diener, Ed and Robert Biswas-Diener. 2008. *Happiness: Unlocking the Mysteries of Psychological Wealth*. Boston, MA: Blackwell. https://doi.org/10.1002/9781444305159

Dossett, Wendy. 2013. 'Addiction, Spirituality and 12-Step Programmes'. *International Social Work* 56 (3): 369–383. https://doi.org/10.1177/0020872813475689

Dossett, Wendy. 2017. 'A Daily Reprieve Contingent on the Maintenance of Our Spiritual Condition'. *Addiction* 112 (6): 942–943. https://doi.org/10.1111/add.13731

Finlay, Steven W. 2000. 'Influence of Carl Jung and William James on the Origin of Alcoholic Anonymous'. *Review of General Psychology* 4 (1): 3–12. https://doi.org/10.1037/1089-2680.4.1.3

Geertz, Clifford. 1974. '"From the Native's Point of View": On the Nature of Anthropological Understanding'. *Bulletin of the American Academy of Arts and Sciences*: 26–45. https://doi.org/10.2307/3822971

Gossop, Michael, Duncan Stewart and John Marsden. 2008. 'Attendance at Narcotics Anonymous and Alcoholics Anonymous Meetings, Frequency of Attendance and Substance Use Outcomes after Residential Treatment for Drug Dependence: A 5-Year Follow-Up Study'. *Addiction* 103 (1): 119–125. https://doi.org/10.1111/j.1360-0443.2007.02050.x

James, William. [1902] 1982. *The Varieties of Religious Experience: A Study in Human Nature*. London: Penguin.

Jung, Carl Gustav. 1961. 'Dr. Carl Jung's Letter to Bill W., Jan 30, 1961'. https://silkworth.net/pages/aahistory/general/carljung_billw013061.php (accessed November 2018).

Kassel, Jon D. and Eric F. Wagner. 1993. 'Processes of Change in Alcoholics Anonymous: A Review of Possible Mechanisms'. *Psychotherapy: Theory, Research, Practice, Training* 30 (2): 222–234. https://doi.org/10.1037/0033-3204.30.2.222

Kelly, John F., Robert L. Stout, M. Claire Greene and Valerie Slaymaker. 2014. 'Young Adults, Social Networks, and Addiction Recovery: Post Treatment Changes in Social Ties and Their Role as a Mediator of 12-Step Participation'. *PloS One* 9 (6): e100121. https://doi.org/10.1371/journal.pone.0100121

Kelly, John F., Robert L. Stout and Valerie Slaymaker. 2013. 'Emerging Adults' Treatment Outcomes in Relation to 12-Step Mutual-Help Attendance and Active Involvement'. *Drug and Alcohol Dependence* 129 (1–2): 151–157. https://doi.org/10.1016/j.drugalcdep.2012.10.005

Kingston, Sharon, Emily Knight, Justin Williams and Hannah Gordon. 2015. 'How Do Young Adults View 12-Step Programs? A Qualitative Study'. *Journal of Addictive Diseases* 34 (4): 311–322. https://doi.org/10.1080/10550887.2015.1074506

Knight, Jonathan, Paul Brand, Peter Willey and Justin van der Merwe. 2016. *'Adult Substance Misuse Statistics from the National Drug Treatment Monitoring System (NDTMS): 1 April 2015 to 1 March 2016'*. London: Public Health England.

Koenig, Harold G. 2015. 'Religion, Spirituality, and Health: A Review and Update'. *Advances in Mind - Body Medicine* (Summer):19–26.

Koltko-Rivera, Mark E. 2006. 'Rediscovering the Later Version of Maslow's Hierarchy of Needs: Self-Transcendence and Opportunities for Theory, Research, and Unification'. *Review of General Psychology* 10 (4): 302–317. https://doi.org/10.1037/1089-2680.10.4.302

Kurtz, Ernest. 1991. *Not-God: A History of Alcoholics Anonymous*. Center City, MN: Hazelden Educational Materials.

Labbe, Allison K., Valerie Slaymaker and John F. Kelly. 2014. 'Toward Enhancing 12-Step Facilitation Among Young People: A Systematic Qualitative Investigation of Young Adults' 12-Step Experiences'. *Substance Abuse* 35 (4): 399–407. https://doi.org/10.1080/08897077.2014.950001

Leighton, Tim. 2008. 'How Can We (And Why Should We) Develop Better Models of Recovery?' *Addiction Research & Theory* 15 (5): 435–438. https://doi.org/10.1080/16066350701450849

Levinson, Daniel Jacob. 1978. *The Seasons of a Man's Life*. New York: Random House Digital.

Mäkelä, Klaus. 1991. 'Social and Cultural Preconditions of Alcoholics Anonymous (AA) and Factors Associated with the Strength of AA'. *British Journal of Addiction* 86 (11): 1405–1413. https://doi.org/10.1111/j.1360-0443.1991.tb01726.x

Maslow, Abraham. 1971. *The Farther Reaches of Human Nature*. New York: Viking Press.

Moreira-Almeida, Alexander, Avdesh Sharma, Bernard Janse van Rensburg, Peter J. Verhagen and Christopher C. H. Cook. 2016. 'WPA Position Statement on Spirituality and Religion in Psychiatry'. *World Psychiatry* 15 (1): 87–88. https://doi.org/10.1002/wps.20304

National Institute of Clinical Excellence (NICE). 2013. 'Drug Misuse-Psychosocial Interventions'. http://www.nice.org.uk/guidance/cg51 (accessed August 2018).

Pennebaker, James W. 1990. *Opening Up: The Healing Power of Confiding in Others*. New York: William Morrow.

Peterson, Christopher and Martin E. P. Seligman. 2004. *Character Strengths and Virtues: A Handbook and Classification.* Vol. 1. Oxford, UK: Oxford University Press.

Rodriguez-Morales, Lymarie. 2017. 'In Your Own Skin: The Experience of Early Recovery from Alcohol-Use Disorder in 12-Step Fellowships'. *Alcoholism Treatment Quarterly* 35 (4): 372–394. https://doi.org/10.1080/07347324.2017.1355204

Rodriguez-Morales, Lymarie. Forthcoming. 'A Hero's Journey: Becoming and Transcendence in Addiction Recovery'. *Journal of Psychological Therapies* 4 (2).

Rodriguez, Lymarie and Jonathan A. Smith. 2014. '"Finding Your Own Place": An Interpretative Phenomenological Analysis of Young Men's Experience of Early Recovery from Addiction'. *International Journal of Mental Health and Addiction* 12 (4): 477–490. https://doi.org/10.1007/s11469-014-9479-0

Ruschmann, Eckart. 2011. 'Transcending towards Transcendence'. *Implicit Religion* 14 (4): 421–432. https://doi.org/10.1558/imre.v14i4.421

Smith, Jonathan A., Paul Flowers and Michael Larkin. 2009. *Interpretative Phenomenological Analysis: Theory, Method and Research.* London: Sage.

Solomon, Robert C. 2002. *Spirituality for the Skeptic: The Thoughtful Love of Life.* Oxford, UK: Oxford University Press.

Wilson, Bill and Bob Smith. 1955. 'The Twelve Steps of Alcoholics Anonymous'. *Alcoholics Anonymous: The Story of How Many Thousands of Men and Women Have Recovered from Alcoholism.* New York: Alcoholic Anonymous World Services

Section Four:
Applied Practice

Chapter 9

Religiosity, Spirituality and Wellbeing in the Perception of Brazilian Health and Mental Health Professionals

Marta Helena de Freitas

What for a Calvinist American, a Puritan Englishman or a Catholic Frenchman would be a sign of superstition and even of cynicism or ignorance, is for us a way of expanding our possibilities of protection. It is also, I think, a way of emphasizing this enormous and moving faith that we all have in the meaning and the eternity of life. Thus, these religious experiences are all complementary to one another, never mutually exclusive. (Da Matta 1986, 77)

Introduction

Brazil currently has a population of more than 208 million inhabitants. According to a survey conducted by WIN / Gallup International (Stoychev 2015) Brazil is the second most religious country in Latin America and 11th as the most religious in the world. 79% of people in Brazil consider themselves religious, 16% consider themselves non-religious, only 2% consider themselves atheists and 3% did not respond). Curiously, however, when asked about the role of religion in their country, 81% of the people interviewed (two percentage points more than the percentage of those of consider themselves religious) considered it to have a positive role and only 7% claimed it has a negative role. If this expresses the positions and impressions of the general population, it will be also important to know and understand how similar or divergent they are from the daily perceptions and experiences of Brazilian health professionals, who work in hospital contexts and mental health services in the country.

In fact, daily experience in Brazilian culture has shown how much and how Brazilians generally value religiosity in their lives, even if they do not attend a weekly religious institution or practise rituals of a specific religion. Everyday expressions such as 'Go with God' or 'God be with you', which serve as farewell wishes to someone, or 'I'm fine, thanks be to God' or 'it will improve, God willing' in response to the traditional 'how are you?', are commonplace. They express people's faith in a transcendent dimension that has a protective and propelling role in their lives, ensuring or promoting their wellbeing. On the other hand, it is known that much of this cultural trend in the country, which is generally passed down from generation to generation, becomes an object of criticism during university training, especially in health courses, which aim to prepare the future professional for the technical care for the welfare of the people, through the prevention and treatment of physical or mental illnesses. Thus, professional training in health care, committed to the technical-scientific model, has, for many consecutive decades, tended to relegate issues related to religiousness and spirituality (RS) to the plane of indifference, suspicion, distrust or pathological diagnoses, as pointed out by several authors (Lucchetti et al. 2013; Inocêncio 2010; Freitas 2007).

On the other hand, the scenario of resistance, prevalent in health contexts, has been changing in recent years and the interest and receptivity about the relationship between RS and wellbeing in the context of health education and care has grown significantly. This is evidenced by several systematic surveys of literature (Melo et al. 2015; Foch, Silva and Enumo 2017; Corrêa, Batista and Holanda 2016; Marques and Rigo 2016), as well as in research conducted directly with students and health professionals from the country (Oliveira and Junges 2012; Borges et al. 2013; Pinto and Falcão 2014; Pereira and Holanda 2016). In the specific field of psychology, where the author's perspective is situated, the Working Group (WG) Psychology and Religion, made up of researchers from several Brazilian universities and linked to the National Association of Postgraduate Research in Psychology (NAPRP), has endeavoured to broaden this openness and receptivity to the subject, especially through qualified bibliographic production and the organization of its biennial international seminars. In the last decade, two of them dealt directly with the RS and health interface, addressing the topic Religious Coping and Health (Freitas 2011), and the theme Religious, Spiritual and Anomalous Experiences: Challenges to the Mental Health (available at http://www.pucrs.br/en/blog/international-seminar-on-psychology-of-religion).

One of the fronts of this WG is precisely carrying out research with health professionals, aiming simultaneously (a) to investigate the way in which these professionals have perceived, handled and approached RS with the users of their services; and (b) to enhance the opportunity to share their impressions and experiences on such an ignored topic throughout their training, as well as to accept questions, anguishes and concerns related to the subject. The relevance of this initiative becomes more outstanding due to the peculiarities of the religious characteristics of the Brazilian population, which led the sociologist Roberto DaMatta

(1986, 76) to affirm 'the variety of Brazilian religious experiences is at the same time broad and limited'. The broadness stems from the great variety of influences that have occurred over time; from Roman Catholicism and the various Protestant denominations that were gradually installed in the country, passing through the traditions of the indigenous peoples who lived there before its colonization, African religious traditions, and later the various other Western and Eastern influences. This variety is shown, although timidly, from a statistical point of view, in the last census of the country (Instituto Brasileiro de Geografia e Estatística 2010): the predominance of Catholicism (64.6%), followed by Evangelicalism (22.2%), non-religious (8%), Spiritism (2%), Afro-Brazilian religions (0.3%) and other religions (2.7%). However, in daily life, these distinctions tend not to present themselves in a clearly defined manner. Thus, among those who call themselves Catholics, many share the beliefs of Spiritism or Afro-Brazilian religions. That is to say, in a certain way all these diverse forms tend to coexist with each other, from the idea of direct relation between two worlds—the visible and the invisible, and the possibility of communication of man with the Transcendent and its various designations: God, spirits, ancestors, among others. In Schmidt's anthropological works, examples of this intense communication and the personal bond between men and spirits are richly described (Schmidt 2016).

This chapter presents and discusses some of the main results obtained so far in three umbrella research projects[1] under the coordination of the author. It presents, initially, the relations between the terms of the trinomial concept: spirituality, religiosity and religion, based on the phenomenological perspective. Then, it describes the method used in the umbrella research projects and presents the main results, choosing as a focus the convergent elements in the perceptions and experiences of the professionals regarding the theme of SR in the context of health, as well as some of its specificities. Finally, as a conclusion, we make some general considerations about the implications of these results for health practices and policies committed to the wellbeing of people in Brazil and beyond.

Conceptual Clarifications and Contributions of Phenomenology

The terms spirituality, religion and religiosity tended to appear in a correlated way in studies considered pioneers in Psychology of Religion. For example, in the work of George Albert Coe (1862–1951), entitled *The Spiritual Life* (Coe 1900), he approached the awakening of religiosity, conversion, miraculous healing and the meaning of spirituality, and the last chapter is entitled *A Study of Spirituality* (Coe 1900, 205). From this perspective, we understand religion as a human experience that necessarily involves personal spiritual adherence. This intersection between the two concepts became even more evident when, later, the same author published another work entitled *The Psychology of Religion* (Coe 1916). However, over the last few decades, this initial spontaneous oscillation between the terms has become the object of polarization between different authors, according to Paloutzian (2003), Paiva (2005), Aletti (2012) and Freitas (2017). As Aletti (2012) points out, the dichotomy arises mainly from the idea that the term religion necessarily refers to dogma, indoctrination, institution and orthodoxy; while the term spirituality would refer to personal inner experience, linked to the demands of existential meaning, but in a free and creative way, without being attached to moralistic, standardized and evaluative elements.

The controversies stemming from the conceptual polarization between spirituality and religion have resulted in the renaming of Division 36 of the American Psychological Association (APA), formerly called Society for the Psychology of Religion (Reuder 1999), and today titled Society for the Psychology of Religion and Spirituality (American Psychological Association 2018). But, the reductionism of that polarization has been critically pointed out by several authors such as Paiva (2004), Carrette and King (2005), Koenig (2006, 9-20) and Aletti (2012). It carries the risk of getting lost in an analytical, scientificist, technological and individualizing fragmentation that ends up alienating itself from the fundamental human experience itself. This conceptual polarization gains relevance here precisely because it has gained space in the common language, and not only between psychologists and researchers in Psychology of Religion. Thus, in the context of the three research projects carried out with health professionals, this polarization was therefore avoided, but, at the same time, we remained aware of its possible presence in the discourse of the interviewed professionals and, also, of the specificities and relationships between both terms. For this, the adoption of the phenomenological perspective was fundamental, either to understand the specific dynamicity of each of the three concepts—spirituality, religiosity and religion—and their reciprocal interrelations, or to understand the experience lived by the professional interviewed, communicated by employing one or the other term during the dialogue established with them in the interview.

In a Husserlian perspective, spirituality is understood as a human manifestation exclusively directed 'towards men as persons and to their lives and personal achievements, as well as, correlatively, to the figures of these achievements' (Husserl [1936] 2008). Now, this implies that in order to understand spirituality effectively, one must also understand its impulse to the figures to which it is directed. For a large contingent of the Brazilian population, this figure of achievement is shaped by religious adherence, as shown by a national survey conducted by Moreira-Almeida et al. (2010). As a result of this, even if one takes religion as an institutional organization, which includes beliefs, values, myths and rites related to the question of the Ultimate, integrated in a hierarchical social body— and to which some people adhere—it constitutes, for religious people, the figure by which the search for connectivity triggered by the quest for meaning (which is characteristic of spirituality) is realized. Thus, if spirituality relates to the pole where the question of the meaning of existence is situated, religion relates to the pole where the collectively shared response is situated, within the context of a church, of an institution, of a community or of a culture.

The term religiosity, in turn, will be reserved to designate how each person, in his or her inner experience, organizes this response, based on a belief in a dimension that transcends it. It may even be that the person conceives of the transcendent dimension as an answer to his or her quest for meaning, but may not be an adherent of a specific doctrine or religion, for the way the person conceives of this transcendence may not entirely correspond to the way in which collective responses are organized institutionally. At any rate, it is worth remembering another Husserlian assertion that recognizes, in turn, the intimate connection and interrelation between human experience and the context of life: 'personal life means living in a communal horizon, as a communalized I and we' (Husserl [1936] 2008, 12). That is, the experiences of spirituality, religiosity and religion always present relations with the existential, social and cultural context of the person that experiences it.

Figure 1, reproduced from Freitas and Vilela (2017), seeks to illustrate the dynamism of the relations between the three terms, characterized in the conceptual notions described above and, at the same time making explicit their specificities and interconnections.

Consonant with the phenomenological approach, this way of defining the three terms—religiosity, spirituality and religion—encourages psychologists and mental health professionals to avoid the tendency of associating spirituality with health and religion with pathology. Instead of that, it allows them to discover:

> a way of assessing, with the user himself, what, in his own way of responding to the demands of existential meaning is legitimately anchored in a religion or is only being "suffocated" or at least "molded" by the imposition of a system of responses not genuinely believed or credited by himself (Freitas and Vilela 2017, 97).

Besides that, the proposed model also allows us to qualify both the singularity and the diversity in finding answers to the quest for existential

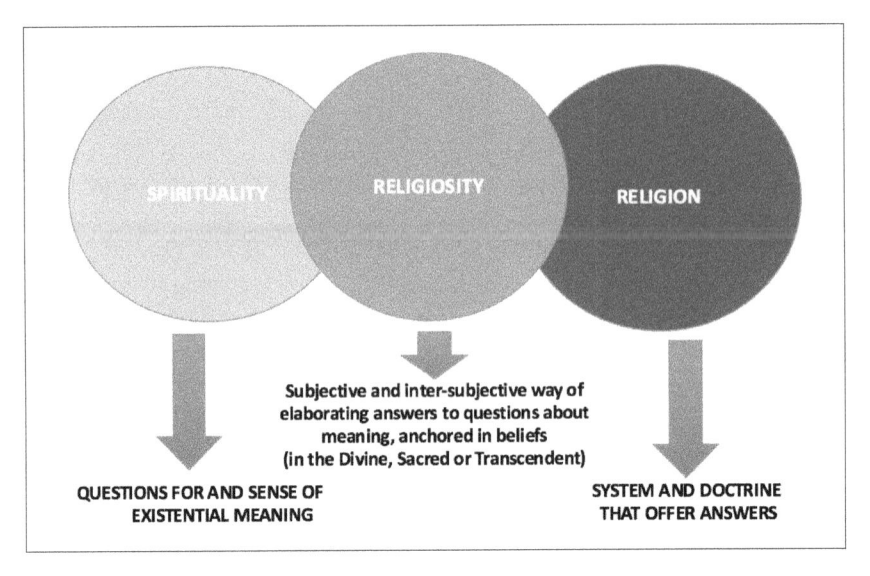

[Diagram: Three overlapping circles labeled SPIRITUALITY, RELIGIOSITY, RELIGION. Arrows below point to:
- SPIRITUALITY → QUESTIONS FOR AND SENSE OF EXISTENTIAL MEANING
- RELIGIOSITY → Subjective and inter-subjective way of elaborating answers to questions about meaning, anchored in beliefs (in the Divine, Sacred or Transcendent)
- RELIGION → SYSTEM AND DOCTRINE THAT OFFER ANSWERS]

Figure 1. Spirituality, Religiosity and Spirituality (reproduced and adapted from Freitas and Vilela 2017, p. 97).

meaning, whether or not they are anchored in a collective system of shared beliefs. To recognize this is fundamental, because the therapist may seek to identify with their patient how much their own belief system has been embraced at the expense of inhibiting their reflective ability about themself and / or the world in which they are situated. Last but not the least, this model also allows us to avoid that the examination of this reflexive capacity is reduced only to the level of rationality, preserving the space for the intuitive and pre-reflexive experiences, for instance, the contact with the sacred, characterized by Pargament (1996) as the connection with ancestors, mystery, hope, surrender, divine purpose, redemption and so on.

Method

Consistent with the phenomenological perspective, the three studies followed an essentially qualitative methodology.[2] A total of 158 professionals were interviewed in their own working contexts, distributed as follows:

(a) According to country region: 68 from the Federal District (Centre-West Region of the country), 21 from Maranhão (Northeast Region), 26 from Rio de Janeiro (Southeast Region), 14 from Rio Grande do Sul (South Region) and 29 from Tocantins (North Region).

(b) According to the place of activity: 102 working in general hospitals and 56 acting in Psychosocial Care Centres (CAPS)[3.]
(c) According to profession: 30 social workers, 47 nurses, 28 doctors, 50 psychologists and three occupational therapists.
(d) According to gender: 36 men and 122 women.

The age range of the interviewees ranges from 30 to 60 years, with a mean of approximately 40 years. All had at least one year of experience in their field of work, with a general average of six years of experience, since many had been in the field for more than 20 years. The average time since their graduation (conclusion of university course) was around 15 years.

Professionals experienced in conducting phenomenological interviews, or duly trained for this, conducted the interview according to a semi-structured script, contemplating the following themes:

(a) Demographic data, previous experiences and specific experience in current context of action.
(b) Context of action (institutional principles, characteristics of the unit, services offered, characteristics of users, routine activities).
(c) How users bring up or demonstrate religiosity and spirituality (RS) related issues in that context (with reports of examples to illustrate that).
(d) Perceptions of professionals about these manifestations and their relationship to health (physical or mental).
(e) How they deal with RS in the context of their actions.
(f) What they consider good or bad practices in the course of handling RS in that context.
(g) Connections or distinctions between their religious / spiritual experience and psychopathology (in the specific case of those who work in the Psychosocial Care Centres).
(h) How they live their own RS experience.
(i) If and how the theme was approached throughout their training.
(j) How they acquired the skill of handling RS in the context of the work place.

With the consent of each interviewee and interviewer, all the interviews were recorded, transcribed, revised and became part of the database of the 'Religion, Mental Health and Culture' Laboratory, coordinated by this author and linked to the Psychology *Stricto Sensu* Post-Graduate of the Catholic University of Brasília—UCB. The analysis of the interviews occurred according to the empirical-phenomenological method proposed by Giorgi (2011, 2012), with priority given to the descriptive processes (based on intuitive rationality modes) about the RS phenomenon as perceived and shared in the interviews by the participants of the three surveys. This process involves three stages, in the course of which each interview is read several times to identify units of meaning (Giorgi 2009). In the first stage, the readings aim to identify, distinguish and retain psychological sensitive meaning, according to the language of each interviewee, as expressed during the interview. In the second stage, each one of these retained expressions is transformed into other expressions that reveal more directly and explicitly the psychological aspect of the given phenomenon (Giorgi 2012). In a third stage, a synthesis of the units of meaning is created, transforming them into phrases that consistently combine the main ideas expressed in the previous ones. Hereby, each unit of meaning can be identified by a consistent wording of the psychological structure of the phenomenon, resulting in a solid declaration on a 'structure of experience', expressed at various levels of profundity and detail.

After the completion of these three stages, it was possible to compare the common or similar (i.e., convergent) and the particular and/or different (i.e., divergent) aspects, perceptions and experiences among all the interviewees and also between those working in general hospital and those working in mental health contexts. The main results of this analysis are presented in the following section.

Perceptions and Experiences of Health Professionals—The Lived Experience Captured in Act

Talking about Religiosity and Spirituality in the Context of Health Work
Being invited to talk about the subject of SR in a work context was very unusual in the experience of practically all the professionals covered in the three surveys. The initial reactions to this experience were far from unanimous. There were those who refused to take part in the research, though quite an insignificant number (most commonly physicians and social workers), even those who interpreted the invitation as a kind of 'sign', through which they would be called upon to come back to an experience they had shunned for years, which was making them 'sceptical' and 'emptied' (this happened with psychologists, doctors, and nurses). There were those who were very tense at the beginning and much more at ease at the end of the interview (more common among nurses), as well as those who, during the course of the interview, were more discreet about some subjects (especially in relation to their own religiosity) but at the end of the interview, after turning off the tape recorder, spoke in a more spontaneous manner, revealing their own religious and spiritual beliefs and experiences more naturally, or expressing their real opinions

about various situations experienced in the work context. There were also those, especially among psychologists, who were so touched during the interviews, to the point of bursting into tears or convulsive crying.

The reactions pointed out above show that, far from being indifferent to them, the subject of RS intensely sensitizes health professionals, mobilizing feelings and attitudes of rejection, doubt, uncertainty and insecurity, but also hope, faith and confirmation of existential meaning. And contrary to popular belief that doctors tend to be atheists or averse to spirituality, experience in all three surveys does not support this. So much so that among the 28 doctors interviewed, only two of them were more sceptical and completely alien to any kind of spiritual or religious activity. Even so, one of them revealed, as the interview unfolded, that what he felt was in fact a kind of 'anger' and 'revolt' against God since the death of his wife, for whom he had true worship, and who died very early. He showed that this anger is deepened every time he encounters misery and suffering around him, and therefore questions the goodness and justice of God. The contradiction of his scepticism is evidenced when he also affirms that he has made a kind of agreement with God: that of helping all the needy around him and, in turn, receiving from Him health and the grace of not being sick or bedridden, depending on other people to be taken care of.

Considerations like the one described above and many others, taken from the interviewees' statements, are in line with Vergote's (1966, 1983) propositions about the conflicts that build faith. In this sense, the clash between science and faith is not exactly what most affects the way in which these professionals perceive and experience RS, but, much more, psychological variables, as shown by the doctor's speech which we reproduce verbatim below:

> ... I have some difficulty believing, right? ... in miracles, in these things ... although, I ... in my heart, I recognize that we need God. In our human frailty, we need God. But, I needed a more concrete God, a God closer to me, a God closer. I find Him very far away. It's up to Him to forgive me, you know? But I needed Him to help more.

Thus, the fact that some health professionals have refused to grant an interview about RS in their work context does not authorize us to interpret the gesture as mere disinterest or distance from the subject at hand. After all, the refusal can rightly point out how much it impacts their affections which are not always easy to express, share and elaborate. In this sense, an avoidance of talking about the subject also means protecting oneself from contact with susceptibilities or from the risks of revealing one's frailties.

Religiosity and Spirituality in the Clinical Context

In addition to the high degree of mobilization in the face of this theme, another convergent factor among the interviewees was the reference to the different ways in which the RS of the patients (or of the patient's family members) are present in their daily context, whether in hospitals or CAPS. In this way, all of them reported the presence of objects considered sacred accompanying the patients in the infirmaries (bibles or gospels, crucifixes, images, Ribbons of the Lord of Bonfim[4], rosaries, medals of Our Lady or Jesus Christ, incense, Spiritism messages, among others), especially in the hospital context. They also referred to the prayers performed by patients or relatives, often inviting or involving other patients who occupy the same ward or hospital corridor (in the case of general hospitals) or requesting the initiation or termination of a group activity with The Lord's Prayer or Hail Mary (in the case of the CAPS). The references to RS are also frequent as reactions to diagnosis, showing gratitude to God when there is news of healing of some disease or faith and hope in healing when facing a serious illness. Thus expressions such as 'God will heal me' or 'I am a person of faith, I know that I will receive a grace from God' have been reported as common examples in the reaction of patients and family members in the face of an unfavourable diagnosis. Religious expressions also appear when visits from religious leaders were requested and received, and these leaders would often perform the rituals of their doctrine in the infirmary itself.

In CAPS, it was common for professionals to report that during group sessions, many patients describe their participation in religious activities during the week—they either ask to sing a hymn of their church during the sessions, or reveal the search for alternative treatment for their problems in specific religious communities, as a complement to what they received from health professionals. In these cases, eventually, the guidance received from the religious leaders may confront those received there. In this way, the health professionals who work at CAPS were almost unanimous in reporting that some patients stop taking psychiatric medications after hearing from the pastor that they would be cured by their faith in Jesus and not by the drugs. Also in this context, it was unanimously reported that RS is very frequent also in the delusional and hallucinatory contents of psychotic patients.

Some of the interviewees' statements were particularly curious because they denote the forcefulness with which RS can manifest itself in the hospital context, given the deep suffering those patients and relatives find themselves in and that sometimes lead them to break the limits and frameworks set by institutional standards. In this sense, it is worthwhile to illustrate here two paradigmatic examples: one reported by several professionals of a hospital in Tocantins, in the northern region of the country, and another reported by a psychologist at a hospital in Brasilia, the capital of the country, located in the Centre-West region.

In the first case, this happened in a children's hospital, where the hospitalization of indigenous children is very common. In this context, some professionals have reported that the families of these children often seek to bring their own healing rituals into the ward, which may involve dancing, smoking, smoking of cigars, and other procedures not authorized by the hospital for reasons of hygiene, routine, organization and asepsis. The families of the children tend to resist this limitation and often camp in the vicinity of the hospital, performing their rituals. On one occasion, the hospital staff were caught unawares by a campfire set up inside the infirmary, which provoked fright and commotion among the team and other users in the face of the danger that this represented for all. In addition to the risks of fire, there was also the risk of suffocation, contamination and burns to other children in that corridor's wards.

In the case of the hospital in Brasília, one of the psychologists interviewed also reported that it is common for some patients of different religions to request that rituals are performed in the hospital, which, according to their belief, aid healing and give spiritual protection. However, the hospital places some limits on the kinds of rituals permitted, for example, not allowing the lighting and smoking of cigars inside the wards and not allowing burning of candles. The psychologist reported the case of a patient who was in a grave condition and had to undergo a delicate surgery. The patient's brother, who was an evangelical pastor, visited every day, and sought to persuade her to convert to his religion so that she could be 'healed' and be 'saved'. To this effect, she needed to be baptized and the baptism ritual involved being immersed in water. The sister agreed, but in keeping with the hospital rules, the baptism was not authorized and she underwent surgery without the proposed baptism. The surgery went well and the sister returned to the infirmary while recovering but still in serious condition, which demanded much care. Taking advantage of the intervals between the visits of the nursing team, her brother entered the infirmary with a small inflatable pool and filled it with water from the bathroom to baptize his sister. When the nurse returned to the infirmary and saw the patient, still with the surgical dressings and stitches, completely immersed in the pool, and her brother preaching aloud the words of Christ according to the rituals characteristic of his Church, a great uproar commenced inside the hospital, and the entire team of that shift was mobilized, trying to hold the young man down, take the patient out of the water, and perform the asepsis of surgery and other cares. The patient did not recover and passed away a few days later.

Extreme situations such as those described above illustrate the complexity of the place occupied by health professionals. For them, reflecting on the theme of RS in the hospital and/or mental health context is not only about the generic character or the personal meaning of their own subjective experience. In this context, their experiences are also and necessarily marked by their responsibilities in the care of the health of others. At this crossroads, they face two demands that do not always complement each other: one of an existential order and the other of a professional order. Perhaps, because of that, from the start, when they seek to answer the question about how RS appears in the context of their performance, none of them restricts themself to just describing how patients bring RS to the hospital or the CAPS. Everyone is almost immediately ready to evaluate how this occurs and how it impacts the health or treatment offered by the staff and the institution. In this way, the vast majority, before being asked about the relationships that are perceived or not between RS and health, already talks about them.

Dealing with the Relationships Between Religiosity, Spirituality and Health
The professionals were unanimous in pointing out positive relationships between RS and health, highlighting the following aspects: promoting faith and hope in healing, good relationship with the team, adherence to treatment, serenity to face the illness, coping with the adversities that accompany the process of being ill and being hospitalized, a sense of life and existential strengthening, as well as other consequences of RS that they consider favourable to health and treatment. But they also mentioned negative relations in both contexts, hospitals and CAPS, especially when religious life is accompanied by rigidity, alienation from treatment, disregard of health, rituals harmful to wellbeing, denial of disease or death, the family's refusal to allow the donation of organs (in the case of brain death), refusal to comply with the clinical procedures indicated by the doctor (e.g., in case of unauthorized blood transfusions for religious reasons), literal interpretation of the sacred texts often accompanied by delusions and religious hallucinations, and so on.

On expressing the way they perceive RS in the context of health, the vast majority of respondents demonstrated ignorance of the contemporary literature concerning the subject, focusing primarily on their own clinical experience. Psychologists eventually came to use expressions such as 'spiritual coping' or 'religious coping' to refer to the role of religiosity in dealing with illness, demonstrating that they had some contact with the term introduced by Pargament (1990, 1997) in the field of Health Psychology, who has been in Brazil a few times in recent years, participating in events in this area. Among those of psychoanalytic formation, the reference to faith, spirituality and religious beliefs as manifestations of 'defence mechanisms'[5] was frequent enough, characterized as a protection for the weakened self in the face of illness and death.

The term most commonly used by respondents of all professional categories and in both hospital and CAPS contexts, in response to the question about how they deal with their patients' RS manifestation was 'respect'. Respect for the vast majority of them means not judging, not imposing one's religion, not giving a value judgment, or trying to change the belief of the patient or family member. And many of them, in making this explicit, make references to the code of professional ethics itself or to the principle of secularity of the State. A minority emphasizes that respecting patients' beliefs goes further, by adding other more proactive initiatives such as: stimulating RS when they feel it can help patients or their family members to cope with the illness or cope with the loss; to know the religious option of the patient and of the patient's family in order to act in harmony with it (in specific clinical procedures or in the preparation of the deceased patient's body); to identify, right from the moment of the patient's admittance to hospital, not only what his or her religion is, but also how much it offers him or her some social support network that could be useful during treatment and social insertion initiatives. These latter alternatives have been reported by a few psychologists from several states. It was also reported by occupational therapists and social workers in São Luis, capital of Maranhão (a Brazilian state located in the northeast of the country).

In spite of a significant predominance in the professionals' discourse of being respectful in their way of handling RS, avoiding influencing patients and their families with their own values, many of them have revealed that in some situations they seek to place limits on religious manifestations, especially when they think that they can be harmful to their physical or mental health. These limits are placed not only when religious rituals can compromise routine and hospital asepsis, as previously reported, but also in several other situations, such as: when, for religious reasons, relatives refuse to authorize the donation of organs of a patient with brain death; when a child needs a blood transfusion, but for religious reasons, the parents do not authorize the procedure; when there is resistance from the patient attending the CAPS to adhere to the medication indicated by the psychiatrist due to the orientation given by a pastor of their Church; and so on. Here, there is a paradox, and a crossover of and a friction between different positions: on the one hand, a commitment to the principle of secularity of the State—which motivates the value standard of respect for the religious diversities characteristic of this culture—and, on the other, the position of a medical-hospital institution—which tends to put the value of life/survival in the foreground and what, from a technical-scientific perspective, is understood as wellbeing. This condition also makes the subject to be considered by a majority of the professionals very delicate and sometimes difficult to manage in the context of their clinical work.

Management of Religiosity and Spirituality in the Health Context: Good and Bad Practices

When invited to characterize what they consider to be good and bad practices in the management of RS of patients in hospitals or CAPS, the term respect again is very prevalent in the discourse of health professionals from all professional categories, reaching 100% of convergence as synonymous with good practice. The specificities appear in the way they describe what a respectful management is. For some, discretion is fundamental and that means not talking about this topic, and if the patient brings it up spontaneously, they consider that one should only listen, sometimes even change the subject, but without interfering or making judgments. For others, respect means more than this, because it also implies legitimizing the experience, sometimes even stimulating it if it enhances wellbeing, faith, hope and existential meaning. These positions were more common among nurses and psychologists. Among the latter, there was eventually a reference, as good practices, to the discernment of the modalities of religious coping, recommending an intervention that helps to enhance positive coping and to demote negative ones. There was also a reference to the importance of RS as a promoter of a social network, indicating it as a good practice to take into account the role of this network and stimulate the social insertion of users, especially in the context of mental health.

Bad practices, by way of contrast, were mainly pointed out as the tendency to impose their own religious values, and there were reports and references to situations in which this type of practice was observed in the hospital context and in the context of mental health. These issues have been more pronounced, with very significant reports, in some specific units, such as services for the care of victims of sexual violence, where, according to the legislation of the country, victims are free to opt for legal abortion. In this context, for example, a social worker reports as an example of bad practice the case of a doctor who, when she saw that a patient was already on the stretcher to perform the clinical procedures for abortion, railed a religious discourse on her, and this generated a situation of much suffering for the patient and great confusion in the medical team.

Less commonly, but relatively common among psychologists, was to point out as a bad practice the absence of an attitude of listening to and welcoming of the religious beliefs of the patients by the professional in the name of a technical discourse, delegitimizing or devaluing what, for the other, is a bearer of existential meaning and promoter of strength, meaning and coping with suffering. Even among psychologists with psychoanalytic training, there was reference to this protective role of RS, considering that these 'defence mechanisms' should not be simply 'dismantled' in the name of a medical, technical and objective discourse.

Distinctions Between Spiritual Experience and Psychopathology
Specifically, with the professionals who work at CAPS, the theme of possible distinctions between spiritual experience and psychopathology, as well as the criteria adopted by them, was addressed. Interestingly, the experiences shared by professionals showed that, although the criteria of form and content still predominate in their conceptions, in line with the principles of classical psychopathology, 100% of professionals (from all areas represented in the research) made references to religious delusions; the great majority also pointed to the criteria of the 'functionality' of religious experience and its suitability or not to the religious values of a community and culture.

In addition, many of them shared situations in which this distinction is not fully assured, either from a technical point of view or from a functional point of view, with references to situations where they have experienced doubts, such as in cases in which the patient or family member reports or experiences *in loco* the 'possession' of spirits. This is illustrated in the vignette below, retained from an interview with a psychologist from São Luis, Maranhão:

> Now I'm going to tell you an issue, it's a very tenuous relationship! ... (...) Because some patients ... they visibly have an issue, for example, it's ... a delusion, something like that, which is visible. But there are other patients, or at least some who I have seen, who bring this very strong spiritual issue; they say, 'no, it's a real spirit, I've already been ...', for example, a patient reported, 'Ah, I've already been in Codó[6] ... I wanted to turn away the spirits'. And some are looking for an evangelical church to do that, and they cannot do that ... (...) I see a very difficult relationship! Why? The health team, the team professionals do not take that into account in any way. I realize that. I feel a bit of difficulty with this ... (...) because I also think the patient has a spiritual side, I think, I do not bring this at all during my clinical care ... (...) but I believe in the spiritual side. (...) ... a question of religion and spirituality, but I think yes, that some patient could also be taken into consideration for that. And those who believe could also be heard; they sometimes need to be heard. And they are not. (...) I think sometimes it is very strong

the question of everything being diagnosed, everything is 'arrived, saw something, passed some form, something of that type, is schizophrenia, heard a voice, it is hallucination!'. I do not know, it depends a lot on the belief of each one and the situation of that patient. And, I particularly, I ... I would listen a little more to them, in some questions ...

However, there were also those who were quite sceptical about the risks of confusion between a religious interpretation and a scientific interpretation, clearly marking the role of the professional, who must be essentially committed to the latter. In this case, the mental health professional tends to be very critical of some religious or spiritual experiences, as is illustrated in the vignette below, from an interview with a psychiatrist from São Luis, Maranhão:

I don't see much comparison. The only comparison I see is that the more religious patients, whatever religion they are in the moment they freak out, for instance, that they have a psychotic outbreak, it becomes very latent in the psychiatric ... (...) When the patient is very attached to a religion, usually the voices he hears are mystical, mystical voices, as I told you, right? It's the only parallel I see. And these voices say, they are religious, they tell the patient that he doesn't need to take medicine, that religion itself will cure him, or that if he is a Umbandist, it is a macumba[7] that was made for him, and so on, it depends a lot on the religion he follows. This is very latent in the psychotic picture mainly. (...) What I see is that when the patient comes a virgin of medication, but a spiritual treatment, the disease is more exacerbated, and because it has mixed the psychiatric illness with that religious work. So it comes more accentuated, it's the only experience I've had.

The different perceptions registered in both previous examples illustrate also that while some of the Brazilian mental health professionals recognize that diagnostic criteria are culturally determined, in consonance with what is argued by different authors (Vieten and Scammel 2016; Amarante and Torre 2017) and institutions (Word Health Organization 2018; Brasil, Ministério da Saúde[8] 2015), others, specially some psychiatrists, seem to see the Diagnostic and Statistical Manual of Mental Disorders (DSM) as the only or the main way of correctly explaining dysfunctional behaviour. The first ones tend to consider, in their speech about psychopathology and religious or spiritual experiences, that mystical experience and spiritual emergencies (for instance, communications with spirit guides; possessions states; and so on) are not the same as psychotic symptoms, although they may reach such levels of intensity and duration that they become similar to mental dysfunctions. This is in consonance with what it is recommended by Vieten and Scammel (2016) as one important competence for mental health professionals: even if these kinds of religious or spiritual manifestations are grounds for concern and care, they may not be confused with delusions and hallucinations and diagnosed as such.

The Skill to Deal with Religiosity and Spirituality: Personal Dimension and the Role of Professional Training

In relation to the previous topic, once again, we have observed the consequences of the challenging friction between the personal dimension, as a person who also believes and has his or her specific spiritual and religious propensities, and the role occupied in that context of performance, where his or her posture needs to be committed to scientific and institutional parameters. In this process, the 'solutions' to dealing with the challenge, are quite complex and there is no shortage of references, direct or indirect, to the conflicts, ambiguities, anxieties, doubts and existential questions that arise from this. After all, as mentioned before, the vast majority of respondents revealed belief in some transcendent dimension and belonged to some religion: Catholic—more frequent, evangelical—also common, or Spiritist, Afro-Brazilian, Buddhist, among others less common. There were also, in particular among doctors and psychologists, those who in the past were very religious, but who, as they went about their formation and professional activity, were moved away from ecclesiastical institutions, becoming more sceptical, but without completely 'extirpating' RS from themselves.

However, regardless of whether or not they moved away from the religious institution and regardless of what religion they professed, the majority of professionals interviewed, especially among doctors, psychologists and social workers, converged in the answer to the question of whether and how the subject was approached throughout their training. Their answers show that, although very present in their daily activities, subjects related to RS were not treated in specific undergraduate subjects. When eventually mentioned, these topics appeared loaded with pejorative, pathological or pronounced connotations in joking tones. Among nursing professionals, it was more common to mention that the subject was eventually approached blandly, especially in professional ethics disciplines or in disciplines dealing with procedures in case of death, where the patient's religiosity had to be taken into account in the process of 'packing' a corpse, among other measures. Several psychologists and a few physicians also mentioned that, although the subjects were silenced during university training, they were later approached in specialization courses, mainly in oncology, hospital psychology, palliative care or gerontology.

A surprising aspect of the research results was the way health professionals claimed to have developed the skills to deal with RS in their respective contexts of action, since the subject tended to be silenced throughout formal training. A significant number of them, in all areas, including psychology, responded that when they began to encounter spiritual and religious manifestations in their practical experience they had to find answers in an almost solitary way. In this process, they emphasized the fundamental role of their personal, religious and family formation, where they could find an anchorage to adopt a sympathetic and welcoming attitude to the spiritual and religious experiences of others, even when these were different from their own. Noteworthy here, and seemingly specific to Brazilian culture, it is the manifestation of something being assimilated by health professionals—their openness to a kind of complementarity, characterizing a tendency towards integration, as described by DaMatta (1986): 'Religious language in our country is, therefore, a language of relation and of connection. A language that seeks the middle ground, the half way, the possibility to save everyone and everywhere to find something good and dignified' (DaMatta 1986, 79). This tendency towards the search for conciliation is a characteristic of the culture, that is still shown in another quite frequent response among the interviewees: that the strategies to deal with their patients' RS were constructed through a summation between what was received from their undergraduate course, what was passed on by their family, what was assimilated in the religion itself and what has been developed during the clinical experience itself. A minority brings a more rational response, reporting that they sought out training on their own account, with a self-taught approach, participating in events, attending complementary training and specialization courses, where they could supply themselves with what was lacking about the subject during graduation.

Conclusion

The perceptions and experiences shared by the professionals during the interviews allow us to conclude that, although relations between RS and health are being contemplated in research and academic productions in Brazil and around the world, a possible integration of this literature as well as the religious experiences of the users themselves, from health services to formal care in hospitals and CAPS, has not yet reached a minimum of systematization and institutional place. The practices that have been reported to us are, in most cases, actions that are disconnected, not recognized or not authorized institutionally. They do not come to characterize a consistent—diverse but integrated—mosaic of initiatives and strategies that are legitimately or formally backed by the humanization guidelines proposed by the country health regulations (Freitas, Turra and Zaneti 2016), despite the evident effort by professionals to give effective answers to the questions that come to them every day in hospitals and mental health services.

The situation described above is particularly colourful in view of the various frictions to which the professional is exposed: on the one hand, immersed in a diverse culture, where different forms of religious manifestations coexist—from Catholicism to Protestantism, from Orisha to Shamanism, from the Western points of view to Eastern cultures; on the other hand, with a professional formation in health that did not contemplate this diversity, and acting in institutions still committed to hegemonic models of health, without effective space for the real integration of issues of cultural, religious, ontological and spiritual nature. The paradox is then constituted when, simultaneously, professionals defend the position of respect for diversity and the integration of knowledge, recognizing in them the potential of good practices, but also showing themselves as reproducers of the medical paradigm, committed to enforcing their norms, their parameters and their rules of asepsis, in the concrete and symbolic sense of the term.

Given this scenario, the development of skills to deal with the spiritual and religious manifestations of the users of health services is entirely in the hands of individual initiatives of the health professionals themselves. In this process, the effort towards an integrative perspective, and even pointed to by themselves as an ideal of good practices, finds anchorage in the 'connecting' culture itself, to use DaMatta's (1986) expression. This cultural characteristic is revealed in the effort of an aggregating and complementary view between the different religions and, more than that, between what has been learned through family, technical-scientific formation, personal religion and clinical experience, with the patients themselves and health services users. In any case, as we have seen, this does not exempt them from experiencing conflicts, doubts and insecurities and paradoxes in the face of such a mobilizing theme. As such, it does not constitute a guarantee of a practice entirely in line with the principles of Humanization of SUS (Unified Health System, the Brazilian universal health care system) and the guidelines of the Psychiatric Reform.[9] That is, it is necessary to invest in training initiatives where the theme of RS is in fact the object of attention, study and reflection, so that it reverts to consistent, systematic and formally institutionalized practices in the Brazilian health system, as well as the other countries.

Despite the specificities of the Brazilian context, as pointed out above, some aspects of the reality in this country is similar to others.

For instance, although there is a rich literature, many papers and books on spirituality and health in the North American context, Koenig (2012), when discussing the clinical implications of this literature, emphasizes that, ideally, in a hospital context, the doctor should take the spiritual history of their patients. That would be one of his attributions. However, only about 10% of physicians in the US usually do that. They tend to leave this task to nurses and social workers. But, even though there is a research lacking in this area, the author believes that 'most nurses and social workers do not take a spiritual history either' and 'simply recording the patient's religious denomination and whether they want to see a chaplain, the procedure in most hospitals today, is NOT taking a spiritual history' (Koenig 2012, 14). That is only one of many examples. It should be pointed out here that the technical professional health competencies in this area is still precarious in the world in general.

It is very relevant here to consider the contributions of Vieten and Scammel (2016), recalling the distinction they made between competence and proficiency as regards the way of handling religiosity and spirituality in clinical context. They consider competence as a general 'set of attitudes, knowledge, and skills in the domains of spirituality and religion that all clinicians should have in order to effectively and ethically' practise in the health context. 'Proficiency, on the other hand, refers to a high degree of expertise or skill'. Considering these distinctions, it is possible to recognize that health professionals, in general (as seen in this and other researches in the health context of many other countries), eventually have some natural competences. However, this is not as a result of some specific professional training they have received on the subject, but rather, due to their personal and clinical experiences over the years in the health context which have made them more sensitive to these issues. There is the need to elaborate manuals for newly trained and unexperienced clinicians in several health areas, as have done the cited authors for psychotherapists and mental health professionals, so as to help them develop skills to handle this delicate and challenging subject. But, it is also necessary to consolidate specific policies, around the world, for hospitals and mental health services, that offer conditions for professionals to act based on specific competencies regarding relationships between religiosity, spirituality and health. These hospitals and mental health services need also to include in the professional team specialists who have specific proficiency in this matter. This will be very necessary especially in cases where medical and psychological competences on their own are not enough to follow up patients that need more qualified services regarding religious or spiritual experiences that deeply affect their health.

Biographical Note

Marta Helena de Freitas has been a professor at the Catholic University of Brasilia—UCB, since 1989. She is a psychologist with a Masters in Social Psychology and Personality and a PhD in Psychology from the University of Brasilia; Post-Doctoral in Psychology of Religion, University of Kent at Canterbury, UK; in Culture Psychology, University of Oporto, Portugal; and in Anthropology of Religion, Alister Hardy Religious Experience Centre, University of Wales Trinity Saint David, Lampeter, UK (in progress). Her research covers: psychology of religion, thanatology, gerontology, the Rorschach psychodiagnostic, phenomenology, training in psychology and mental health. Marta Helena de Freitas is Coordinator of the Psychology and Religion Working Group of the National Association of Post-Graduation and Research in Psychology—ANPEPP, and a member of the International Association for the Psychology of Religion—IAPR.

Acknowledgement

The author is grateful to the team of researchers of the Religion, Culture and Mental Health Laboratory linked to the Post-Graduate Programme in Psychology of the Catholic University of Brasília, who collaborated in the projects that resulted in this chapter, especially to the Doctorate degree student, Emmanuel Ifeka Nwora for its final revision.

Notes

1. Identification of the three umbrella research projects:
   a) Religiosity and Spirituality in the Hospital Context: perception of multi professional teams (RESCH); funded by the National Council of Development in Science and Technology (CNPq) and the Ministry of Science, Technology, Innovation and Communications (MCTIC), through the Spontaneous Demand Announcement 2013.
   b) Religiosity of the Immigrant—Health or Symptom: perceptions of Brazilian and Portuguese mental health professionals (RISS); funded by Santander Universities (Phase I) and CNPq / MCTIC (Phase II), through the Universal Announcement 2014.
   c) Mental Health in Psychosocial Care Centres: perceptions of professionals about the role of religiosity (RESMCAPS), funded by the Foundation for Research Support of the Federal District (FAP-DF), through the Spontaneous Demand Announcement 2015.
2. The three research projects were carried out in the context of health professionals, with the prior authorization of hospital institutions or health services and after submission and approval of their respective Research Ethics Councils.
3. CAPS is a modality of mental health service implemented in the country since the Psychiatric Reform, constituting a place of reference for treatment and follow-up of people suffering from mental disorders, replacing the former

hospital-centred and asylum model. It functions as a daily, interdisciplinary, personalized device and promoter of family and social integration in the communities where it is inserted, linked to the Unified Health System—SUS (Brasil, Ministério da Saúde, 2004).

4. A ribbon of the Lord of Bonfim is a coloured ribbon, which is a lucky charm, originally typical of the city of Salvador in the State of Bahia, but now spread all over the country. It is usually attached to the wrist or ankle, accompanied by a request addressed to Lord of Bonfim, and allowed to wear out naturally over time for the request to be granted. Tradition holds that the use of these ribbons comes from the ancient custom of wearing strips of clothing of saints for luck or protection.

5. In psychoanalyses, the expression 'defence mechanism' is used, since Freud, to refer to an unconscious psychological mechanism that reduces anxiety arising from unacceptable or potentially harmful stimuli. A defence mechanism may result in healthy or unhealthy consequences depending on the circumstances and frequency with which the mechanism (denial, projection, regression, reaction formation, rationalization, sublimation, and so on) is used. Strictly speaking, in each defence mechanism there is a complex psychic process that aims to remove an ego-generating event of anxiety from conscious perception.

6. Codó is a city in Maranhão, Brazil, very rich in religious rituals of indigenous and Afro-Brazilian traditions. It has therefore already been represented by contemporary media as the 'World Capital of Sorcery' and the 'Black Magic' (Lindoso, 2014).

7. Macumba is a type of spiritual practice in some African-Brazilian religions, as well is a term to nominate witchcraft.

8. In the fifth volume of its thematic and periodic journal on National Humanization Policy (PNH), published in 2015, the Ministry of Health in Brazil, through the Secretariat of Health Care, devoted itself to systematizing the experiences and debates that the Psychiatric Reform (PR) has produced in the country. The title of this volume—Humanization and Mental Health: Humanized Care is Care in Freedom— as well as the content of the articles, experience records and various reports, clearly establishes the institutional commitment to a comprehensive, humanized health system for the population that suffers psychic disorder. And also that the realization of this commitment goes through the recognition of these subjects as citizens who enjoy the right to seek help when they judge it necessary, to have a network of attention with different services to be accessed in different circumstances of their lives.

9. The Psychiatric Reform began in Brazil at the end of the military dictatorship in the late 1970s. In this context of democratization, experiences of other countries were instrumental in the Brazilian Psychiatric Reform, including: Therapeutic Communities and Anti-Psychiatric movement, England; Psychiatry of the French Sector and Institutional Psychotherapy, France; Preventive and Community Psychiatry, United States; Democratic Psychiatry,

Italy. Other important contributions in this context in Brazil were: The Health Reform Movement, the contributions of Social and Preventive Medicine, the Human Rights Movement and the Movement of Workers in Mental Health. Although it started later, this movement also went through several stages, and became known as the Anti-Asylum Movement, which reached its so-called third era from the 1990s. This process resulted in an initiative to de-institutionalize and to invent new practices in mental health, supported by a paradigm shift where, at least theoretically, the treatment is no longer centred on the doctor who sought to 'cure' the 'evil' of the so-called mentally ill, becoming an interdisciplinary and expanded assistance, which received the name of 'social rehabilitation'. From this new perspective, it was institutionalized new practices officially regulated by the Ministry of Health in the country, for instance, CAPS (see note 3).

Bibliography

Aletti, M. A. 2012, 'Psicologia diante da religião e da espiritualidade: questões de conteúdo e de método', in *Religiosidade e cultura contemporânea: desafios para a psicologia*, edited by M. H. Freitas and G. J. Paiva, 157–90. Brasília, Brazil: Universa.

Amarante, P. and E. H. G. Torre. 2017. 'Madness and Cultural Diversity: Innovation and Rupture in Experiences of Art and Culture from Psychiatric Reform and the Field of Mental Health in Brazil'. *Interface (Botucatu, Brazil)* 21 (63): 763–74. Available at: http://www.scielo.br/pdf/icse/v21n63/1807-5762-icse-21-63-0763.pdf (accessed May 2019).

American Psychological Association (APA). 2018. *Div. 36 Bylaws*. Available at: http://www.apadivisions.org/division-36/about/index.aspx (accessed May 2019).

Borges, D. C., G. L. A. Anjos, L. R. Oliveira, J. R. Leite and G. Lucchetti. 2013. 'Health Spirituality, and Religiosity: Medical Students' Views'. *Rev Bras Clin Med* 11 (1): 6–11.

Brasil, Ministério da Saúde, Secretaria de Atenção à Saúde, Departamento de Ações Programáticas Estratégicas. 2004, *Saúde mental no SUS: Os Centros de Atenção Psicossocial*. Brasília: Editora do Ministério da Saúde. Available at: http://www.ccs.saude.gov.br/saude_mental/pdf/sm_sus.pdf (accessed May 2019).

Brasil, Ministério da Saúde 2015. *Saúde Mental, Cadernos HumanizaSUS Vol. 5*, Brasília, Brazil: Ministério da Saúde, Secretaria de Atenção à Saúde, Departamento de Ações Programáticas Estratégicas.

Carrette, J. and R. King. 2005. *$elling Spirituality: The Silent Takeover of Religion*. London: Routledge. https://doi.org/10.4324/9780203494875

Coe, G. A. 1900. *The Spiritual Life: Studies in the Science of Religion*. New York: Eaton & Means.

Coe, G. A. 1916. *The Psychology of Religion*. Chicago, IL: The University of Chicago Press.

Corrêa, C. V., J. S. Batista and A. F. Holanda. 2016. 'Religious/Spiritual Coping in Health and Disease Processes: A Review of the Brazilian Literature (2000-2013)'. *PsicoFAE* 5 (1): 61-78.

DaMatta, R. 1986. *O que faz o brasil, Brasil?* Rio de Janeiro, Brazil: Rocco.

Foch, G. F. L., A. M. B. Silva and S. R. F. Enumo. 2017. 'Spiritual / Religious Coping: A Systematic Literature Review (2003-2013)'. *Arquivos Brasileiros de Psicologia* 69 (2): 53-71.

Freitas, M. H. 2007. 'Quando o silêncio transborda, calaboca já morreu: religiosidade, cientificidade e formação em psicologia'. In *As vozes do silenciado: Estudos nas fronteiras da antropologia, filosofia e psicologia*, edited by M. H. Freitas and O. P. Pereira, 187-205. Brasilia, Brazil: Universa.

Freitas, M. H. 2011. 'News: Seminar Psychology and Religious Sense – Religious Coping and Health'. *Psicologia: Teoria e Pesquisa* 27 (2): 257. Retrieved from http://periodicos.unb.br/index.php/revistaptp/article/view/17532

Freitas, M. H. 2017. 'Psicologia religiosa, psicologia da religião / espiritualidade, ou psicologia e religião / espiritualidade?'. In *Psicologia da religião no Brasil*, edited by M. R. Esperandio and M. H. Freitas, 61-76. Curitiba, Brazil: Juruá.

Freitas, M. H., V. Turra and N. B. Zaneti. 2016. 'Religiosidade, saberes tradicionais e saúde no Brasil'. In *Na fronteira da Psicologia com os saberes tradicionais: práticas e técnicas*, edited by L. E. V. Berni, 73-77. São Paulo, Brazil: Conselho Regional de Psicologia de São Paulo.

Freitas, M. H. and P. R. Vilela. 2017. 'Phenomenological Approach of Religiosity: Implications for Psychodiagnostic and Psychological Clinic Praxis'. *Phenomenological Studies - Revista da Abordagem Gestáltica* XXIII (1): 95-107. https://doi.org/10.18065/RAG.2017v23n1.10

Giorgi, A. 2009. *The Descriptive Phenomenological Method in Psychology*. Pittsburgh, PA: Duquesne University Press.

Giorgi, A. 2011. 'Sketch of a Psychological Phenomenological Method'. In *Phenomenological and Psychological Research*, edited by A. Giorgi, 8-22. Pittsburgh, PA: Duquesne University Press.

Giorgi, A. 2012. 'The Descriptive Phenomenological Psychological Method'. *Journal of Phenomenological Psychology* 43 (1): 3-12. https://doi.org/10.1163/156916212X632934

Husserl, E. [1936] 2008. *A crise da humanidade europeia e a Filosofia*. Covilhã, Portugal: LusoSofia.

Inocêncio, D. 2010. 'Medicina e religião: a visão do profissional médico'. *Revista Pandora Brasil* No. 25, *Ciências sociais e religião na América Latina*. Accessed May 2019. http://revistapandorabrasil.com/revista_pandora/religiao/texto_10.pdf

Instituto Brasileiro de Geografia e Estatística. 2010. *Censo Demográfico 2010 - Características gerais da população, religião e pessoas com deficiência*. Brasília, Brazil: Ministério do Planejamento, Orçamento e Gestão.

Koenig, H. G. 2006. *Medicine, Religion, and Health: Where Science and Spirituality Meet*. West Conshohocken, PA: Templeton Foundation Press.

Koenig, H. G. 2012, 'Religion, Spirituality, and Health: The Research and Clinical Implications'. *International Scholarly Research Network* 2012: 1-33. https://doi.org/10.5402/2012/278730

Lindoso, G. C. P. 2014. 'Codó e o Terecô na fé: a festa de Santa Bárbara'. Paper presented at the 29th Brazilian Anthropology Meeting, 3–6 August 2014, Natal, Brazil. Available at http://www.29rba.abant.org.br/resources/anais/1/1401896697_ARQUIVO_ARTIGOABA2014.pdf (accessed May 2019).

Lucchetti, G. et al. 2013, 'Medical Students, Spirituality and Religiosity—Results from the Multicenter Study SBRAME'. *BMC Medical Education* 13 (162). Available at https://bmcmededuc.biomedcentral.com/track/pdf/10.1186/1472-6920-13-162 (accessed May 2019). https://doi.org/10.1186/1472-6920-13-162

Marques, L. F. and R. M. Rigo. 2016. 'A produção científica atual (2008–2014) em Psicologia da Religião e da Espiritualidade no Brasil', In *Psicologia, Religião e Espiritualidade: Estudos contemporâneos no contexto brasileiro,* edited by M. H. Freitas, N. B. Zaneti and S. H. N. Pereira, 19–41. Curitiba, Brazil: Juruá.

Melo, C. F., I. S. Sampaio, D. L. A. Souza and N. S. Pinto. 2015. 'Correlation Between Religiousness, Spirituality and Quality of Life: A Review of Literature'. *Estudos e pesquisas em Psicologia* 15 (2): 447–464. https://doi.org/10.12957/epp.2015.17650

Moreira-Almeida, A., I. Pinsky, M. Zaleski and R. Laranjeira. 2010. 'Envolvimento religioso e fatores sociodemográficos: resultados de um levantamento nacional no Brasil'. *Rev Psiq Clín.* 37 (1): 12–15. https://doi.org/10.1590/S0101-60832010000100003

Oliveira, M. R. and J. R. Junges. 2012. 'Mental Health and Spirituality/Religiosity: Psychologists' Understandings'. *Estudos de Psicologia* 17 (3): 469–476. https://doi.org/10.1590/S1413-294X2012000300016

Paiva, G. J. 2004. 'Espiritualidade e qualidade de vida: pesquisas em psicologia'. In *Espiritualidade e Qualidade de Vida,* edited by E. F. B. Teixeira, M. C. Müller and J. D. T Silva, 119–130. Porto Alegre, Brazil: EDIPUCRS.

Paiva, G. J. 2005. 'Psicologia da religião, psicologia da espiritualidade: oscilações conceituais de uma (?) disciplina'. In *Psicologia e espiritualidade*, edited by M. M. Amatuzzi, 31–47. São Paulo, Brazil: Paulus.

Paloutzian, R. F. 2003. 'Psychology Of, And, For, In and Against Religion (and Spirituality?): Pragmatism Works'. *Psychology of Religion Newsletter, American Psychological Association Division 36* 28 (2): 17–19.

Pargament, K. I. 1990. 'God Help Me: Toward a Theoretical Framework of Coping for the Psychology of Religion'. In *Research in the Social Scientific Study of Religion*, edited by D. McIntosh, B. Spilka, D. Moberg and M. Lynn, vol. 2, 195–224). Greenwich, CT: JAI Press.

Pargament, K. I. 1996. 'Religious Methods of Coping: Resources for the Conservation and Transformation of Significance'. In *Religion and the Clinical Practice of Psychology*, edited by E. P. Schafranske, 215–239. Washington, DC: APA Books. https://doi.org/10.1037/10199-008

Pargament, K. I. 1997. *The Psychology of Religion and Coping: Theory, Research and Practice*. New York: Guilford Press.

Pereira, K. C. L. and A. F. Holanda. 2016. 'Spirituality and Religiousness for Psychology Students: Ambivalences and Expressions of the Lived-Experience'. *Rev. Pistis Prax.* 8 (2): 385–413. https://doi.org/10.7213/revistapistispraxis.08.002.ds07

Pinto, A. N. and E. B. M. Falcão. 2014. 'Religiosity in a Medical Context—Between Receptivity and Silence'. *Revista Brasileira de Educação Médica* 38 (1): 38–46. https://doi.org/10.1590/S0100-55022014000100006

Reuder, M. E. 1999. 'A History of Division 36 (Psychology of Religion)'. In *Unification Through Division: Histories of the Divisions of the American Psychological Association, Vol. IV*, edited by D. A. Dewsbury, 91–108. Washington, DC: American Psychological Association. Available at http://www.apadivisions.org/division-36/about/history.pdf (accessed May 2019). https://doi.org/10.1037/10340-004

Schmidt, B. E. 2016. *Spirits and Trance in Brazil: An Anthropology of Religious Experience*. London: Bloomsbury.

Stoychev, Kancho (Ed.). 2015. *Voice of the People 2015*. Zurich, Switzerland: WIN/Gallup International. Available at http://www.gallup-international.com/wp-content/uploads/2017/10/GIA-Book-2015.pdf (accessed May 2019).

Vergote, A. 1966. *Psychologie Religieuse*. Brussels, Belgium: Dessart.

Vergote, A. 1983. *Religion, foi, incroyance. Etude Psychologique*. Psychologie et sciences humaines 126. Brussels, Belgium: Pierre Mardaga.

Vieten, C. and S. Scammel. 2016. *Spiritual and Religious Competencies in Clinical Practice: Guidelines for Psychotherapists and Mental Health Professionals*. Oakland, CA: New Harbinger.

Word Health Organization 2018. *Cultural Context of Health and Well-Being: Culture and Reform of Mental Health Care in Central and Eastern Europe*, Workshop Report. Copenhagen: World Health Organization (WHO), available at https://apps.who.int/iris/bitstream/handle/10665/312314/9789289053075-eng.pdf?sequence=1&isAllowed=y

Chapter 10

Compassionate Presence: Buddhist Practice and the Person-Centred Approach to Counselling and Psychotherapy

Becky Seale

In my work as a counsellor I spend my days listening to the suffering of others. I hear people who are feeling unloved or uncared for. Some are feeling hopeless and powerless to change their lives, wondering what purpose their life has; some regularly hurt themselves physically to try to relieve the emotional pain they are finding so hard to live with. I hear these human beings wondering if their life is worth living; wondering if the world would be better off without them, with some even thinking of taking their own lives. All of the people I currently work with, however, are young people under the age of 18. Recent studies suggest that what I am hearing in the counselling room is not unusual; the UK is experiencing a marked decline in the mental wellbeing of young people (Slawson 2018), and suicide is one of the main causes of death in older teenagers worldwide (WHO 2018). Addressing the causes and solutions for improving mental health and wellbeing is, therefore, an urgent concern both for now and the future. For me, how I can best help on a day-to-day basis is an ongoing consideration. Working in any helping profession has many challenges and it is often difficult to manage caring for others in distress and taking care of oneself. Many helping professionals such as counsellors find there is a high cost to the work of listening to others who are suffering. Burnout, vicarious trauma and compassion fatigue are often consequences of being empathic (Beaumont et al. 2016) and counsellors may find over time that they become unable to do their work safely or effectively and may become ill themselves as a result of the impact of this work (Rothschild 2006). I have found that it has been essential for me in doing this work to develop a way of working in which I can help others find solace and a greater sense of wellbeing in their lives in a way that sustains rather than drains me. Counsellors with a spiritual practice, as well as those who are able to cultivate therapeutic presence, can perhaps protect themselves from burnout and develop a greater sense of wellbeing (Geller and Greenberg 2012; Hardiman and Simmonds 2013) and I have found having a Buddhist practice is one way in which I can gain sustenance to do this work. My practice primarily enables me to sit and listen and to be with another who is suffering. It also gives me perspective, enabling me to find some meaning, value and purpose in the face of the suffering I hear. Hence, my therapeutic practice as part of this process becomes a spiritual one.

The philosophy that underpins my work as a counsellor is that of the Person-centred approach (PCA). This humanistic approach developed by Rogers (1957) offers a way of working for me that not only is in line with my values but, I believe, integrates with and complements my Buddhist practice. The Person-centred approach can be described as a 'way of being' with clients, which Rogers (1980, 129) described thus:

> I find that when I am closest to my inner, intuitive self, when perhaps I am in a slightly altered state of consciousness, then whatever I do seems to be full of healing. Then, simply my presence is releasing and helpful to the other.

The concept of 'presence' or 'therapeutic presence' (Geller and Greenberg 2012) for me describes the essence of the work of a person-centred counsellor and also the essence of my Buddhist practice, and may be considered as the meeting place of these two approaches. For many years, the relationship between the two was an intuitive one that I did not even question. However, in recent years I have watched the increasing dominance of mindfulness within therapy in the form of mindfulness-based cognitive therapy (MBCT) and mindfulness-based stress reduction (MBSR) with the relationship between the PCA and mindfulness being little known. This led me to question what had been implicit for me and to consider making more explicit the relationship between Buddhist practice and the PCA. In this chapter, therefore, I will explore aspects of spirituality through Buddhist practice and wellbeing within the context of Person-centred counselling. As well as reflecting on my own experiences, I will also draw from my small-scale qualitative research study using interpretative phenomenological analysis (IPA, Smith, Flowers and Larkin 2009) with four therapists who have a Buddhist practice.

Bringing Together East and West

In many ways, synthesizing my Buddhist practice with my work as a counsellor is encapsulated in Rogers' (1980, 129) words when he writes that 'simply my presence' is helpful. Yet in examining the ideas and concepts underlying a Buddhist and psychological worldview, this synthesis becomes increasingly complex.

The medical model dominates current discourse in the field of psychopathology; a predominance which perhaps reflects a deeper, centuries-old undercurrent: the relationship between science and spirit. Despite its etymological roots (the 'psyche' in psychotherapy deriving from the Greek for 'soul'), psychotherapy and counselling are generally placed within the domain of science rather than the spiritual. Where once priests and spiritual teachers would provide solace in times of distress, today, in the West at least, it is most likely to be counselling and psychotherapy that provide this kind of help. Freud, in developing the field of psychotherapy in the early twentieth century, was keen to advance it as a 'new science of the psyche' (Needleman 1983, 4). Consequently, as Needleman (1983, 7) argues, human experiences of the great mysteries of life, death and search for meaning have been left to flounder in an existential vacuum of meaninglessness leaving many not knowing 'whether they need psychological or spiritual help'. The split between medical science and the soul remains at the heart of many differences in approaching mental health and wellbeing and placing mental health within a scientific, medical model has far-reaching implications.

Mindfulness

Whilst the spread of mindfulness in the field of therapy could be seen as a synthesis of the scientific with the spiritual, this synthesis is not as straightforward as it seems. Walsh and Shapiro (2006) suggest bringing the East and West together in this way leads to a clash of paradigms that on closer examination becomes more apparent. Reconciling a Western emphasis on strengthening the ego through therapy with the notion of transcending the self in a Buddhist practice is one example of clashing worldviews.

Bringing mindfulness to Western therapy is also problematic. It is unlikely that mindfulness would be so well-known and widespread today without the work of Kabat-Zinn (1994) in introducing MBCT in the 1980s. In doing so, however, Kabat-Zinn was keen to present a sterilized version of mindfulness, removing the Buddhism from it which he felt many would see as 'new agey' or 'just plain flakey' (Booth 2017). In Buddhist terms, mindfulness is just one aspect of the eightfold path, which includes a wider, ethical context for the practice. Divorced from this wider context, mindfulness can easily become a 'health gimmick' (Welwood 2000). For some, there is a concern that the current proliferation of mindfulness may be based on too narrow an understanding. The context of an existential inquiry underpinning mindfulness may be missed or else it becomes oversimplified as a 'reprogramming' tool (Bazzano 2010, 36), as exemplified by its use in training US marines, something clearly antithetical to Buddhist teaching (Williams and Penman 2012). Purser (2015) also questions the role of mindfulness to reduce stress without addressing its origins. Stress, he argues, becomes the fault of the individual suffering it rather than the socio-economic conditions to which they may be subjected. Batchelor (2015, 255) writes that a secular approach to meditation could end up losing 'any sense of sublimity, mystery, awe or wonder', therefore, mindfulness is in danger of being simply a technique to feel better rather than a spiritual practice.

Buddhist Practice

Buddhism may be considered the least religious of all the major world religions, if it can even be considered a religion at all (Batchelor 1997). Being Buddhist does not necessarily require belief in a God and may lack the dogma and restrictions of many religions. Rather than being something to believe in, the Buddha's teaching emphasizes action. Hence, in this chapter as in my research study (Seale 2016), I have specifically chosen to use the term 'Buddhist practice' rather than mindfulness. Buddhist practice usually, but not always, includes some form of meditation but with the main intention being to practise 'the moment-to-moment flourishing of human life within the ethical framework of the eightfold path here on earth' (Batchelor 2012, 1). I have also steered away from the term 'Buddhism' here: three of my four research participants, for example, were keen to stress that they wouldn't call themselves Buddhist. One, Hannah, is Jewish and is keen to retain this identity alongside her Buddhist practice. As Goenka (Hart 1987, 18) says, the Buddha 'never taught any "ism" or sectarian doctrine... [A]nyone can practise this technique and find benefit. A Christian will become a good Christian, a Jew will become a good Jew, a Muslim will become a good Muslim, a Hindu will become a good Hindu, a Buddhist will become a good Buddhist. One must become a good human being'. In Buddhist practice, therefore, the emphasis is on the practice itself rather than the belonging to any particular religion.

Buddhism and Wellbeing

Other difficulties in bringing mindfulness to a Western mental health setting are seen in differences at the heart of a Buddhist view of wellbeing as opposed to a psychological one. Although Buddhist teaching has been interested in wellbeing for 2,500 years, the notion of wellbeing is seen very differently by psychology and Buddhism (Wallace and Shapiro 2006). Paradoxically, the path to wellbeing from a Buddhist perspective begins with the task of fully knowing suffering or 'dukkha'. Wellbeing is not a hedonistic experience to be found through the pursuit of pleasure but rather an inner state not contingent on transient external experiences. Unlike a Western psychological perspective which views the 'ordinary' person as being mentally healthy, a Buddhist perspective views this ordinary human experience to be full of suffering rather than wellbeing. It doesn't take long sitting on a meditation cushion to experience how hard it is to be with things as they are. The desire to push away the unpleasant and cling to the pleasant is constant. Yet the Buddha taught that it is possible to train to balance the mind to be with our experience as it is and it is through becoming aware of the transience of experiences and gaining insight into the nature of reality that true enduring '*sukha*' or wellbeing can be found (Wallace and Shapiro 2006; Ekman et al. 2005).

Huntington (2018) also suggests that it is a misunderstanding to see mindfulness as a way to find the kind of happiness sought through the 'fulfilment of desire'. Wellbeing, or an 'ultimate promise of liberating insight', from a Buddhist perspective is to be found in 'renunciation, and unqualified self-surrender'. In the final analysis, a lack of wellbeing from a Buddhist perspective has its roots in seeing ourselves as 'separate beings' (Morgan 2006, 26). In bringing together the psychological with Buddhist thinking, it is perhaps necessary to take into account that whilst the psychological may help us 'find ourselves', the spiritual 'takes a further step, helping us let go of ourselves' (Welwood 2000, 97). As Brazier (1995, 39) suggests, a Western perspective may view wellbeing in terms of getting rid of things that stop us from getting what we feel we need in order to be happy. This, he argues, will inevitably lead to conflict and suffering, however. Yet, Brazier highlights that we are inseparable from the universe in which we live: 'we are it and it is us'. Wellbeing can be found through staying awake to an inherent desire to 'live in harmony with the universe'. This concept points to the ethical underpinning of Buddhist practice; in seeing and knowing our inseparability in this way, living an ethical life becomes inseparable from our wellbeing.

The Person-Centred Approach and Wellbeing

Wellbeing, from the perspective of the Person-centred approach to counselling, as Pilgrim (2017, 7) points out, is also not to be found through a hedonistic experience of happiness or bliss but rather reflects an Aristotelian emphasis on eudemonia, namely the pursuit of finding meaning in life. Rogers (1961, 196) talks of the 'good life' as 'enriching, exciting, rewarding, challenging, meaningful', rather than in terms of contentment. The 'good life', he suggests, is 'launching oneself fully into the stream of life ...', with all the ups and downs this may entail. Wellbeing, from this Person-centred philosophy, is understood through the description of a 'fully-functioning person' which Rogers (1961) describes as someone who trusts and is 'open to their experience' as it is in the moment. Human functioning is impaired, Rogers advocates, when our experience in the moment is denied. Through what are termed 'conditions of worth' (Rogers 1959), human thoughts, experiences and feelings become acceptable only through socially acceptable conventions. As such, a person loses trust in their own experience of themselves. Fundamental to the Person-centred view of wellbeing is the capacity for humans to heal themselves, to reclaim their own expertise on their lives and to 'promote their own well-being' (Bohart 2017, 2). The assumption underlying this view is the belief that human beings have a natural self-actualizing tendency generally considered positive, towards self-expression and development. This somewhat optimistic view of human nature is further exemplified by the centrality of the concept of 'unconditional positive regard' (UPR), (Rogers 1957; Bozarth 1998) within the therapeutic practice. According to Rogers, being able to genuinely understand and accept clients, without trying to change them or mould them in any way, is all that is required for successful, effective therapy. Rogers later described this as a 'way of being' (1980) with clients rather than a 'doing to' or attempt to fix or educate in any way.

Some of these key elements can be seen in the following extract from a recorded session between Rogers and a client, Gloria in 1965.

> Gloria: And I, I, I have a feeling that you are just going to sit there and let me stew in it (laughs) and I- I want more. I want you to help me get rid of my guilt feeling. If I can get rid of my guilt feeling (...) I can feel more comfortable.
>
> Rogers: Mhm. And I guess I'd like to say, 'No, I don't want to let you stew in your feelings', but on the other hand, I, I also feel that this is the kind of very private thing that I couldn't possibly answer *for* you. But I sure as anything will try to help you work toward your own answer. I don't know whether that makes any sense to you, but I mean it.

In his response, Rogers shares something of how he is feeling about what she has just said. He aims to do this in a real way, without professional artifice. At the same time, he communicates that he understands how she is feeling, without judging her. In addition, Rogers refuses to accept that he has the answer for her; refuses to take the role of expert. Rogers' philosophy implies that the therapist is there to be alongside the client; rather than lead the way, he accompanies them on the journey to wellbeing.

The Person-Centred Approach and Spirituality

Within the theory of the PCA, therefore, the self-actualizing tendency is the key force, the motivational direction of human beings, and for the therapist, fundamentally the work is not to *do* anything for the client but rather be with, or even, get out of their way; to trust the client's inherent self-direction. In many ways, this notion requires some faith in human capacity; although Rogers doesn't talk in terms of good or bad, he nevertheless sees this tendency in humans towards growth as inherently prosocial. Rogers stresses the importance of being non-judgemental, and for some Person-centred theorists, this unconditional positive regard is a revolutionary aspect of the approach which offers the cure itself. Bozarth (1998), for example, suggests that UPR is the key condition in facilitating change in the PCA and for Freire (2001, 145–154) it is what makes the PCA a 'unique and revolutionary approach in the field of psychotherapy', making it distinct from other therapies. For Thorne (2002), the practice of offering a client unconditional positive regard, the commitment to do so—the willingness to meet an 'Other' at depth, becomes a spiritual discipline.

This view of spirituality within the approach remains controversial, however, (Kalmthout 2013) with many practitioners uncomfortable with any relationship to a spiritual worldview. Yet, there is no doubt that for many, the spiritual aspects of the approach are pronounced. In his later work, Rogers' language becomes increasingly mystical in describing the depth of experiences possible within the therapeutic relationship. Sometimes the quality of the relationship is such that in Rogers' words, 'it transcends itself and becomes part of something larger' (Rogers 1980, 129). Kalmthout (2013, 144) asserts that spirituality is an inherent part of the PCA, suggesting that 'if spirituality means anything at all, it can be found in the essence of Person-centredness: empathy, unconditional love and authenticity', which he suggests are in themselves key qualities of spirituality. These qualities, known as the core conditions necessary for therapeutic relationships (Rogers 1957) form the basis of what has also been termed 'therapeutic presence'; a concept which may be considered as a meeting point between the PCA and Buddhist practice. As such, it became one aspect of my research exploring this relationship.

Therapeutic Presence

The ineffable, subjective quality of presence does not lend itself easily to investigative research (Tannen and Daniels 2010) yet Geller and Greenberg (2012, 9) argue it is a key therapist quality and 'essential for good psychotherapy'. Their definition of it as 'being completely in the moment on a multiplicity of levels, physically, emotionally, cognitively and spiritually' (ibid., 70) suggests it is a holistic experience to which the therapist brings their whole self rather than having any special, transcendental quality. In proposing that it is 'more than the sum of its parts', it could be considered a foundation to the core conditions or a fourth condition in its own right (ibid.). Therapeutic presence in many ways may also be seen as a synthesis of the core conditions of the PCA (Mearns and Cooper 2005).

Presence seems to be a quality that has significance in both the PCA and Buddhist practice. Many in the field of the PCA consider presence central to the approach, Merry (1999), for example, seeing it as a summation of the therapist qualities underlying the approach. For Freire (2001, 150), it is presence that 'turns unconditional regard into unconditional positive regard. Warmth rather than cold regard' and ultimately, Natiello (2001, 155) contends that the PCA 'cannot be practised without passionate presence'; and is therefore fundamental and essential to effective Person-centred therapy. Presence clearly encapsulates what Rogers termed a 'way of being' with clients rather than doing something to them (Geller and Greenberg 2002). For Buddhist teachers, presence may also be considered a key aspect of Buddhist practice. Vietnamese monk Thich Nhat Hanh (2009, 35), for example, writes that it is in the 'present moment that life, peace, joy, happiness and well-being are possible'.

Moore and Purton (2006, 10) point out that although Rogers did not have a spiritual discipline he was able to cultivate the ability to be present through years of 'disciplined professional practice'. For Brazier (1995) the ability of the therapist to be still and create internal space enables them to listen deeply and accept their clients. He proposes that it is this quality of stillness that allows clients the opportunity to heal. Mearns (2003) also writes of the benefits of developing a quality of stillness, whilst others call for a greater emphasis on developing this quality rather than the teaching of techniques (Andersen, 2005; Tannen and Daniels, 2010). Thorne (2003) believes it to be the responsibility of the counsellor to develop a spiritual discipline that will cultivate the ability to be present and Welwood (2000, 117) writes of creating space within ourselves and suggests that 'unconditional presence' is the most important 'powerful transmuting force there is' and therefore an important quality for therapists to develop. It seems clear to me, therefore, that therapeutic presence enables the PCA

Research into Buddhist Practice and the Person-Centred Approach

This sense of congruence between my Buddhist and Person-centred practice through the practice of being fully present with my clients led me to an enquiry into the experiences of other therapists. I wanted to know whether my experience is unique or whether others too, felt drawn by the qualities that seem to draw these concepts together. A qualitative, phenomenological approach is well suited to an enquiry of this nature. As Bazzano (2011, 116) highlights, phenomenological principles are central to the PCA as well as a Buddhist practice involving meditation, an experience which itself is 'rooted in phenomenological observation'. Batchelor (2011, 134) stresses that the Buddha's teaching is a direction 'to pay close penetrating attention to the rise and fall of the phenomenal world itself', rather than being a transcendental experience. Welwood (2000) and Brazier (1995) also highlight the relationship between the phenomenological interest in experience and Buddhist practice.

Interpretative phenomenological analysis (IPA, Smith, Flowers and Larkin, 2009) as a methodology emphasizes the in-depth analysis of individual experience. Whilst experience is stressed, however, the notion of 'logos' or analysis, is also drawn out of the word 'phenomenology'. The meaning given to experience is given prominence and the communication of ideas and experience is considered a necessary element of this process. This methodology requires the interpretation or translation of lived experience into language that can be shared. The hermeneutics of empathy, interpreting texts in order to stay close to experience as expressed by participants, is highlighted as well as an emphasis on the idiographic. Providing a space to hear a few individual voices in-depth is valued within IPA, rather than having many participants who might only be considered superficially.

I developed an interview schedule around the question of the extent to which the PCA may be considered a Buddhist practice with consideration of presence as a bridge between the two approaches. My initial questions also aimed to explore whether there is a connection between what draws my participants to their therapeutic approach and to their Buddhist practice. In my experience, there are aspects of both that attract and interest me and I wondered if the attraction to both is similar for others.

The interviews with four research participants, Andy, Caroline, Sally and Hannah (names changed) who are all experienced therapists, took place over a three-month period. Prior to the interviews, participants were asked to reflect on their experience of presence in their Buddhist and therapeutic practices for approximately a week. The purpose of this was to emphasize the phenomenological experience of presence in the moment and to encourage participants to convey more accurately their in-the-moment experience of the phenomenon. Semi-structured interviews of approximately one hour took place via Skype. They were recorded, transcribed and anonymized in order to protect the identity of participants. The transcribed interviews were subsequently analyzed for themes arising out of a descriptive, linguistic and conceptual investigation of the texts. Emergent subordinate themes were grouped together creating superordinate themes. Four themes of *Inner Authority*, *Compassion and Acceptance*, *Wholehearted Engagement* and *Therapeutic Space* emerged from the data collected through this research process which highlighted the key aspects of the relationship between Buddhist practice and the PCA through therapeutic presence.

Inner Authority

Challenging the medical model within mental health is also a fundamental concern of the PCA and many of its practitioners question the validity of an objective approach above human experience. The term 'mental illness' may be better considered in terms of metaphor as, unlike physical diseases, it is not subject to objective diagnoses (Sanders 2017). Diagnoses of mental illnesses instead rely on expert opinion with the patient's own judgement and experience given little weight. For the Person-centred therapist, there is a strong commitment within the approach to support an individual's 'existential freedom in deciding whether, when or how to process their own experience' (Warner 2017, 99). This concept is reflected in the first theme identified in the research study of '*Inner Authority*'. The emphasis in the PCA on the client as the expert on their own lives is something that three of my research participants felt particularly drawn to.

Andy highlights that the PCA is an approach that '*goes against the medical model*'. It is important for him to work with clients in a way that is not '*taking control of someone, but working alongside someone, journeying with them rather than sending them on a journey or sending them on a task*'. Caroline originally trained as a nurse and rails against the paternalism of medical professionals who '*were trying to order people's lives for them*'. For her, an approach to therapy that respects clients' views is essential. She stresses that: '*I would hit the roof if somebody was telling me how to live my life. I realised that, that I wanted to work with people in a way that enabled them to trust themselves*'.

This theme is also reflected in what draws my participants to their Buddhist practice as well as the PCA. Three of my four participants are also drawn to the lack of dogmatism within Buddhist teaching. Batchelor (2011) writes of the Buddha encouraging self-reliance and the importance of trying out what he taught rather than believing in any doctrine. Unlike other religions, there are no commandments or imperatives to behave a certain way. Instead, the Buddha encouraged questioning and critical inquiry: 'Just as a goldsmith assays gold, by rubbing, cutting, and burning ... so should you examine my words. Do not accept them just out of faith in me' (Batchelor 2011, 33), he urged.

One participant, however, does not highlight the importance of inner authority either in her therapeutic or Buddhist practice. In her therapeutic practice, she is further away from a Person-centred way of working than other participants. In addition, out of the four, she is the only one to call herself a Buddhist and also emphasizes her belief in a higher power. This anomaly, therefore, suggests to me that this emphasis on 'Inner Authority' may be particular to a synthesis of the PCA and Buddhist practice.

Compassion, Acceptance and Suffering

As outlined earlier, the path to wellbeing in Buddhist terms is through fully embracing suffering. *Dukkha* or unsatisfactoriness (Batchelor 2011) may be experienced simply through everyday discomforts or through more challenging experiences of physical pain, disease and the loss of loved ones. Ultimately, though, it is the knowledge of our own mortality, the uniquely human consciousness of the nature of existence that inevitably leads to the search for meaning and purpose.

Suffering is usually something that as living beings we aim to avoid and the restlessness of body and mind which becomes instantly apparent when meditating, for example, shows how this avoidance is a constant process for us. Yet, as the Buddha taught, it is through being with things as they are that we may come to know the transience of all experiences, and from which opens up the possibility of transcending suffering.

As shown earlier in responding to Gloria, Rogers does not try to reassure or take away her feelings. She feels she is being 'left to stew' in her feelings and whilst Rogers doesn't wish this on her, he also knows there are no shortcuts. There is a sense here in which he allows her to be with or embrace her suffering. As in a Buddhist practice or meditation practice, sitting with the feelings may be the key to releasing them. Whilst Rogers believes he has no choice but to be with Gloria whilst she has these feelings, he doesn't do so heartlessly. His care and concern for her suffering are evident; he strives to be with her almost sharing in her suffering—the very definition of another key teaching of Buddhism, that of compassion. Compassion literally means 'to suffer with' and from a Buddhist perspective, seeing ourselves as separate beings only enhances our suffering. Being able to recognize our deep connection to the universe and all beings within it is what leads us to be compassionate (Morgan 2006). To be with another with compassion first requires us to be still and the 'more we learn to sit still, the more we are able to hear, because we no longer need to avoid or fear suffering' (Morgan 2004, 48). Buddhist monk Thich Nhat Hanh (2001, 93) describes deep listening as 'compassionate listening'; listening that does not seek to analyze or fix things, but rather to provide conditions so that others may simply 'suffer less'. These words from these Buddhist teachers resonate strongly for me in my practice as a Person-centred therapist and similarly for all the participants in my study the concepts of compassion and acceptance were significant aspects of both their Buddhist and therapeutic practice.

Andy has many years' experience as a therapist and has spent many of them working with survivors of torture. Being compassionate is something that deeply concerns Andy in his work as a therapist. For him, it is this *'journeying with'* his clients, being alongside them, therefore, *'connecting to people, hearing them, being with them, working with them, um, sharing with them, engaging humanly with them'* that feels greatly important. Caroline, an experienced therapist, supervisor and lecturer in counselling, talks of being motivated by wanting *'people to not suffer'* and emphasizes that she sees compassion fitting well with the notion of unconditional positive regard in her therapeutic work.

Hannah, a Jewish therapist and artist with a background in social work felt drawn to Buddhism by the sense of acceptance she felt, saying, *'maybe other religions are maybe more punitive? In some ways? I think. Whereas I think Buddhism accepts your flaws'*. For Sally, a writer, therapist and Buddhist priest, her Buddhist faith allows her to *'relax knowing that something else has already accepted me ... somehow I am seen completely and accepted completely'*. This sense of nurture being not only for the clients but also the therapists is also a significant aspect of the study. Therapists and counsellors spend a lot of time with people who are lacking in wellbeing and for many therapists this can also have a big impact on their own sense of wellbeing over time. For the therapists in my research, as well as for myself, having a Buddhist practice not only supports us in our daily lives but also supports us in the work we do being with the pain and suffering of others.

Andy, in his work with survivors of torture, reflects on his ability to be able to cope and engage with hearing *'terrible things'* from his clients. His Buddhist practice helps him stay present and not be overwhelmed. He stresses how somehow pushing himself to engage deeply with his client leads him to be '*more alive in that moment*' and that '*the incredible intensity of our clients, um, pushes me to be more intensely present*' in a way that he feels he even benefits from his clients by engaging at depth with them.

Hannah feels that her Buddhist practice offers her a way to become more accepting of herself, '*it allows me to accept my layers and my frailties, in the sessions*' without having to be a '*perfect therapist*'. For Sally, having a Buddhist faith gives her a sense of grounding, enabling her to '*lean a little bit into something bigger*'; she experiences a solidity in her work that enables her to '*tolerate discomfort*' more. For Caroline, the Buddhist practice feels nurturing and enables her to both give to others and feel compassion for others whilst nourishing herself. Compassion and acceptance are not experienced one-way however and as Caroline explains: '*It's a kind of sense of that kind of cyclical kind of nurture. Um, acceptance of others, acceptance of self; acceptance of self, acceptance of others*'.

Wholehearted Engagement

Feeling compassion towards and acceptance of both themselves and their clients can be seen as one aspect of being present with clients. In addition, the theme of '*Wholehearted Engagement*', which emerged from the research data, also suggests another aspect of the experience of therapeutic presence.

It is striking how many times Andy uses the word '*try*' throughout his interview and in doing so strongly conveys the depth of his desire to be completely there for his clients. '*I am trying to be as fully present as I can be for the client*' he says, and in listening to him speak I am aware of the effort he puts into his work, '*it's a constant pressure to try to be engaged as well as I can be*'. Andy stresses that this is something he has to work at, '*I don't want to lose a sense of engagement with what's around me. Um, I feel like I could be on autopilot but I don't want to be*'.

Connection with others and the ability to cultivate human relationships of depth is an aspect that emerged as significant in both Buddhist practice and therapy with all participants. In Person-centred terms, this aspect correlates closely to the core condition of authenticity and could be considered an aspect of being fully present. Caroline considers '*a sense of wholeness in ... the encounter*' with her clients to be essential. She explains that otherwise, '*there would be bits I'd leave in the kitchen or bits that I would be pushing under the chair or something*'. Embodied experience as well the cognitive are also highlighted within this theme through the participants' wish to bring their whole selves to the experience of the moment and with their clients. Hannah explicitly conveys this in talking of the impact of her Buddhist practice on her as a therapist: '*It, it, um, enables me to ... be ... more ... present and embodied, actually in my body*'. Her hesitance and struggle for words when talking also indicate less of a cognitive experience. When Caroline talks, she moves physically as she describes her experience; she is almost dancing. The embodied experience comes first for her, which she then tries to make sense of: '*Something gets translated between here and to being spoken, to being voiced*'. In using the word 'translated' here, she evokes the sense of needing a new language to express herself. For Caroline, it is as if the physical experience is directly related to her ability to be present. When she lacks presence, she becomes '*much more heady*' and '*wordy*' leading her to '*offer more than is needed*' to her clients. There is some evidence to suggest that therapeutic outcomes are more positive for clients the more present a client perceives their therapist to be, regardless of the modality of therapy provided (Geller and Greenberg 2012) and this is something that my research participants seemed well aware of in their own work. Andy, for example, in working with survivors of torture, notices that, '*the intensity of their trauma experience means if you're not present you're really letting them down*'.

This sense of '*Wholehearted Engagement*' therefore suggests a desire to connect with the moment and with others in a way that is embodied as well as cognitive, as suggested by Geller and Greenberg's (2012) definition of therapeutic presence. The ability to be present with clients in this way allows the therapist to be more authentic in the relationship and, as Caroline's words imply, to *be* more and *do* less.

Creating Therapeutic Space

Each research participant describes ways in which their Buddhist practice helps to create spaciousness in their therapeutic work. Andy's Buddhist practice becomes integral to his working day when he tries to create spaces in which he can '*capture being present*'. He uses the image of an astronaut going into an airlock before going out into space to describe the minutes he has between clients. This image offers a sense of Andy trying to create an actual sense of space from the metaphorical, in order for him to become more available for his clients.

Caroline describes her Buddhist practice as setting '*the foundation for ... for ... for having that space just to be and having that space to settle my mind*' so that when she is with clients '*there's just a kind of sense of being there that kind of has some space in it*'. She uses the image of '*crystal balls*' filled with '*different coloured gases*'. She is keen to emphasize it as a space which holds and contains but allows for movement within: '*it feels like that kind of a space that things can move around in, but can't jump out of*'.

For Hannah, the concept of space is also a key aspect of therapy: '*You know, it's the ... you know, just the ritual of being there and the sacredness of creating a space is enough in itself sometime*s'. The religious language she uses of '*ritual*' and '*sacredness*' further reflects the relationship between her therapeutic and Buddhist practice.

Sally describes this sense of space in the therapeutic relationship as something that emerges through her being '*able to lean a little bit into something bigger, even though it's an unknown thing*'. She goes on to say that therapists can allow '*clients to be able to lean into [us] and for [us] both to be able to lean*'. The image of both her and her client '*leaning*' conveys a sense of comfort and safety for both in being able to let go and feel held within the therapy.

My research participants found it easy to talk about the relationship between their Buddhist practice and their work as a therapist. Although the themes identified above are described separately, I see them as different facets of a whole experience. The desire to respect deeply individual clients' experience and autonomy as described by the theme '*Inner Authority*', seems to be one way in which '*Compassion and Acceptance*' of another might be expressed. Creating a safe '*Therapeutic Space*' for clients to be themselves is a precious gift in a busy world; and the wish to be fully present for clients as expressed by the theme '*Wholehearted Engagement*', also suggests to me a strong desire to connect deeply and unreservedly with the experience of others who are suffering.

Conclusion

After many years' practice as a counsellor, I still feel surprised when I hear from clients that I have been helpful. Rarely do I actually 'do' anything, other than be attentive. Listening openly and carefully, I try to be as fully present to my clients as I can. In this way, I see my Person-centred counselling practice as an extension of my Buddhist practice. Rather than sitting on a meditation cushion drawing my attention back to *my* experience in this moment, in the counselling room I am including my client's experience of this moment alongside my own. This letting be, allowing what is, accepting that I can't fix anyone or make anyone feel better (Shainberg 1983) seems in itself to have the power to transform. As Geller and Greenberg (2012) propose, cultivating therapeutic presence is beneficial to both my clients' and my own wellbeing. In the act of letting go and becoming more present I too gain sustenance; I can relax into the flow without trying to swim against the tide. Thus, practising presence with 'what is' in meditation, becomes a therapeutic presence when practised in the counselling room.

Through my research, the concept of a compassionate presence has come into focus for me as fundamental to creating the conditions for cultivating emotional wellbeing. Yet a therapeutic approach such as this, which for me is a spiritual practice, a sensibility or an art rather than a collection of techniques or a science, may be hard to justify within health or educational settings requiring 'sound' evidence of effective practice for the allocation of resources. With the increasing dominance of technology in our everyday lives, the simple act of *being with* another human being may seem at odds with a mechanized and medicalized world. As Thorne (2006, 44) writes, 'to be fully present person-to-person in the moment and in the flesh seems now almost counter-cultural'. The modern world questions what it means to be a human being when there is no scientific evidence of the existence of the human soul (Harari 2015) and we face a future in which artificial intelligence could replace many human relationships. There is some evidence to suggest, for example, that people feel more open, trusting and less fearful of judgement when talking to a robot instead of a therapist (Galvão Gomes da Silva et al. 2018). However, despite the opportunities for connection offered by modern technology, a recent study into loneliness (Loneliness Results, 2018) highlights that probably the most technologically connected generation (16–24 year-olds) report feeling the loneliest. It seems to me, therefore, that emotional wellbeing remains very much dependent on human connection and that a therapeutic space offering a compassionate presence underpinned by spiritual values as described in this chapter, still has much to offer current and future generations.

Biographical Note

Becky Seale is a lecturer in counselling at Coleg Sir Gâr on the University of Wales Trinity St David validated foundation degree and BA in counselling in Ammanford, Wales, UK. Becky has a Buddhist practice and also works as a school-based Person-centred counsellor working with children and young people.

Bibliography

'Loneliness Results'. 2018. *All in the Mind*. BBC Radio 4, 2 October [Online]. Available at https://www.bbc.co.uk/programmes/m0000m8s (accessed October 2018).
Andersen, D. T. 2005. 'Empathy, Psychotherapy Integration, and Meditation: A Buddhist Contribution to the Common Factors Movement'. *Journal of Humanistic Psychology* 45: 483. https://doi.org/10.1177/0022167805280264
Batchelor, S. 1997. *Buddhism Without Beliefs*. London: Bloomsbury.
Batchelor, S. 2011. *Confessions of a Buddhist Atheist*. New York: Spiegel & Grau.

Batchelor, S. 2012. 'A Secular Buddhist'. Available at https://gaiahouse.co.uk/wp-content/uploads/Stephen-Batchelor-A-Secular-Buddhist.pdf (accessed June 2018).

Batchelor, S. 2015. *After Buddhism*. New Haven, CT: Yale.

Bazzano, M. 2010. 'Mindfulness in Context'. *Therapy Today* 21 (3): 38–39.

Bazzano, M. 2011. 'The Buddha as a Fully Functioning Person: Towards a Person-Centred Perspective on Mindfulness'. *Person-Centered & Experiential Psychotherapies* 10 (2): 116–128. https://doi.org/10.1080/14779757.2011.576560

Beaumont, E., M. Durkin, Martin C. Hollins and J. Carson. 2016. 'Measuring Relationships Between Self-Compassion, Compassion Fatigue, Burnout and Well-being in Student Counsellors and Student Cognitive Behavioural Psychotherapists: A Quantitative Survey'. *Counselling and Psychotherapy Research* 16 (1): 15–23. https://doi.org/10.1002/capr.12054

Bohart, A. 2017. 'A Client-Centred Perspective on "Psychopathology"'. *Person-Centered and Experiential Psychotherapies* 16 (1): 14–26. https://doi.org/10.1080/14779757.2017.1298051

Booth, R. 2017. 'Master of Mindfulness, Jon Kabat-Zinn: People Are Losing Their Minds. That is What We Need To Wake Up To'. *The Guardian*, October 22, 2017. https://www.theguardian.com/lifeandstyle/2017/oct/22/mindfulness-jon-kabat-zinn-depression-trump-grenfell (accessed June 2018).

Bozarth, J. 1998. *Person-Centred Therapy: A Revolutionary Paradigm*. Ross-on-Wye, UK: PCCS Books.

Brazier, D. 1995. *Zen Therapy*. London: Robinson.

Ekman, P., R. J. Davidson, M. Ricard and B. A. Wallace. 2005. 'Buddhist and Psychological Perspectives on Emotions and Wellbeing'. *American Psychological Society* 14(2): 59–63. https://doi.org/10.1111/j.0963-7214.2005.00335.x

Freire, E. 2001. 'Unconditional Positive Regard: The Distinctive Feature of Client-Centred Therapy'. In *Unconditional Positive Regard, Rogers' Therapeutic Conditions Evolution Theory & Practice*, edited by J. Bozarth and P. Wilkins, 145–154. Ross-on-Wye, UK: PCCS Books.

Galvão Gomes da Silva, J., D. Kavanagh, T. Belpaeme, L. Taylor, K. Beeson and J. Andrade. 2018. 'Experiences of a Motivational Interview Delivered by a Robot: Qualitative Study'. *Journal of Medical Internet Research* 20 (5): 628–639. https://doi.org/10.2196/jmir.7737

Geller, S. and L. Greenberg. 2002. 'Therapeutic Presence: Therapists Experience of Presence in the Psychotherapy Encounter in Psychotherapy'. *Person-Centered & Experiential Psychotherapies* 1 (1 and 2): 71–86. https://doi.org/10.1080/14779757.2002.9688279

Geller, S. and L. Greenberg. 2012. *Therapeutic Presence: A Mindful Approach to Effective Therapy*, Washington, DC: American Psychological Association. https://doi.org/10.1037/13485-000

Hardiman, P. and J. G. Simmonds. 2013. 'Spiritual Well-Being, Burnout and Trauma in Counsellors and Psychotherapists'. *Mental Health, Religion & Culture* 16 (10): 1044–1055. https://doi.org/10.1080/13674676.2012.732560

Harari, Y. N. 2015. *Homo Deus: A Brief History of Tomorrow*. London: Harvill Secker.

Hart, W. 1987. *The Art of Living, Vipassana Meditation as Taught by S. N. Goenka*. Mumbai, India: Embassy Books.

Huntington, C. W. 2018. 'Are You Looking to Buddhism When You Should Be Looking to Therapy?' [Online]. Available at https://tricycle.org/magazine/buddhism-and-psychotherapy/ (accessed March 2018).

Kabat-Zinn, J. 1994. *Wherever You Go, There You Are*. New York: Piatkus.

Kalmthout, M. V. 2013. 'A Person-Centred Perspective on Spirituality'. In *The Handbook of Person-Centred Psychotherapy and Counselling*, 2nd edn, edited by M. Cooper, M. O'Hara, P. F. Schmid and A. Bohart, 136–146. London: Palgrave Macmillan. https://doi.org/10.1007/978-1-137-32900-4_9

Mearns, D. 2003. *Developing Person-Centred Counselling*. 2nd edn. London: Sage. https://doi.org/10.4135/9781446279779

Mearns D. and M. Cooper. 2005. *Working at Relational Depth*. London: Sage.

Merry, T. 1999. *Learning and Being in Person-Centred Counselling*. 2nd edn. Ross-on-Wye, UK: PCCS Books.

Moore, J. and A. C. Purton (Eds.). 2006. *Spirituality and Counselling: Experiential and Theoretical Perspectives*. Ross-on-Wye, UK: PCCS Books.

Morgan, D. 2004. *Sitting Buddha*. Hexham, UK: Throssel Hole Press.

Morgan, D. 2006. 'The Process of Transformation Within Buddhism'. In *Spirituality and Counselling: Experiential and Theoretical Perspectives*, edited by J. Moore and A. C. Purton (Eds.), 26–34. Ross-on-Wye, UK: PCCS Books.

Natiello, P. 2001. *The Person-Centred Approach: A Passionate Presence*. Ross-on-Wye, UK: PCCS Books.

Nhat Hanh, T. N. 2001. *Anger: Buddhist Wisdom for Cooling the Flames*. London: Random House.

Nhat Hanh, T. N. 2009. *You Are Here: Discovering the Magic of the Present Moment*. Boston, MA: Shambhala.

Needleman, J. 1983. 'Psychiatry and the Sacred'. In *Awakening the Heart: East/West Approaches to Psychotherapy and the Healing Relationship*, edited by J. Welwood, 4–17. Boston, MA: Shambala.

Penman, D. 2012. 'Meditate Just Like the U.S. Marines'. *Psychology Today*. https://www.psychologytoday.com/us/blog/mindfulness-in-frantic-world/201207/meditate-just-the-us-marines (accessed April 2013).

Pilgrim, D. 2017. *Key Concepts in Mental Health*. London: Sage.

Purser, R. 2015. 'Confessions of a Mind-Wandering MBSR Student: Remembering Social Amnesia'. *Self & Society* 43 (1): 6–14. https://doi.org/10.1080/03060497.2015.1018668

Rogers, C. R. 1957. 'The Necessary and Sufficient Conditions of Therapeutic Personality Change'. *Journal of Consulting Psychology* 21 (2): 95–103. https://doi.org/10.1037/h0045357

Rogers, C. R. 1959. 'A Theory of Therapy, Personality and Interpersonal Relationships as Developed in the Client-Centered Framework'. In *Psychology: A Study of a Science, Vol. 3: Formulations of the Person and the Social Context*, edited by S. Koch, 184–256. New York: McGraw Hill.

Rogers, C. R. 1961. *On Becoming a Person*. London: Constable.

Rogers, C. R. 1980. *A Way of Being*. New York: Houghton Mifflin.

Rothschild B. 2006. *Help for the Helper: The Psychophysiology of Compassion Fatigue and Vicarious Trauma*. New York: W W Norton & Co.

Sanders, P. 2017. 'Principled and Strategic Opposition to the Medicalisation of Distress and all of its Apparatus'. In *The Handbook of Person-Centred Therapy and Mental Health*, edited by S. Joseph, 11–36. Ross-on-Wye, UK: PCCS Books.

Seale, B. 2016. 'Compassionate Presence: Buddhist Practice and the Person-Centred Approach'. *Self & Society* 44 (1): 3–12. https://doi.org/10.1080/03060497.2015.1053256

Shainberg, D. 1983. 'Teaching Therapists How To Be With Their Clients'. In *Awakening the Heart: East/West Approaches to Psychotherapy and the Healing Relationship*, edited by J. Welwood, 163–175. Boston, MA: Shambala.

Slawson, N. 2018. 'Young Britons Have Never Been Unhappier, Research Suggests'. *The Guardian*, April 5, 2018. https://www.theguardian.com/society/2018/apr/05/young-people-have-never-been-unhappier-research-suggests?CMP=share_btn_link (accessed June 2018).

Smith, J. A., P. Flowers and M. Larkin. 2009. *Interpretative Phenomenological Analysis*. London: Sage.

Tannen, T. and M. H. Daniels. 2010. 'Counsellor Presence: Bridging the Gap Between Wisdom and New Knowledge'. *British Journal of Guidance and Counselling* 38 (1): 1–15. https://doi.org/10.1080/03069880903408661

Thorne, B. 2002. *The Mystical Power of Person-Centred Therapy*. London: Whurr.

Thorne, B. 2003. 'Developing a Spiritual Discipline'. In *Developing Person-Centred Counselling*, 2nd edn, edited by D. Mearns, 45–48. London: Sage.

Thorne, B. 2006. 'The Gift and Cost of Being Fully Present'. In *Spirituality and Counselling: Experiential and Theoretical Perspectives*, edited by J. Moore and A. C. Purton, 35–47. Ross-on-Wye, UK: PCCS Books.

Wallace, A. and S. Shapiro. 2006. 'Mental Balance and Well-Being: Building Bridges Between Buddhism and Western Psychology'. *American Psychologist* 61 (7): 690–701. https://doi.org/10.1037/0003-066X.61.7.690

Walsh, R. and S. Shapiro. 2006. 'The Meeting of Meditative Disciplines and Western Psychology: A Mutually Enriching Dialogue'. *American Psychologist* 61 (3): 227–239. https://doi.org/10.1037/0003-066X.61.3.227

Warner, M. 2017. 'A Person-Centred View of Human Nature, Wellness and Psychopathology'. In *The Handbook of Person-Centred Therapy and Mental Health*, edited by S. Joseph, 92–115. Ross-on-Wye, UK: PCCS Books.

Welwood, J. 2000. *Toward a Psychology of Awakening*. Boston, MA: Shambhala.

WHO. 2018. 'Adolescents: Health Risks and Solutions'. [Online]. Available at: http://www.who.int/news-room/fact-sheets/detail/adolescents-health-risks-and-solutions (accessed June 2018).

Index

acceptance 6, 8, 52, 74, 138, 142, 146, 152, 190, 234-7, 239
actualizing tendency 13, 82
addiction 11, 67, 113-17, 119-20, 125, 128-9, 180-3, 185-6, 188, 190
adverse effects of meditation 30-34, 37, 54
Afro-Brazilian religion 143-4, 149, 154, 201, 215, 220
Al-Anon 130
Alcoholics Anonymous (AA) 11-12, 113-32, 181-92
alcoholism 116, 119, 130-1, 183-4
Alister Hardy Religious Experience Research Centre (AHRERC or RERC) 1, 14, 85, 129, 155, 219
altered states of consciousness 59, 87, 108, 162, 226
American Transcendentalism 124
anomalous experience(s) 7-9, 23, 44, 46-53, 57-59, 158, 163, 166, 200
anxiety 26-29, 32, 34, 47, 54, 67, 79, 102, 120, 189, 220
asceticism 70-71, 84, 95-96
authenticity 48, 81, 107-8, 189-91, 231, 237
autoethnography 9, 158-64, 171-3

Bach, Richard 125
Beattie, Melody 125
Behar, Ruth 158, 160
bereavement 46-47, 56
bio-medical 142, 153
Bolivia 138
Brazil 8, 14, 20, 24-25, 28-29, 38, 137-8, 141-55, 199-201, 203, 210, 216, 220-1

Buddha 31, 89, 93, 95, 101, 104, 228-9, 233, 235
Buddhism/Buddhist 10, 71, 83, 87-90, 93-94, 96, 100-8, 124, 128-9, 131, 144, 150, 215, 225-40

Candomblé 153, 155
Cartesian dualism 13, 69-70
Casey, Karen 125
Catholicism 143, 150, 153, 201, 215, 217
childhood trauma 28-29
Chödrön, Pema 124
Christian/Christianity 13-14, 25-26, 55, 67-77, 81-84, 95, 107-8, 114, 118, 123-4, 126, 128-9, 143-4, 150, 153, 228
clinical parapsychology 44, 51, 53, 58
Coelho, Paul 125
compassion 88-89, 93-94, 98, 102, 104, 187, 225, 235-9
conditions of worth 78-79, 81, 230
congruence 6, 78, 80, 82, 233
counselling 6-8, 14, 47-52, 56, 60, 75, 84, 225-9, 236, 239-40
Covington, Stephanie 125
cultural commentary 159

Dalai Lama, The 1, 2, 88, 124, 139
Darwin, Charles 125
Dawkins, Richard 125
Deism 23, 76-77, 87-88, 90, 96-99, 102, 106, 109, 114, 125, 128, 130, 142
déjà-vu 162
depression 20, 27, 34, 47, 54, 67, 75, 147, 151-2
Desiderata 123
Dick B 114, 118, 122

discipline 3, 13, 70–71, 74, 114–5, 126, 128–9, 139, 173, 215, 231–2
disease model of addiction 116, 149, 184–5
dissociative symptoms 28–29
divinization 13
Dukkha 229, 235

ecstatic 162
Ecuador 138
Eddy, Mary Baker 124
Eightfold Path 227–8
Ellis, C and Bochner, A 158–60
embodied 76, 96, 139, 153, 160–1, 173, 237–8
embodiment 77
empathy 79, 231, 233
epilepsy 9, 158–73

faith 2, 5, 7, 10, 19, 27, 69, 72, 75–76, 99, 104, 121, 138, 141–2, 144, 147, 149, 152–4, 187–8, 199, 200, 207–8, 210–12, 231, 235–7
fellowship 5, 113, 115, 118, 123, 126, 129–31, 182–4, 186, 189–91
feminist self-care spirituality 124, 158
Fenwick, Peter 162–3, 165
first-hand account 1, 163
Fox, Emmet 123
Freud, Sigmund 36, 220, 227
Fry, Stephen 125

Gervais, Ricky 125
Greer, Germaine 125

hallucination 28, 30, 32, 34, 147, 159, 163, 210, 214–15
happiness 2–4, 10, 21, 27, 47, 54, 87, 100, 109, 137–8, 143, 145–6, 166, 229, 232
Hardy, Alister 1, 6, 14, 129, 155, 219
harmony 10, 19, 108, 137, 144–5, 153, 162, 166, 181, 211, 229
Harris, Sam 30, 125
Hay, David 6
Hazard, Rowland, III 119
Hazelden Foundation 125

healing 7, 13, 20, 23, 46, 50, 77, 90, 138–40, 142–3, 153, 181, 183, 188, 201, 208–10, 226
health 1–4, 7, 10–14, 20–22, 26–28, 30, 36–37, 54, 67, 75, 83–84, 94, 115, 129, 139–40, 142, 144–6, 148, 151, 159, 161, 163–64, 173, 181, 187, 191, 200, 203, 205, 210–12, 217–8, 227, 229, 234
Higher Power 11–12, 115–8, 120–9, 183, 185, 189, 235
Hindu/Hinduism 70–72, 144, 228
Hitchens, Christopher 125
homosexuality 74
humanistic psychology 6, 68, 77, 83, 181, 226

illness 9, 49, 56, 91, 94, 116, 140, 152–3, 159, 161, 168–9, 171, 182–3, 188, 200, 208, 210–11, 214, 234
incarnation 13, 76–77, 84, 94
individuation 5, 10–11, 14, 21, 35–37
insider-perspective 158
integration 24, 52, 63, 77–80, 82, 84, 97, 159, 216–7
interpretative phenomenological analysis (IPA) 54, 57, 226, 233
introjection 78, 83
Islam 70

James, William 5, 22, 36, 118, 123, 139, 163, 183, 187, 189, 191–2
Judaism 68, 153
Jung, Carl Gustav 5, 10–11, 21, 35–37, 68, 118–21, 129, 181, 183, 192

Kardecism 144, 147
Kelly, John F. 129, 186
Kornfield, Jack 30–33, 124
Kurtz, Ernest 114, 116–8, 125, 183

Latin America 14, 137, 155, 199
Leonardi, Jeff 1–2, 9, 13–14, 84, 141, 155
life satisfaction 4–5, 7, 57, 137, 140
lived experience 158, 161, 163, 173, 206, 233
living well 5, 137–8, 143, 145

Index

Llewellyn, Dawn 122
Lord's Prayer 130, 208

magical cures 161
Mearns, D. & Thorne, B. J. 82, 232
medical 7, 9, 27, 32, 35, 50, 52, 95, 113–4, 116, 138–42, 147–54, 158, 160, 162–4, 166–7, 169, 171, 173, 211–3, 217–8, 227, 234
medicine 7, 89, 119, 139, 152–4, 214
meditation 13, 20, 22, 24, 30–35, 56, 102, 113, 124, 127, 139, 150, 153, 184, 186, 191, 228–9
mediums 53–59, 151, 153
mediumship 25, 46, 53–54, 56, 138, 149–51, 154
mental health 20–22, 26, 28, 36–37, 48, 54, 140, 181, 191–2, 199–200, 203, 205–6, 210–2
mental illness 56, 161, 200, 234
mindfulness 10, 12, 22, 33, 83–84, 124, 226–9
Mitchell, David 125
moral inventory 113, 126–7, 184
Moral Re-Armament 118
mortification 71, 84
mutual aid 113, 129–30
Myss, Caroline 125
Mysticism 9, 22–23, 76, 125, 129, 157–9, 162, 166, 172, 214, 231

narcissism 161
New Age 22–24, 227
New Thought Religion 123
non-linear states 158

organism/organismic awareness 13, 78–81, 83–84
original sin 69
Orthodox churches 76
Ouspensky, P D 125

paranormal beliefs 23, 59
parapsychology 23, 44–47, 51, 53, 58–59
pathology 7, 32, 46, 52, 54, 58–59, 203, 205, 213–4, 227
Peck, M. Scott 125

Pentecostalism 22, 143
perennialism 114
Person-centred approach (PCA) 1, 13–14, 68, 78–79, 81–84, 108, 141, 225–6, 229–39
phenomenology, phenomenological 9, 31, 51, 54, 57, 59, 70, 83, 158, 166, 171, 173, 191, 201–5, 226, 233–4
presence 2, 49, 79, 98, 117, 145, 148, 162, 192, 202, 208, 225–6, 231–4, 237–40
psychic change 118
psychosis 159, 163, 167, 173
psycho-spiritual 13, 68
psychotherapy 6–7, 51, 58–59, 75, 77–78, 80, 149, 160, 173, 218, 225, 227, 231–2
psychotic symptoms 33–35, 167, 173, 208, 214
purity 71–73, 84, 105, 118
purpose in life 6, 10, 21, 23, 25–26, 36, 108

recovery (from addiction/alcoholism) 11–12, 113–6, 119–20, 124–31, 181–91
reflexive, reflexive writing 160, 204
relaxation-induced anxiety 34
religion 1–2, 5, 7, 10, 13, 19, 21–25, 36, 55, 72–73, 84, 88, 96, 102, 104–5, 113–4, 118–9, 122–3, 126, 129, 138–54, 169, 190, 199, 201–3, 209, 211, 213–8, 228, 235–6
Religious Experience Research Centre (see Alister Hardy Religious Experience Research Centre)
Rogers, Carl. R. 5–6, 13, 77–81, 108–9, 181, 226, 230–2, 235
Rohr, Richard 77, 81–82, 123
Rumi, Jalaluddin 125

Sacks, Oliver 162, 172
sacred disease 161
Schmidt, Bettina 1, 7–8, 12, 14, 23, 137, 141, 144, 154–5, 163, 201
Schucman, Helen 124

self 2, 5-6, 8, 10-13, 21, 24, 28, 30, 34-36, 52, 57, 78-83, 100, 108, 118, 127, 146, 158, 160-1, 165, 172-3, 181, 186-7, 190-1, 211, 226-232, 235, 237
Serenity Prayer 123, 130
sexuality 3, 67-68, 73-74, 77, 88, 92, 105, 163
shaman(s) 92, 163, 171, 217
Sir Halley Stewart Trust 130
Smith, Robert (Dr Bob) 117-8, 120, 183
sobriety 116-20, 131
social desirability bias 28-29
socio-cultural 159-60
Solignac, P. 75
soul 71-72, 74, 90, 92, 192, 227, 240
South America 2, 138
Spiritism / Spiritist 142-3, 146-7, 150, 152-4, 201, 208, 215
Spiritual 2, 8, 10-13, 19, 21, 23-24, 26-30, 36-37, 46-47, 49, 54, 56, 58-59, 67-77, 81, 84, 87-88, 90, 94, 97, 100, 102-3, 106-9, 113-20, 122-29, 139, 141-54, 162, 173, 182, 184-91, 202, 206-18, 225-232, 240
spiritual experience(s) 1-3, 6, 9, 12, 22-23, 26, 29, 51, 59, 119, 120, 122, 142, 149-52, 158-66, 169-73, 181-3, 192, 205, 213-4, 218
Spiritualism 55
spirituality 1-14, 19-29, 35-38, 47, 71, 77, 83-84, 88, 90, 95-96, 98, 102, 105, 107-8, 113-5, 121-9, 138-54, 159, 164, 172-3, 181-2. 185-6, 189-91, 200-7, 211, 213, 218, 226, 231
spiritus contra spiritum 113, 119, 129
stigma 50, 52, 162, 170, 172
suffering 7, 46, 58, 71, 83, 91, 94-95, 104, 113, 118-9, 127-8, 131, 140, 182-3, 189, 207-8, 212-3, 219, 225-9, 235-6, 239

Sumedho, Ajahn 124
Swedenborg, Emanuel 124

Taves, Ann 118
Teilhard de Chardin 76, 108
temporal lobe epilepsy 162-3, 170
Thatcher, Ebby 119
theosis 76
therapeutic presence 225-6, 231-2, 234, 237-9
therapeutic space 234, 238-40
Tolle, Eckhart 124
transformation 2, 13, 22, 24, 87-90, 97, 99, 107, 161, 181-3, 186, 190-1
Twelve Step fellowships 113, 115, 118, 123, 130-1, 182-3, 186, 190-1
Twelve Step programme 118, 126, 132, 184-6, 190

Umbanda 25, 143-4

vernacular religion 122
vicarious trauma 225
Vieten, C.& Scammell, S. 9, 12, 214, 218
voice hearers 57

Walshe, Neal Donald 125
wellbeing 1-14, 19-30, 35-38, 46-47, 52-54, 58, 67, 75, 79, 81-84, 87-90, 98, 100-3, 108-9, 114-5, 126, 128-9, 137-47, 151-4, 159, 161-2, 164, 173, 181-2, 189, 191-2, 200-1, 210, 212, 225-31, 235-6, 239-40
wholeness 35, 77, 79, 80-81, 98, 108, 181, 237
Williamson, Marianne 124
Wilson, Bill (Bill W.) 117-20, 183, 192

young adults, young people 11, 182, 186, 190-1, 225